CREATIVE AGING

A Meaning-Making

Perspective

Mary Baird Carlsen, Ph.D.

W • W • NORTON & COMPANY
NEW YORK · LONDON

By the same author
Meaning-Making: Therapeutic Processes in Adult Development

Excerpts from *Condemned to Meaning* by Huston Smith. Copyright © 1965 by Huston Smith. Reprinted by permission of HarperCollins Publishers, Inc.

Excerpts from *Understanding Mourning: A Guide For Those Who Grieve* by Glen W. Davidson, copyright © 1984 Augsburg Publishing House. Used by permission of Augsburg Fortress.

Excerpts from *The Challenge of Aging*, by John A.B. McLeish, copyright © 1983 Douglas & McIntyre. Reprinted by permission.

Excerpts from *Enjoy Old Age*, by Skinner & Vaughan. Copyright © 1983 by B.F. Skinner and Margaret E. Vaughan. Reprinted by permission from W.W. Norton & Company, Inc.

Excerpts from *Conceptual Blockbusting*, by James Adams. Copyright © 1974, 1976, 1979 by James L. Adams. Reprinted by permission from Stanford Alumni Association.

Excerpts from *The Measure of My Days*, by Florida Scott-Maxwell, copyright © 1968 by Florida Scott-Maxwell. Reprinted by permission from Alfred A. Knopf, Inc.

Excerpts from *Turning Points*, by Clark Moustakas. Copyright © 1977 by Clark Moustakas. Permission to publish from Clark Moustakas.

Excerpts from *The Courage to Grow Old*, by Phillip Berman. Copyright © 1989 by The Center for the Study of Contemporary Belief. Reprinted by permission from Ballantine Books and Phillip Berman.

Excerpts from "Final Days," by Nancy Burson, 1990. Permission to quote from Nancy Burson.

Excerpts from *The Once and Future King*, by T.H. White. Copyright © 1987 by T.H. White. Permission to quote from The Putnam Publishing Group.

Quotes from letters to the editor in *Modern Maturity*, Aug-Sept, 1987, and June-July, 1989. Permission to quote from *Modern Maturity*.

Quotes from editorial essay by Frances Lear, *Lear's*, Jan/Feb. 1989. Permission granted by Frances Lear.

First published as a Norton paperback 1996.

Printed in the United States of America.

Library of Congress Cataloging-in Publication Data
Carlsen, Mary Baird, 1928–
   Creative aging : a meaning-making perspective / Mary Baird
Carlsen.
      p.   cm.
   Includes bibliographical references and index.
   ISBN 0-393-70226-X
   1. Psychotherapy for the aged.   2. Aging—Psychological aspects.
I.   Title
RC480.54.C37   1991   155.67—dc20   91-24641

W.W. Norton & Company, Inc., 500 Fifth Avenue, New York, NY 10110
W.W. Norton & Company Ltd., 10 Coptic Street, London WC1A 1PU

2 3 4 5 6 7 8 9 0

To Jesse Hays Baird
Father, Mentor, Friend

A birthday —
Like yesterday,
And Sunday,
And all the rest —
Lasts 24 hours,
Just as long.
Though you know
The hands on the clock move,
You cannot see it.

Suddenly,
The meter flips over
And a whole year drops away.
If you look quickly,
All time comes into sharp focus,
And you are aware of your long fall
From the past
Into the future,
Continually gathering a life.

— Phil Carlsen, 1975

CONTENTS

SECTION II

Cognitive Interruptions in Creative Aging

SECTION III

Therapies and the Therapeutic

9. Narrative as Meaning-Making   154

To shape one's story requires an attention to what matters. Whether used as a therapeutic tool or as an adventure in private meaning-making, narrative process can make an important contribution to creative aging.

10. Meaning-Makings Unto Death   167

This thought piece asks each of us to consider our stance along a continuum from detached observer to involved participant in the dramas and meaning-makings of death. This exploration also highlights ways we can learn about death, facilitate palliative care for the dying, and help survivors through the processes of grief.

SECTION IV

Learning From Our Elders

11. Pioneers in a New Prime of Life   187

Here are real world experiences of a remarkable group of older people who are serving as pioneers in a new prime of life. Volunteering, lifelong learning, traveling, entering new careers — all these and more are included in this synthesis of a variety of late life adventures.

12. Our Elders at the Conference Table   208

Observations, insights, and bittersweet wisdoms from this select group of elders can help us open our eyes to the practical, the conceptual, and the spiritual, in matters of age. Their courageous examples can illustrate how much we can learn by listening to those who precede us.

Belief in our mortality, the sense that we are eventually going to crack up and be extinguished like the flame of a candle, I say, is a gloriously fine thing. It makes us sober; it makes us a little sad; and many of us it makes poetic. But above all, it makes it possible for us to make up our mind and arrange to live sensibly, truthfully and always with a sense of our own limitations. It gives peace also, because true peace of mind comes from accepting the worst.

—Lin Yutang, 1937, p. 158

PREFACE

I WRITE FOR ALL of us who are growing older. I write because I believe in the potential for lifelong, creative development until the day we die. I write because I believe we do gain true peace of mind if we face our mortality by considering the worst and exploring the best. To do all this has been for me and can be for you a "gloriously fine thing."

These are meaning-makings—a set of thought pieces on age, aging, and the aged—the state, the process, and the person. I write with an emphasis on the creative because I believe it is all too easy to adopt a posture that treats the older person as an object of our studies rather than a human participant in the human journey; all too easy to see only the negative aspects of aging, forgetting the courage, spirit, and determination which enable many older people to work actively with the dilemmas of age; all too easy to see older people as just so many gray-haired, bland, uninteresting members of a class rather than as individuals going through the processes of aging in a multitude of differing ways.

In this spirit, I launch this book. As I do so I also initiate an accompanying dialogue which I will maintain throughout this book—a dialogue between more objective, formal material and that which is personal and subjective; between research findings and the findings that come from anecdotal materials of every sort; between the therapist as professional and the therapist as aging person. Using this approach I model the duality of being both outside our aging and within our aging as we work with friends, family, and clients who are facing the realities of getting older. Validation and modeling of this dual role have been provided by the older professionals whom I cite throughout this book. Their example gives me courage for what I do here.

Initiating the dialogue, then, I share here some late night wonderings stimulated by the juxtaposition of this writing and the anniversary of my mother's death:

Writing about "creative aging" is touching many feelings in me. I think I expected this, but I am finding emotional responses that are unpredicted, strangers to my ways of feeling and of thinking.

To read about death is to think about my own death, about my mother's death, about my father's death. It is to imagine the closings of life and to wonder about my own scenario and that of my husband. When? How? Where? To feel the fear and the questioning which is being stimulated and sharpened by this writing. So, this book is painful, but I think the process is enlightening and that I will find some answers within its search.

As my thoughts circled around these issues, I moved into questions of the stereotyping of aging, questions that have always concerned me, particularly in my research into the matters of gender identity and prejudice:

One of the bigger questions I am finding here is the question of ageism—of how we discriminate against the old in quiet, unnoticed ways, until we ourselves pass through the portals of age and discover that we are victims of our own stereotypes and discriminations! I remember a colleague who often puzzled and offended me with her rather pat statements about other colleagues who were growing older: "Oh, she is so old!" (when really the woman was not so old, was still attractive and active in her work), or "He's an old man," a judgment which negated all the important contributions of this distinguished psychologist, a friend and strong influence in my life. Where did her hypersensitivity to age originate? And how on earth was she going to deal with her own aging?

Indeed, the puzzles of perception in the matters of age are collecting in my current awarenesses—and they disturb me a great deal. I feel the same rage and urge to protest as I do at simplistic labels of sexism. I find the same dynamics operating in aging in ways that I had somehow barely fathomed until now.

And, finally, the reality of my own feelings breaking through:

I think the reason I am feeling a bemused ambivalence these days is that I am indeed walking through a perceptual portal, adjusting my sights and emotional responses as I peer through the windows of age.

"As I peer through the windows of age." Those words are key to this book as I assemble differing perspectives on aging — from the demographer, the gerontologist, the anthropologist and sociologist, from the psychologist, the therapist and helping professional, from a wide variety of people of all ages. Very particularly, with my theme of "creative aging" as a guide, I am actively searching for those perspectives, attitudes, expectations, and involvements that are likely to bring constructive, creative approaches to the problems and potentials of age.

What is my purpose in all this? To orient us to the differing ways we can look at aging. To argue the definitions and possibilities for "creative aging." To consider the powerful influence of our patterns of meaning-making on how we age. To set forth a therapeutic attitude and outlook which I consider supportive of the uniqueness of the person within the universals of life. And finally and most importantly, to learn from those older than we who are serving as our guides, as our pioneers in a new prime of life.

ACKNOWLEDGMENTS

I acknowledge here those who have both taught me and are actively teaching me about positive, creative aging. These mentors, colleagues, models, family members and friends, have included so many that I can't name them all, but I would cite particularly Dorothy Strawn, Marian Mowatt, Robert and Laura Lowe, Bonnie Genevay, Helen Ansley, Ruth and Art Farber, Win and Callie Stone, Leonard and Louise Jones, Neva Waggoner, Bob Deits, Roy and Verna Fairchild, Jerald Forster, Roger Axford, Lawrence Brammer, John Brubacker, Henry Maier, Robert Kastenbaum, Nancy Hooyman, C. Gilbert Wrenn, Charles Mitchell, Ronald J. Manheimer, Robert Kegan, Maurice Friedman, Jan Lawry, David LaBerge, Michael Mahoney, Michael Basseches, Sandra Elder, and Karen Martin.

I also thank the variety of persons in a variety of settings who have provided supportive interest and informed, practical response: the staff of the Farmington, Maine, library; the educators, board, and staff of the Center for Creative Retirement of the University of North Carolina in Asheville; students and staff at the School of Communications at Arizona State University in Tempe (and what an important time that was in Kastenbaum's "Death" class); the staff of the East Valley Psychological Center, Apache Junction, Arizona; the pastors, staff, and librarians at Velda Rose Methodist Church, Tempe, Arizona; the Department of Cognitive Sciences at the University of California, Irvine; staff and residents of Regents Point Retirement Community in Irvine, California; and the staff of the Social Work Library at the University of Washington.

Particular thanks go to Susan Barrows, my editor at W.W. Norton, for her continuing support of my efforts, and to Dorothy Bestor, who not only reviewed the structures of my writing but contributed her unique insights about aging. I also thank Pamela Goad whose many hours of patient sorting of bibliographic material not only supported me but helped bring this book to its completion.

Finally, I thank James, my partner in these processes of aging, for his willingness to step aside when my writing moved to center stage. His thoughtful wisdom and caring responsiveness have stimulated my creativities even as they continue to sustain me.

I dedicate this book to my father, who was a model for me of the adventuresome spirit as he continued to sort and shape his meanings of life, even as he suffered his way into death. To his last living moments he was sorting questions of personal faith as he wrestled with questions of "heaven and hell," the Eastern and the Western in world philosophy, the rapturous and the tragic, the human and the divine. His awe and wonder were stimuli for my deep consideration of what we do know and what we do not know about living and dying, and of the amazing and complex capacities of the human being to face the challenges of the unknown while keeping the creative spirit active to the very end. In my father's approach to death I witnessed forms of meaning-making which were unique to him and which dared me to look through his windows into the processes of death. There I found dramatic illustration that human "beings-and-becomings" can continue unto death.

CREATIVE AGING

A Meaning-Making Perspective

I consider the old who have gone before us along a road which we must all travel in our turn and it is good we should ask them of the nature of that road.

—Socrates, *The Republic*

When you get to be older, and the concerns of the day have all been attended to, and you turn to the inner life—well, if you don't know where it is or what it is, you'll be sorry.

—Joseph Campbell, 1988, p. 3

When those interested in the care of the aged gather, there often is one vacant chair at the conference table. Absent is the individual about whom all are talking, the very one all want to make happy—the old person himself. It is *Hamlet* without Hamlet.

—George Lawton, 1943, p. 160

By Way of Introduction

M Y THESIS OF CREATIVE aging draws heavily on theories of creativity and human development. I named these carefully in my earlier book, *Meaning-Making*, where I proposed a concept of a "better way" for aging—a better way that widens the images of aging as it builds upon cognitive, developmental, dialectical perspectives which have been enriched by the theories of people like Erik Erikson, Robert Kegan, Michael Basseches, George Kelly, and Michael Mahoney.

With that concept and attitude shaping my approaches to aging, I continue to search for and highlight models of creative aging which encourage the personal growth of:

- wisdom and integrity over ignorance and despair;
- generativity and care over self-aggrandizement and narcissistic preoccupation;
- open-mindedness over rigid, closed thinking;
- a willingness to entertain new ideas over opinionated self-righteousness;

1

- transcendent relationship over the extremes of either self-absorption or of absorption within the identity of another. (see
  Carlsen, 1988, p. 228)

This thesis of a "better way" is incorporated into a therapy for
creative aging as it offers what Aaron Antonovsky calls a "salutogenic"
perspective and approach that points us towards the healthful rather
than the pathological. Here primary attention is paid to "ways of going
right" over ways of going wrong; to proactive, vital, intentional kinds of
living over passive, reactive, predetermined living. With that attention
comes a search for models of health which go beyond those of the
"OK," the average, the well-adjusted, or the reasonable, to those which
reflect an ideal of what human living can be about (see Korchin, 1976).

As a person incorporates these creative attitudes and approaches,
flexibility of thought and action is often the result. With this cognitive
and behavioral flexibility comes an enhanced ability to explore alternatives within the disappointments and tragedies of life, to transcend
despair while shaping personal integrity, and to incorporate originality
and a greater tolerance for unusual ideas and circumstances while
facing the risks, losses, and dilemmas of advancing age.

I agree, therefore, with Frank Barron (1963) that as a person grows in
personal, cognitive complexity, as he or she works towards a higher-
order synthesis, as he or she finds patterns within diversity — that "such
a person is not immobilized by anxiety in the face of great uncertainty."
Though optimism may sometimes be very difficult for the older person, "pessimism is lifted from the personal to the tragic level, resulting
not in apathy but in participation in the business of life" (p. 199).

*I have pondered this quotation from Barron after a professional
colleague asked, "What does he mean by that?" I think what he means
is very much like what Erikson means when he juxtaposes integrity
with despair. We do not lose despair — we simply gain a new perspective
that enables us to step outside of despair. To acknowledge and accept
the tragic in life is to transcend it, to gain a new perspective on it that
makes it a companion to meaning rather than a source of our meaning.*

Barron's language of the "participation in the business of life" is an
ordering language for my writing. This is a participation which sees life
not as an arrival or a completion, but as a journey into the very moments of death. It is a participation of the sort described by a 92-year-
old man just a few months before his death. When his dinner companion suggested that "it must be hard to grow older," he responded: "Yes, it
is difficult to be old, but after all, this is what it is all about. I simply
have to keep working with what I have." In such words are the wisdoms
and meaning-makings of old age.

The vocabularies of meaning and meaning-making join the languages of creativity and active participation in coloring my thinking and writing. And yes, these words are slippery, ill-defined, often eluding our grasp. "The meaning of meaning is meaning" obviously does not tell us very much. But, on the other hand, if we begin to see meaning and meaning-making as the shapers and sharpeners of experience, as the ordering and reordering of personal reality and significance, then the concepts of meaning begin to take shape.

I have found solution for some of these semantic/cognitive problems in an adoption of a systems perspective on meaning-making. What I find helpful is to conceptualize meaning on a ladder of abstraction, which suggests steps from the simplest to the most complex, from the concrete basics of life to the abstract reaches of the spiritual and divine (whatever that means to you). What gives meaning to aging, then, can be traced from the practical, day-to-day processes of eating and sleeping, of learning, working or playing, into the interactive processes of personal relationships, and on to more overarching perspectives on the world as a community of interconnection and the transcendent as a movement into mystery. This image of a ladder of abstractions fits well with Kenneth Boulding's open systems perspective, which sees systems within systems: the cellular within the person; the person within the family and the community; the community and the nation within a global connectedness; the physical systems within the "metaphysical" system of transcendence (1985).

In the case of aging, meaning-making can include the taking of what we have to make of it what we can. Here is the creation of the self, the telling of the personal story, the arranging of the symbols that make sense of who and what we are. Here is the translation of personal decline into the expandings of insight, which can give us meaning as we pass through a succession of psychological doorways, as we approach the perplexities of personal turning point—yes, as we approach our very moments of death.

The meaning-making therapist works with these self-creations, these story tellings, these rearrangings of "who and what we are" in ways that go beyond treatment paradigms, in ways that respect the integrities of the person, which conceptualize the individual as an open, expanding system, which perceive human aging as much more than a pathology. Maintaining these perspectives, the meaning-making therapist considers it essential to appreciate the "intimate interdependence of all realms of functioning"—the physiological, psychological, and socioeconomic—"if the well-being of the elderly is to be protected" (Kastenbaum, 1978, p. 63).

Additionally, this structuring of the therapeutic role means facing an array of questions about purposes and meanings in old age. Even further, it asks for clear definitions of better ways to grow older—whether in the physical practices of exercise and nutrition, in the cognitive/emotional practices of opening perceptions to imagination and possibility, or in the willingness to engage the mysteries and meaning-makings of life. What is helpful? What is defeating? What is stimulating? All this to guide clients more effectively through the maze of physical decline, diminishing power, and current cultural reaction to the state of being old. It is the process of attending to a more proactive, constructive vision of life.

As we define our purposes and perspectives we may need to reshape a "core vision." In the words of Robert Kastenbaum:

Limitations and distortions in our core vision of what it means to be a person become starkly evident in old age. If to be an old person is to suffer abandonment, disappointment and humiliation, this is not a "geriatric problem." It is the disproof of our whole shaky pudding, technology, science, and all. If our old people are empty, our vision of life is empty. (1978, p. 63)

Taking hold of these challenges means turning about tendencies in the helping professions to speak from outside of the experience of older people. It means to raise some pointed questions: Why have psychology programs and gerontological research been slow to challenge and inform the clinician? Why has gerontology been slow to pinpoint and emphasize the generative capacities of the older adult? Why has a life-span, developmental perspective been slow to inform the professional of the perspective of aging as a lifelong process, as a "seamless whole" (Neugarten, in Fisher, 1985), instead of focusing on divisions and categories that place the older person in a very peculiar place vis-à-vis other human beings? These are questions that point to dilemmas within the disciplines of psychology and of gerontology—dilemmas of language and focus, of outlook and attitude, of fragmentations and "islands of densely packed information with few bridges" (Birren, 1988, p. 147), of a state of affairs where "no consensus has emerged on either the definition of *gerontology* or on its scope and boundaries" (Achenbaum & Levin, 1989, p. 393).

But gerontology as a discipline is changing. Achenbaum and Levin (1989), in a careful review of the meanings of *gerontology*, arrive at some hopeful conclusions: Gerontology is going beyond the reductionist and pathology-oriented approaches that have so dominated its research scenes. There appears to be increasing respect for gerontology's dual role as an applied science and a basic science, for a multidisciplinary interaction of approaches, and for goals for the study of aging that go beyond the extension of life to increasing the quality of life. Here, too, are trends toward widening the study of aging to broader and broader perspectives (National Institute on Aging, *Age Words*, 1986). All this is happening as gerontology expands its definitions of purpose to include "applications of knowledge for the benefit of mature and aged adults" (Kastenbaum, 1987).

Greater attention is being given to clinical training. Social work is continuing its thoughtful, innovative studies in the field of aging (a notable example is the current effort to help caretakers, many of whom are quite old themselves); clinical psychology is awakening to its task with older people (as evidenced by increasing attention in the journals of the American Psychological Association); and medicine continues to tackle the difficult questions of ethics in matters of life and death, studying and evaluating ways to meet more effectively the needs of aging patients. Here I am particularly impressed with contributions from thoughtful, well-informed members of the nursing profession.

Within the many varieties of psychotherapy I see increasing attention to the person as a meaning-making self, as a unique individual who is being defined as more than a stimulus-response machine, as a creative, active, involved, human *being*. Increasingly, the constructive, cognitive developmental outlook is shaping therapies that are more than treatments and symptom-fixing, more than medical models which confine themselves to the languages of pathology; therapies that are indeed proactive, involved, sensitive to the healthful and the creative potential of the aging.

In naming models for creative aging and the vital involvements of old age (see Erikson, Erikson, & Kivnick, 1986), I do not ignore the reality that many clients will be unable to go very far in realizing the ideal, whether because of lack of health or personal capability, because they have been deeply hurt or abused, because they are lost in impoverished environments, because their attitudes and beliefs lock them into negative patterns of life, or because they do not agree with this particular ideal.

But this is not an either/or—this is a continuum from less to more which can point to the improvements in living, however slight, that can be made if we maintain a creative outlook and courage and conviction about what it is we are suggesting and doing. As clients and therapists join in a mutual stimulation of the creative, they are acting on life in a constructive, forward-looking manner. By studying and building creative experiences, therapists and clients may override some of the expectations that society has handed them, even as they demonstrate the possibility of vital involvements in old age.

Within this perspective on creative aging, therefore, it becomes an important therapeutic challenge to help clients name and understand the processes of their own aging, to guide them in developing skills in advance of being old, and to join them in the meaning-makings that go with being old. This builds on an important suggestion:

From here on, old age must be planned, which means that mature (and, one hopes, well-informed) middle-aged adults must become and remain aware of the long life stages that lie ahead. The future of these long-lived generations will depend on the vital involvement made possible throughout life. (Erikson, Erikson, & Kivnick, 1986, p. 14)

This means, too, that we join our aging clients in considering everything from the practical day-to-day arrangements of life-style, health care, and meaningful activity to the more global realms of that which can be called spiritual. This means that the therapist goes beyond behavioral management to deal with the less definable realms of emotion, meaning, and purpose—the stuff of "sleeping, dreaming, imaging, fantasizing, meditating, creating, loving, grieving, and dying ... processes that involve the inner core of human experience" (Kastenbaum, 1973, pp. 699–700). It thus means, as the sage Lin Yutang so wisely suggested, that the therapeutic experience faces directly the widening shadow of old age and death without running away from that shadow.

As I write for readers who are both professional and nonprofessional, I ask each of us to acknowledge and name our own aging without running from the physical, emotional, psychological jolts that alert us to its processes. By doing so we enhance our abilities to enter our aging clients' worlds of meaning. Certainly one of the dilemmas of working in the field of aging is that we only begin to perceive, by fits and starts, the worlds of clients who are older than we are. We simply are not there yet. Indeed, because it *is* difficult to comprehend the strange mix of positive and negative in the aging experience until we experience it ourselves, it means we open our minds to frame helpful, imaginative questions that help our clients tell us what it is about.

We gain, I believe, by examining our own particular stance towards age—our definitions, biases, prejudices, our denials and fears of death, our emotional reactions, our beliefs or disbeliefs about the degree of creative potential available in the final years of life. This means that we need to probe the contemporary and historical images planted by the media, literature, medical models, depictions of death and dying, and family ideologies. There are a lot of cruel, harsh stereotypes out there.

Finally, I believe that we gain therapeutic sensitivity by taking a hard look at our own disgusts at and aversions to the aging body—to wrinkles and age spots, to sagging muscles and curving backs, to the faltering step and the shaking voice. By doing this we face again our own prejudices and automatic responses; it is to be hoped that we will come to a perspective that can bypass the degeneration of the body to the regeneration of the human spirit.

Throughout this book I turn to older people for their stories and commentaries as I include readings, conversations, observations, and participations from a variety of sources and a variety of places—everything from casual conversations in a corner restaurant or at a dance in an RV park, to autobiographical materials, to concerns of clients, to letters to the editors in such magazines as *Modern Maturity* and *New Choices*. In doing this I want to correct an all too common tendency of all of us to neglect the stories of older people, to forget to study "old people as people"—a theme so simple, yet so surprising to some, that anthropologist Jennie Keith (1982) has centered her research and writing upon it.

The first section of this book explores current happenings, perspectives, definitions, and attitudes that form a theoretical foundation for the considerations of creative aging. This includes reflection on the dialectics of aging, the naming of theories of the "salutogenic" and the creative, consideration of the meanings of meaning-making and developmental process, and finally, articulation of my therapeutic approach in working with the questions of aging. In this articulation I will summarize the cognitive, developmental "meaning-making therapy" that I have developed fully in *Meaning-Making* (1988).

The second section assembles some of the cognitive patternings and conditions that can interrupt creative thinking, distort perceptions of human possibility and growth, and seriously negate the individuality of the aging person. Here are contributors to the erosion of the human spirit, of self-esteem, of the continuities of the self. Here are the structurings of ageism and defeatism, of the negation of pupose and meaning for the closing years of life.

Section III offers an eclectic gathering of therapies chosen to facilitate creative process, the "turnings to take next" in midlife, the narrative processes which help us tell our story, and finally, the meaning-making challenges associated with death, dying, and the loss of self.

In the fourth and last section I seat a select group of older people at the conference table. These wise people share their discoveries about aging as they give us a set of insights into how they are grappling with their personal edicts of time and age. Here are lessons, examples of that which can be called "therapeutic." Modeling these may be individuals continuing the same work that they did earlier: writers still writing (and hoping that the next book will be the best); artists still painting, sculpting, and working their clay; and small business owners appearing in their offices to continue running the show. But then there are the many models of kinds of living seldom if ever seen before. Here, for example, are the RV people creating their worlds of activity and community; the lifelong learners out beating the bounds; the volunteers and social activists demonstrating Erik Erikson's concept of care—people who are working on behalf of minorities, of environmental concerns, of other older people, of children in search of nurture and love. Some of these people have a great deal to teach us, and their wisdom and learning will be offered as models of outlook, attitude, and behavior in the business of constructive aging.

Throughout these four sections I continue to address the concerns of the therapist and to introduce examples of therapeutic activity with older people. I also maintain my dialectical perspective so as to reinforce my thesis that a major task of the therapist working with creative aging is to continue actively his or her own dialogue with aging.

SECTION I

Perspectives on Aging

Far from being a disease, normal human aging may simply be nature's way of telling a person to slow down and smell the roses, appreciate the wonder of life, and bequeath to younger generations a legacy of maturity. Old age is also a time for new fulfillments, particularly involving the use and sharing of knowledge and experience that has accumulated over a lifetime.

—Baltimore Study, 1989, p. 43

We are much too much inclined in these days to divide people into permanent categories, forgetting that a category only exists for its special purposes and must be forgotten as soon as that purpose is served.

—Dorothy Sayers, 1938, p. 33

CHAPTER 1

Perspectives on Aging

AN EMERGING CHALLENGE for the helping professional comes in the interaction with what is happening to older people in our country. These seniors are growing in numbers and in proportion. At the same time they are becoming better educated and more aware, healthier, more active and vocal, as they name and proclaim their needs. These people are "pioneers in a new prime of life" (Donahue et al., 1958), the ones who are not going to stand for the "kind of nonsense" that older people had to contend with just a few years ago (Eisdorfer, 1974, p. 67).

Living a quiet revolution, many of these older people are bypassing the contemporary negative expectation of what aging is about. They are altering normative portraits as they actively model new ways to grow older: in the formation of communities, in the experiences of being mentors and teachers, in entrepreneurial ventures to meet the needs of other older people, in activism and volunteering—in all the ways that show that many older people are not willing to adopt paths of least resistance in dealing with the challenges of life.

Comparative statistics from the AARP booklet, A *Profile of Older Americans* (1988), show how dramatically the demographics of aging have changed since the turn of the century:

Since 1900, the percentage of Americans 65+ has tripled (4.1% in 1900 to 12.3% in 1987), and the number increased over nine times (from 3.1 million to 29.8 million).

By the year 2000, persons 65+ are expected to represent 13.0% of the population, and this percentage may climb to 21.8% by 2030.

The most rapid increase in the older population is expected between the years 2010 and 2030 when the "baby boom" generation reaches age 65.

Robert Butler calls this the "Age of Aging," writing that it is the "first century in which a human being can be expected more often than otherwise to live out what we presently think of as the life course. It is the first period in history when any child can expect to attain old age" (Butler & Gleason, 1985, p. 1). This phenomenon is occurring not only in the First and Second Worlds, but in Third World countries as well. In its forward thrust it is already altering the worlds of advertising and marketing, of housing and recreation, of health care services and systems, and now, in new and important ways, it is changing the helping professions across a range of disciplines and specialties in medicine, psychology, and social work.

This is where the concept of creative aging comes in — we as helping professionals are being asked to foster, encourage, and reinforce creative outlooks, activities, and attitudes not only in our older clients and patients, but in ourselves. If we are to do more than perpetuate the negative equations that make aging equal disease, uselessness, and hopeless passivity, we need to take a hard look at our definitions of the aging person. We also need to learn from older people at the same time we weigh our definitions and interpretations of what aging is about — all this to avoid naive and presumptuous intervention in the name of therapy for the "old."

To open our definitions of aging to broader conceptualization is to open our eyes to the self as active meaning-maker. It is to know the self as vitally involved in "interpreting, managing, rationalizing, readjusting, copying, and planning new modes of action" (Breytspraak, 1983, p. 149), a self continually organizing and ordering its meanings. Here is the person, the manipulator of experience, the intervenor working to influence, negotiate, and manage the business of life, the person who is a self searching for some sort of continuity to unite the very beginnings of life with its very endings.

And we are those selves building a life. In my preface and introduction I have already pondered this mind-boggling dual position, which makes our work with aging our work with ourselves. I continually remind myself of this even as I find my mind fighting the neat little classifications that all too easily push older people off into little corners by themselves. I find the dual perspective a most interesting cognitive challenge—to keep perspectives clear, emotions and stereotypes untangled. At the same time I keep reminding myself that "only by first knowing how the elderly view themselves, their lives, and the nature of old age can we hope to fashion a meaningful present and future for them and for those who follow" (Kaufman, 1987, p. 4).

A dual perspective honors the expertise of older professionals and draws them into the therapeutic action in the business of aging. They have unique opportunities not only to share insights born of growing older, but to serve as practicing therapists and researchers. Highlighting these contrasts, Joan and Erik Erikson name the dual role that older persons can serve, especially those, like themselves, who have achieved old age while remaining actively involved in the study of human development. At a conference on the humanities and aging they observed: "We were the seniors in the senior group and thus, in a discussion on aging, were not only participant observers but also participants under observation" (1978, p. 1). With a touch of irony they asked, "Is it too personal to assume that in this function we represent not only our professional concern with the 'elderly,' but also this newly discovered human subspecies itself?" (p. 2).

It is to this "newly discovered human subspecies"—these "pioneers in a new prime of life" that we are addressing ourselves. Counselor/educator C. Gilbert Wrenn, speaking from within his own aging, writes:

It's about time! Some of us on the older side have been wondering when counselors, and before that, counselor educators, would realize that we are a significant and rapidly growing segment of this country's population. We are significant in terms of numbers and significant in terms of unique psychological needs and unique potentials for further contribution to our society. Recognition has begun. . . . (1989, p. 9)

Let us hope that the recognition has *indeed* begun.

DEFINITIONS OF AGING

"Definitions are tools, often weapons, not truths" say Achenbaum and Levin (1989, p. 395), a conclusion that seems to be illustrated by current struggles with the labels of age. This welter of language demands a continual sorting of our terminologies, lest we lock older people into simplistic labels and broadly encompassing categories, thereby losing the uniqueness of the person. Dorothy Sayers' words at the beginning of this chapter were written in protest of sexist language and classification, but are indeed pertinent to the matters of age.

But who, what, and when is an older person? This is not an easy question to answer, for definitions become entangled with the rules and regulations of bureaucratic structure and perspective. Just consider this set of definitions, for example:

The World Health Organization provided the following definitions: 45–59, middle-aged; 60–74, elderly; 75+, aged. The U.S. Administration on Aging, the federal agency which administers the Older Americans Act (OAA), defines "older" as age 60 and above, though a person under the age of 60 married to one over 60 is eligible to participate in OAA services with his or her spouse. The Social Security Administration refers to persons as "older" when they are 62, if they want "reduced retirement" benefits. Full retirement benefits may be received at the age of 65, or at any age when they acquire a disability. (Myers, 1989, p. 16)

In sharing this summary Jane Myers asks us to take note of the "not-so-subtle equation of 'aging' and 'disabled' [that] commonly occurs in the wording of federal legislation."

Warner Schaie categorizes three groups: (1) those in their 60s and early 70s who are most similar to persons in middle age, although many are no longer in the work force; (2) those in their late 70s and early 80s, a group which is "composed largely of people who still live in their communities, but it also contains an increasing proportion of individuals whose health and behavioral competence are beginning to fail"; (3) the "very-old," who are people in their late 80s and beyond. This group, says Schaie, "contains the largest proportion of frail and institutionalized elderly persons, many of whom fit the adverse stereotypes of old age even though a significant minority continue to function remarkably well" (1988, pp. 179–183).

In a letter to her colleagues in the American Psychological Association, developmental psychologist Marie Jahoda (who was in her 80s) rather threw up her hands in negative reaction at such finely delineated divisions. Whether we agree with her or not, there are real dangers that we will set up false definitions and false limitations in the name of chronological age.

As a person who has just recently entered her 60s I have found it jolting and perplexing to be handed the title of "senior" even when I feel just great and don't think I am any different from what I was a year ago. The peculiarities of labeling and definition plague me as well as other older people as they thrust us into arbitrary categories. And they certainly affect interactions with our own expectations as well as with those of others—not a welcome situation at all.

Certain of my gerontologist friends protest when someone is identified by age. But you will find me identifying individuals by age in this writing—not to put them into neat little slots of the "young-old, middle-old, old-old, and very old" but to acknowledge that we are in a remarkable historical period where older people are setting the stage for new possibility. As they experiment and explore their personal options they offer a massive research project whose results are not yet fully known.

I find it quite reassuring to know that an 83-year-old is learning to paint, or that a 100-year-old is living with relatively good health and retains an alert and probing mind. By naming chronological age I am able to orient myself to the problems unique to a child or an adolescent, to a middle-aged adult, a retiree, or to an aging politician, active beyond what we would normally expect of someone in his 80s (and the late Claude Pepper certainly comes to mind). To ignore the age variations in the later years of life would seem to foster a kind of reverse discrimination which says we should ignore some of the pertinent biographical information helpful in examining the stretching of the limits of life.

A point on which I do agree strongly is that simple categories don't fit the vast permutations of age. Simple categories can close perception. As Willing (1981) reminds us, "This is what Korzybski called elementalism, the habit of explaining complex things as resulting from single causes (whatever older people do, they do because they are old) and of reducing people to a single characteristic (older people are only old, they are nothing else)" (p. 171). As we sort, then, we sort with care.

FURTHER DELINEATIONS AND TITLES

What is to be emphasized is that each of us contains within us a number of agings. We can be at different levels of aging depending upon which process we look at, whether it be what James Birren has called our *senescing,* our *eldering,* or our *geronting. Senescing* is the biological dimension of our aging involving those processes that increase our vulnerability and our probabilities of dying. *Eldering* is the living out of social roles which have traditionally been age-graded, normative kinds of aging. *Geronting* is about our self-regulation—our choices, our meaning-makings, our interactions with others.

How we grow up and grow old is never an exclusive product of any single set of determinants. It is a consequence of our phylogenetic background, our unique individual heredity, the physical and social environments in which these genetic predispositions are expressed, and, for complex mammals like man, the effects of thinking and choice. (Birren & Cunningham, 1985, p. 8)

Like Birren and Cunningham, Neugarten has suggested that aging is not just aging: Aging occurs through meaning-making and reflection as the person sorts the inputs of life through the "inner eye of the mind." Aging has physical and psychological patterns affected by how we cope with life stresses and how we come to terms with demanding life situations. Aging can mean a pulling away from social interaction — yet at widely differing rates according to personal temperament, opportunity, and exposure to particular environments and interactions. By shaking loose our images and timetables of aging we gain a "richer context for understanding the changes in behavior and in self-assessments that occur as the individual moves through adulthood" (Neugarten, 1972b, p. 14).

Neugarten calls the older person a "translator and interpreter of experience, a person who creates a future and recreates a past." And, pertinent to the titles and assignments of age, she suggests that we reconsider and reintroduce the concept and title of "elder." In a conversation with Arthur Flemming on matters of public policy for older people she made this point:

I think we need to create a 20th-century version of the "elder." We often think that in the 20th century we don't have any place for the older person, that the "elder" disappeared when agricultural society disappeared. Can we create a society in which older people are once again a mainstay? (1983, p. 313)

In that spirit I share some humorous suggestions from a few of these "elders." These are responses sent to *Modern Maturity* after the editor made the whimsical suggestion that the word "elderly" be changed to "emeritan":

"Emeritan" — an excellent suggestion. . . . If you use it in your excellent publication and we readers do the same, it should be in general use in about five years.

Fie on "emeritan"! Here in Boston the word around town is "prime timer."

. . . and while we're on the subject, the "retired" in AARP is outmoded. Many of us are still working or actively involved in some enterprise and would rather belong to the American Association of Mature Persons.

Let's *not* find another word for "elderly." We are born, we are babies, we are children, we are men and women. We grow, we age, we are old. We live, we die. Let's not change any more good, honest words that say what they mean.

Just drop the word "citizen'" "senior" implies everything . . .

"Emeritan," sounds like a proprietary pharmaceutical, of which there are already far too many. (*Modern Maturity*, 1987, p. 7)

Within these responses I find deeper thoughts to consider: the variety of older persons, their differing perspectives and meanings, and the reality that they are people reading, reacting, and arguing points of view just like the rest of us. Consider this letter to *Modern Maturity* which protests their editorial emphasis:

Your magazine is beginning to depress the daylights out of me. Do you realize there are those of us in our 60s who smoke, drink, dance, exercise, golf, travel and work, who do NOT have diabetes, high cholesterol, high blood pressure or arthritis? I wish you'd lighten up your ads and articles and consider us. (August–September, 1988, p. 8)

Or consider the protest of editor Frances Lear in reading Ken Dychtwald's 1989 *Age Wave*. Although this book has been highly praised by many critics for its optimistic approach to the concerns of aging, Lear believes there is a danger of new stereotypes in the name of such optimism:

Not since *Megatrends* have we seen such commercial promise from a futurist's pen. Dychtwald's aging society is nifty indeed. We can expect romance till we drop, any work and leisure pattern that suits us. Smaller steps. Soft tubs. One can hardly wait to go gray. (1989, p. 168)

A reader echoes Lear's comments, "I, too, resent the trend to establish new stereotypes based on so-called statistics. Grouping by age or Zip Code robs each of us of our uniqueness."

These, then, are differing perspectives on aging from within the experiences of being older, perspectives that illustrate that older people are living, learning, and reacting in a variety of ways, just like the rest of us. They are not a separate and "exotic breed," writes anthropologist Jennie Keith, as she calls attention to the strange "psychological quirk" which cognitively places older people outside the pale of ordinary experience and understanding:

I am often asked the following rather querulous question: But isn't everything you're saying about old people just like students in dorms, or soldiers in camps, or anyone who's suffered a loss, and so on? Of course it is—which pleases me, but seems to annoy the audience. Our expectation that old people are different is so strong that it is annoying to be told, and difficult to believe, that they behave very much as other human beings under similar conditions and in similar cultural contexts. We don't need special "old-people theory" to understand what old people do and feel. We apparently do need a great deal of evidence to persuade ourselves that old people are people. . . . (1982, p. 2)

I reiterate, older people are simply living life as a "seamless whole" (and I credit Neugarten for offering and reinforcing this concept). They are unique and they are not. They represent the normal and the far from normal. They are persons living in a wide variety of neighborhoods, reacting to the news of the world, sorting the strange positions they find themselves in as older persons, grieving the losses that come with age.

They are more likely older versions of what they have been in earlier, younger years: The person who has never learned to think clearly is going to be the person in old age who does not gather new ideas or stimulation to keep the mind alive and growing. The person who forgets names at age 35 is going to continue to forget names when he is 65. The person who enjoys learning at 45 will no doubt continue to learn. If vision should fail there are talking books and electronic devices to fill the gap.

There are various agings, then, which makes us realize we are not talking about AGING; we are talking about "aging1," "aging2," "aging3," ... ad infinitum. Whichever aging we might describe, these forms of growing older come in as many sizes and flavors as there are persons. These agings come within our bodies, in our minds, between ourselves and others, and in culturally defined patterns. And these agings come within all the differing ways we have of making meaning, of creating sense, of shaping and determining personal significance, of sorting that which we believe to be true.

VARIATIONS ON THE THEME OF AGING

Gerontologist Robert Atchley writes of researchers who "focus on sickness, poverty, isolation, and demoralization. The theories they develop seek to explain how people arrive at such an unhappy state. And they tend to see aging as a social problem" (Atchley, 1983). But, then, he adds, there are other researchers who pay attention to the positive. "They look at the elderly and see that most have good health, frequent contact with family members, adequate incomes, and a high degree of satisfaction with life. The theories they develop try to explain how aging can have such positive outcomes. They see the social problems of aging as applying to only a minority of the elderly" (1983, p. 10). Which is to say, we can look at aging from differing angles, and unless we keep the broader perspective we may lock into one side to the neglect of the other.

Age *is* a complex mix. And there are as many opinions and reactions as there are individuals. Take, for example, the words of psychologist Eda LeShan, who doesn't mince any words in stating her position:

There is nothing wonderful about getting old ... old age is the time when we begin to understand that we each have a terminal disease. Aging forces us to face mortality as we have never faced it before. ... I worry about being sick and dependent; I agonize most of all over the possibility of becoming widowed. It frustrates the hell out of me that things I did easily ten years ago—bicycling, gardening, walking ten miles—are now painful, exhausting; the subject depresses me; it makes me feel agitated. ... Everything about it shocks me. (1986, pp. 4-5)

Not many of us state our feelings so clearly!

And then there are the words of composer David Diamond, who writes of "Dark Years and Difficult Questions" in Phillip Berman's remarkable collection of essays, *The Courage to Grow Old* (1989):

I have come to approach the last years of my life with an attitude of irony and pity, for to me, there is no dignity in growing old. We are born, we mature. We feel sadness and happiness. We praise and we mourn. We age, sicken, and die. Is that worth a lifetime on earth? (Berman, 1989, p. 85)

Is it not easy to criticize those who voice their despair? To turn our backs as we search for nuggets of hope and alternatives to the darker sides of our last years? I think so. Isn't this our dilemma? Which way to look, what to believe, what to hope for?

Certainly, the manifestations of the negative are there to be seen in the lives of the many disadvantaged older persons who have economic, physical, social, and psychological dependencies. "Unfortunately," writes James Birren, "this population, already in the millions, seems destined to grow and will require attention from many professions, including psychology" (1983, p. 298). In this population are those older persons who are disabled physically and/or mentally, who face aging either alone or with sick partners, who have inadequate funds, and who face the dilemmas of complex, confusing bureaucratic structures, and the experiences of dealing with a health industry that is increasingly expensive and all too often unresponsive to their needs.

And then there are women who must face the gender prejudices that all too often compound the problems of ageism. Robert Kastenbaum sees the older woman as an all too common victim of a "definite bias in favor of males in most of the cultural traditions that flow into our own" (1979). Frequently poor and alone, without shared advocacy to help her fight battles for housing, financial security, health benefits, or personal respect and acknowledgment, the older woman often becomes entangled with health problems unique to women: osteoporosis, breast disease, particular forms of heart disease, and hypertension (Older Women's League, 1987). These discriminations and complications further show up in "disturbing evidence of gender-based distinctions in the way that medical personnel treat older women. Studies show that doctors often bring preconceptions to their treatment of these patients . . . when treating older women, doctors take less time with their patients, give less full explanations, and prescribe drugs more often" (Older Women's League, 1987, p. 2). To undo such misinterpretation and neglect the aging woman "still requires a special advocacy beyond a basic commitment to gerontology and geriatrics" (Kastenbaum, 1979, pp. 70–71).

Addressing this need for a special advocacy for older women, Robert

Butler has called for a "close alliance with the women's movement, especially emphasizing the powerful twin facts of the feminization of aging and the feminization of poverty" (Butler & Gleason, 1985, p. 10). To further the exploration of this concern, Butler drafted Betty Friedan to the cause of ageism, asking her to use her unique understanding of sexism to study the problems of "the mystique of age." Butler stated the problem this way: "The policies and the research on aging in America are formulated mostly by men, based on the lives of men and the experience of men, but most of the aged are women" (Friedan, 1985, p. 40). But what really caught Friedan's attention—what, in her words, started her "Geiger counter" clicking—was the question, "Why were men dying so young?" Betty Friedan joined the search into the problems of ageism not to work only on the concerns of women, but *because she was also concerned about men*:

It had become clear that there was an enormous discrepancy between the life expectancy of women and men, and it was getting worse and worse. I had also begun to wonder how far women could go just by themselves. A lot of these vibrant women were complaining that there were no men. Men seemed to be stuck in dreary routines. They were tired, rigid, uptight, threatened, and, if they were my age, they often were dead. Something must be seriously wrong with the role of men. If menopause was no longer traumatic for women, why were there now all these new traumas of the male midlife crisis? Why were men dying so young? (Friedan, 1985, p. 41)

So here we have to be careful about what we are saying. Although Butler summoned Friedan, a feminist, to the concerns of aging, and although our researchers above have named many of the difficulties of older women, we come back around to the concerns of *both* men and women in the business of old age. The search for new understandings of the intertwinings of age and gender combine with all the other intertwinings of the negatives and positives. What I gain from studying all this is to appreciate even more our search for finer and finer distinctions in the study of old age.

THE POSITIVE AND THE NEGATIVE — A DELICATE BALANCE

Our perspectives on aging can be couched in black or gray, or we can turn in another direction toward some clearly stated positives that are affirmed by a number of current studies. Three of these studies have been summarized by James Birren (1983), who concludes that the "quality of life for most older adults is far from bad."

The first study is one by J.D. Flanagan who explored the lives of three cohorts of subjects, ages 30, 50, and 70, with 1,000 individuals in each cohort. The results of this study showed that three factors were particularly important in maintaining quality of life: (1) what might be called the "bread and butter" issues of life—material comforts, work, and health; (2) "intimacy, the existence of close friends and opportunities for socializing;" and (3) ongoing opportunity to exercise cognitive capacities and creative expression. Birren reports that the majority of those people who were studied reported that their lives were "good, very good, or excellent." And this included the oldest group. Birren closes his summary of Flanagan's study by emphasizing psychology's important role in helping older people meet their vital needs (Birren, 1983, p. 298; Flanagan, 1978, pp. 138–147).

Birren then cited a 1975 Harris survey that showed that problems of loneliness and dreary lives are not unique to old age but are a problem for certain percentages of every age group. Indeed, these percentages do not differ significantly when categorized by age. To illustrate: This survey "showed that the proportion of those over 65 who said they had no close person to talk to was 8%, whereas for those under 65 it was 5%. This slight increase in loneliness is hardly justification for assuming that the average older adult is lonely" (Harris, 1975).

The third study that Birren cited was a 1981 Harris poll that showed that "poor health was a serious problem for 8% of the individuals age 18–54, 16% of those age 55–64, and 21% of those over 65." Again, although the figures show differences, they are not large differences; they indicate that at every period of life a certain proportion of the population will be afflicted with some kind of disability or illness.

The more complex problem in the processes of aging is that low income, poor health, and limited education seem to go together—a reality that becomes an important challenge for cultural rearrangements in the matter of public policy. Psychology has shown evidence of paying increased attention to these public policy issues. Take note of the March 1983 *American Psychologist*, for example. In a lead article, Birren stated that this was the first time the *American Psychologist* had focused on aging as a policy concern. In that article, he called for psychologists to become informed about these matters—about the "'bread and butter' issues of money, health insurance and health care" (p. 298). But, in acknowledging the concerns of the needy adult, he also asked that psychologists raise their sights to what is possible for the older population. "Above all, we must recognize that this growing population in the future is going to be increasingly well educated and will increasingly demand options for working or retiring, options for volunteering, and options for personal growth" (p. 299).

What is needed is a clearer definition of what health means and of how it can be facilitated. This challenge is a guiding impetus for much speculation, research, and application, at the present time. A proliferation of new materials and programs are daring us all to look at aging with fresh perspectives. With the decade of the '90s well under way, many professional organizations are making health and wellness central themes for their conferences. For example, the 1991 annual meeting of the American Society on Aging (New Orleans, Louisiana) was organized under the banner of "A Good Old Age," and offered pre-conference workshops on health care, housing challenges and choices, spiritual journeys in aging, and business and aging. Another professional convention—the 1991 annual meeting of the American Association for Counseling and Development (Reno, Nevada)—took as its theme, "Wellness Throughout the Lifespan." Content sessions focused on a wide range of wellness topics organized within categories of the emotional, intellectual, social, occupational, physical, and spiritual. How refreshing it is to see case studies in health taking their place alongside case studies in pathology!

A SALUTOGENIC PERSPECTIVE

In all this excitement it remains important to look for research that anchors hopes and speculations in carefully developed studies. A contemporary researcher who emphasizes this care is Aaron Antonovsky whose books, *Health, Stress, and Coping* (1979) and *Unraveling the Mystery of Health* (1988), reveal a story of his search for understandings of health. In his first book he developed the concept of *generalized resistance resources* (GRRs)—money, ego strength, cultural stability, social supports, and the like—that he defines as "any phenomenon that is effective in combating a wide variety of stressors" (1988, p. xii). But this was not enough, he discovered. There had to be some "culling rule" that would help understand why certain factors contributed to the ability to handle stress. The answer for Antonovsky came in his concept of a *sense of coherence* (SOC): "a global orientation that expresses the extent to which one has a pervasive, enduring though dynamic, feeling of confidence that one's internal and external environments are predictable and that there is a high probability that things will work out as well as can reasonably be expected" (1979, p. 123). As Antonovsky's research has further evolved, he has widened the definitions of SOC to include the three core components of comprehensibility, manageability, and meaningfulness. That last, of course, is a central theme in my own writings on meaning-making.

In using the terminology of a "sense of coherence," Antonovsky is very specific and very careful. He is not describing a simplistic sense of "I'm in control," but rather, a sense of meaningfulness about the situation one is in and the direction one is going. This meaningfulness contains a belief that the situation is understandable and will indeed "work out as well as can reasonably be expected." The sense of coherence constitutes a "generalized, long-lasting way of seeing the world and one's life in it. It is perceptual, with both cognitive and affective components." Not only does the person orient towards meaningful stimuli with a conviction that the inputs of life will continue to be meaningful, he or she also has a level of confidence that "the stimuli one sends will be received without undue distortion" (p. 126).

To maintain a sense of coherence — to be received and seen "without undue distortion," to have some influence in the comprehensibility, manageability, and meaningfulness of one's order of things — certainly has powerful meaning in our dealings with dependent older people. If they have to turn over their control to a caretaker or to an institution, their sense of coherence can be encouraged by allowing them to participate in the ordering of things, by respecting them as individuals, and by including them as worthy participants in decision-making (Langer and Rodin's studies on control and "mindfulness" are highly pertinent here).

Another of Antonovsky's ideas is particularly helpful: In contrast to a dichotomous perspective of sickness vs. health, Antonovsky suggests a "health ease/dis-ease continuum." Thus, rather than viewing the person as either sick or well, this orientation suggests an image of moving the individual along a continuum towards a pole of health (1988, p. 4). This image of the continuum makes the salutogenic approach both process and dialectic. To interpret stressor events through this theoretical perspective takes them beyond the quantitative listings of the Holmes and Rahe stress scale (1967). Rather than treating a stressor event as adding to a cumulative total, a stressor is placed against the backdrop of the meanings and coherence of the individual person, of individual capacities to deal with stress. This enlarged interpretation of stressor events fits Lazarus and DeLongis' thesis that "we must abandon the simplistic notion that stress is adequately described by life events, however psychometrically sophisticated, and that it is sufficient to treat coping as a stable, overarching style with which people address the myriad sources of stress in their lives" (1983, pp. 245–254).

Antonovsky's perspective incorporates Hans Selye's idea of "good stress" or "eustress," which we all need if our lives are to include excitement, stimulation, and dynamic interactions within the happenings of life. This is the kind of stress that stimulates us, energizes us, and awakens us. When we try to avoid stress, when we settle into a peaceful, laid-back, waiting kind of existence, we may actually be adopting a lifestyle antithetical to the kinds of vital, involved agings that we are naming here. The challenge is to reinforce and support involved participation in the evolving dramas of one's life, the invested activity in the processes shaping one's destiny as well as one's daily experience — in the movements along a continuum towards health.

I close this discussion with a colorful metaphor that Antonovsky uses to convey the flavor of the salutogenic image of life and to counter what he calls "the bias of the downstream focus." Reminding us that it is all too easy to blame those who get sick as somehow failing—what I call the flunking of "Aging 101"—he challenges us to see the interactions between the many variables that affect our place along the "health ease/dis-ease continuum."

Contemporary Western medicine is likened to a well-organized, heroic, and technologically sophisticated effort to pull drowning people out of a raging river. Devotedly engaged in this task, often quite well rewarded, the establishment members never raise their eyes or minds to inquire upstream, around the bend in the river, about who or what is pushing all these people in. . . . [A new school of thought might inadvertently tend] to assume that people are jumping into the river of their own volition and refusing to learn to swim. . . . My work has been devoted to confronting the question: "Wherever one is in the stream—whose nature is determined by historical, social-cultural, and physical environmental conditions—what shapes one's ability to swim well?" (1988, pp. 89–90)

BUT WHAT SHAPES ONE'S ABILITY TO SWIM WELL?

Part of the experience of "swimming in one's own river" is facing the many forces outside of oneself: neighborhoods, relationships, culture and history, stereotypes and prejudice, economic conditions, job opportunity, living arrangements. Then, of course, there are all those other matters, such as genetics, accidents, and patterns of health and decline in the history of one's family. The fruit that one is handed from the family tree is not always good for one's health. But one has some choices in how one processes that fruit.

Consider here the aging of those people who come out of the late 1800s and early 1900s. These are the people who survived in an era when life expectancy was 45 years and only 10% of the population was middle-aged (Desmond, in Vedder, 1965). These folks grew up through major world wars, through the Depression, through an era of enormous changes in science and technology as well as in social customs and contexts. These people also lived within a population of people who were less educated, less introspective, less psychologically aware, whose needs were more frequently on a survival level than a self-actualizing, self-enriching level.

I was alerted to the qualities of this generation when I gave a retirement workshop to a group of retired music educators. Though I had a few ideas to share with them I ended up being the one who learned from a group of older, wiser folks. One thing they declared strongly and proudly was that they were "survivors"—survivors of the years of hardship and self-discipline which were a part of the Depression experience.

They felt that this very experience and all the learning that it had brought were helping them to grow older more effectively as they genuinely appreciated all that they had. (Whether other members of their cohort feel this way is another question. It is the interaction between their history and their attitudes—the choice for a positive story vis-à-vis a negative story—which is of significance here.)

In contrast to these survivors of the two World Wars and the Depression era, contemporary middle-aged adults grow up in a totally different world with entirely different dilemmas to be resolved—dilemmas of drugs and nuclear weapons, of attitudes and values that reflect an increasing dominance by philosophies of the "bottom line" and of a market economy. These aging populations will not be the survivors of a Depression; they will be survivors of a society that is increasingly complex, that has a high incidence of divorce and separation, that highlights its technology, that is ruled by a philosophy of dominance (see Eisler, 1987, for thoughts on this), and that is not noted for tempering its needs for instant gratification.

In conclusions drawn from his research studies, Martin Seligman believes that people in their mid-40s (and younger) are experiencing more depression than former generations at this age. He theorizes that the "sharp rise in depression since World War II is largely the result of the 'waxing of the individual and the waning of the commons'. . . . In other words, more people have suffered depression—the loss of hope and faith—as a result of an exalted sense of commitment to the self and a concurrent decline in commitment to religion, family, the nation and community. Traditional institutions, Seligman said, despite their demands of conformity, buffered people when they failed, and kept them from sinking into despair" (Buie, 1988, p. 18).

In my search for those human qualities that can heighten effective, creative living, I have found Lawrence Al Siebert's profile of the "survivor personality" and John A.B. McLeish's descriptive formulation of the "Ulyssean Adult" particularly helpful. Here I share Siebert's model and introduce ideas from McLeish as we move through future discussions.

THE SURVIVOR PERSONALITY

During the early 1950s Siebert trained as a paratrooper with a unit which had been trapped and practically wiped out during the Korean War. In spite of the hell that these combat veterans had been through, they demonstrated qualities suggesting they had survived not because of fate or luck but because that they had particular attitudes and attributes that coalesced into a style of handling life and its crises. These soldiers started Siebert on his study of life's best survivors. In his search

Siebert discovered a "small fraction of individuals made stronger by extreme circumstances and torturous conditions" — in other words, people who have been able to work through crisis in a constructive fashion. In looking back over their crisis experience, these people showed:

- They had surmounted the crisis through personal effort.
- They emerged from the experience with previously unknown strengths and abilities.
- In retrospect, they found value in their experience.

These individuals don't have simple personality profiles. Rather, they carry *repertoires* of personal traits that are biphasic and paradoxical — traits that don't fit into neatly arranged psychological categories. They combine such personality "opposites" as seriousness and playfulness, self-confidence and self-criticism, diligence and laziness, introversion and extraversion, thus contradicting thinking in psychology which conceptualizes personality traits as unidimensional. According to Siebert (1983), this paradoxical mix is the most prominent characteristic of survivors, for it enables them to adapt to a wide spectrum of situations.

Consolidating his findings from over 30 years of careful study, Siebert has constructed the following set of guidelines for handling life pressures, adversity, and change (and what a great list this is for creative aging!):

1. Be curious, ask questions, laugh, and play.
2. Develop self-confidence, self-esteem, and professional pride.
3. Value being paradoxical.
4. Develop intuition.
5. Practice empathy.
6. Become increasingly synergistic.
7. Defend one's self well.
8. Acquire a talent for serendipity.

The outcomes of all this? The ability to:

Read reality rapidly. Become increasingly life competent. Get better and better — more humorous, resilient, durable, playful, and free. Constantly "grow," adapt, evolve, and transform. Heal and recover better. Spend less time surviving than others and survive major adversity better. Enjoy life more. Develop high level psychological fitness.

Siebert agrees that creative aging overlaps with the survivor personality but cautions that if all these traits are included "you've also reduced your description down to a very small percent of the population" (personal communication, 1990). This can either discourage us or challenge us to enter people's lives much sooner — in childhood, if possible — to teach them the skills to field life's "curve balls" as effectively as possible.

STIMULATING WELLNESS

Incorporating methods and orientations complementary to a meaning-making, salutogenic perspective, a variety of "wellness" programs are turning their sights to problems and process in human immune systems. As they do this they are sorting disease and disuse processes from those of normal aging. Combining the psychological and the physiological, acknowledging the spiritual, this growing field of psychoimmunology is actively exploring methods of helping older adults adopt more healthful habits for living. For example, in the combined medical programs of San Francisco State University and Pacific Presbyterian Medical Center, older people are being drawn into programs of health evaluation and self-management that encourage physical, emotional, and spiritual fitness. At the same time, the training curricula are encouraging medical students to "think interdisciplinary" as they are allowed to explore both traditional and nontraditional approaches to health and healing. These explorations can include everything from psychic healing to holistic medicines that emphasize biofeedback, autogenic training, and meditation. While students are given the opportunity to open their minds to healing possibility, no value judgments are being placed on their explorations (Schmidt, 1989).

A number of other programs have been set in motion to educate older people about health practices that can reduce risks of disabling illness and increase their prospects for more productive, active lives. The Office of Disease Prevention and Health Promotion of the U.S. Public Health Service is sponsoring a "Healthy Older People Program." In an informational bulletin they state that their purpose is to encourage "older adults to improve their health by eating right, exercising regularly, using medicines safely, giving up smoking, and preventing injuries."

Then there are the innovative "Healthwise" programs in Boise, Idaho. Healthwise is a "nonprofit organization dedicated to helping people succeed in making positive health changes." Medical self-care workshops, videotapes, and other instructional aids encourage physical and mental wellness. Under the leadership of Donald W. Kemper, Molly Mettler, and other staff members, this very active program is modeling what can be done in stimulating the optimism and involved participation of older people in their own wellness programs.

The emerging emphasis on wellness and psychoimmunology offers excitement in the field of aging just because it *does* draw in the older person to work actively on his or her own behalf, just as it *does* join the psychological, the emotional, and the spiritual with the biological. Such collaboration gives hope for further fruitful interactions between basic and applied science, between experimental and ecological, anthropological approaches, between the scientist in the laboratory and the therapist in his or her office, between the person who is older and the person who is younger—all as we sort the amazing developments in this new prime of life.

And this indeed is how creativity works: through a motivated, purposeful, acting *self* using imagination, reason and the astonishing human ability to put experience into words.

—Frank Barron, 1988, p. 78

. . . the ageless self maintains continuity through a symbolic, creative process . . . its definition is ongoing, continuous and creative.

—Sharon Kaufman, 1987, p. 14

Attack old age as a problem to be solved. Take all possible steps to increase the chances that you will enjoy it. We even venture to suggest that the steps you take can be among the things you enjoy. Instead of complaining of the sere, the yellow leaf, you can enjoy the autumn foliage. Instead of learning to bear the taste of bitter fruit, you can squeeze that last sweet drop of juice from the orange.

—B.F. Skinner and M.E. Vaughan, 1983, p. 20

CHAPTER 2

Creativity and Aging

AS I STUDY THE CONCERNS of aging I sometimes think it would be quite easy to abandon a concept of *creative aging*—especially when facing the dilemmas of ageism, poverty, disease, and negative cultural attitudes. When I visit a nursing home where so many people sit slouched in attitudes of despair, where vacant stares and aimless motions are often the rule, I wonder if this idea of creative aging is a cruel illusion to offer those who are growing older. And then, when I am told by a noted psychologist, who is himself growing older, that the predominant moods of older persons in his retirement park are "discouragement, lassitude, and lack of purpose," I wonder even further how principles of creative aging can jar loose such negative outcomes.

But then I read the words of Silvano Arieti, whose research demonstrates that creativity can "occur at any age, even the most advanced, and seems to have a salutary effect on the creative person." Further, "memory impairment does not seem to be prominent in creative people who reach a very advanced age; or if it exists, it is easily compensated

29

for by a broader vision of life and easy associative powers" (1976, p. 383). Creativity, in the eyes of Arieti, is both a possibility and a healing potential for people of every age, and thus, in answer to my concerns and wonderings, available as a resource when people become old.

I find my own evidence of this, doing a bit of a double take, as I go into the activities room of a well-run retirement home. Here is a small group of people, in their 70s, 80s, and 90s, deeply engaged in a class discussion on "A Search for Meaning." Guided by a sophisticated teacher, using a well-written source book, it is not long before these people are in active dialogue using ideas from Sartre and Camus. I am stimulated by the creativity of their questions and their thinking (and catch myself when I realize my double take is evidence of some deeply internalized stereotypes). I grab hold of the wisdom of the distinguished older man who ponders self-discovery and self-creation. And I smile in appreciation as the woman next to me leans over to tell me rather proudly, "He is 94 years old," as if to confirm her own hopes for old age.

As I look around, I see people sitting in what looks like apathetic postures who spring to life with the introduction of a new idea. On the outside they are models of varying stages of physical decline, but their attitudes and outlooks give evidence of curiosity, an openness to ideas and questionings, and a certain "mindfulness," which both Bonnie Strickland and Ellen Langer have identified as an important ingredient in creativity.

But even as these people demonstrate creativity they also give evidence that it isn't all so easy. One woman in this class reports the death of her husband during the past week. Another woman tells the story of her entrance into this home when surgery made it necessary for her to retire from her job. At that time, she says, she lost one of her major reasons for living when she was no longer able to work with little children. But, then, illustrating the capacity of the human spirit to recreate itself in the middle of difficult circumstances, she tells of her discovery of new meaning in the satisfactions and enjoyments of friendship and of opportunities to help those worse off than herself.

Not only is there evidence here of creativity in action, but there is also an illustration of a principle I learned a number of years ago.

IS THERE ANYTHING NEW UNDER THE SUN?

My philosophy professor once asked, "Is there anything new under the sun?" After much consideration of this intriguing and somewhat troubling question, my class came to the following conclusion: "No, there is nothing new under the sun, but there are infinite themes and variations of that which is under the sun." That simple statement has enriched my thinking about meaning-making, and it enters now to interact with thoughts and wonderings about creative aging.

I go to music for illustration of these principles: Music, in all of its potential combinations of symphony, rock, and minimalism, is a mix of notes within scales, sounds within a large variety of timbres, rhythmic patterns within all levels of complexity from Western music's straightforward 4/4 to a Bulgarian pattern of 11/8. All these interesting and varying ingredients—elements of the "somethings under the sun"—can combine and recombine in an infinite number of ways (making it extremely unlikely that composers will ever run out of ideas and combinations).

In like manner, consider the person. What about all the unique human combinations within the universals of life and destiny? Here are the givens that are combined and recombined at differing periods of life. Here are the evolutions of the self: the shifting recipes of attitude, opportunity, and purpose; the shifting mixtures of talent and possibility; the shifting combinations of the ongoing, the continuous, and the creative.

We are those creative meaning-makers. Managing and rearranging our personal ingredients in the tellings and enactments of our personal stories, we are constantly mixing and matching the particulars of our storyline. We compose and perform our stories within the dramas of the ordinary: in the choosing of a partner, in discovering a place to live, in grappling with health problems and genetic limitation, in arguing with a spouse, in determining what activities will go into a day. To make our meaning is to sort purposes, feelings, and physical reactions in choosing whether to stay in bed or to run seven miles before breakfast. It is to decide whether to retire at 65 or to build an entirely new career at 67. Or, in a more encompassing manner, to search for an organizing principle for life which enables us to find purpose and significance in our many various acts—all the way from the simplest act of viewing a sunset to the drama of joining a Peace Corps program in Africa.

This creativity of meaning-making is a handling and a manipulating of the varying crisis experiences that life can throw our way. In crisis, life is shaken as systems of belief and activity are interrupted and challenged. The Chinese had it right when they called crisis a mix of "danger and opportunity." But what we do with this danger and opportunity i. up to us. (Erik Erikson has suggested that crisis is a major turning point when we can lock into our current trouble or when we can set in motion new programs of growth and development.)

This brings me to a second principle of creativity: the idea that our freedoms are born of our limits, an idea which was seeded in my thinking when I read Rollo May's *Freedom and Destiny* (1981). (This idea complements Allen Wheelis' conclusion that the more we know we are determined, the less we are determined (1973).)

CREATIVITY: FREEDOM BORN OF LIMITS

John Brubacker, the professor I cited earlier, made a further contribution to my thinking when he talked of the unique qualities inherent within a block of wood, for example, or a piece of marble, qualities waiting to be set free by the artistry of the wood carver and the sculptor. He believed that in order for this to happen, the artist must respect the inherent limits and integrity of the material by allowing the essence to be revealed. It is a kind of dialogue between the creator and that which is being created. Paradoxically, the freedoms of the material are born of the limits of the material.

That is really what all creativity is about—a taking of the material at hand, the givens, the structures already present, the limitations of the raw materials, to make of them what you can. To do this requires discipline and perseverance, as well as a certain "courage to create" that allows for the confusions and the anxieties that go with creative process (May, 1975).

Creativity also involves searching and grappling, researching and learning, facing chaos in order to bring diverse elements into some kind of new whole. Such creative activity requires a willingness to risk, an openness to the experience itself, a recognition of patterns, the making of connections, the challenging of assumptions, the taking advantage of change, and the seeing of a new way (Barron, 1988, p. 78). These same outlooks, approaches, and processes can and must operate if creative aging is to be a part of life.

As we grapple with our limits we can come to appreciate just how much we are shaped by what May (1981) calls our "destiny." This isn't a lot of vague metaphysical stuff; this is our set of genes, our family heritage, our relationships, our physical condition, our temperament, our learnings, our place in history, our location and dynamics within a neighborhood, our jobs, our culture. Then there are the further "stuffs" of money and opportunity, of accident and decline. Again, there are life circumstances over which we may not have a lot of control, our raw material for our present and ever emerging "destiny."

There is a certain built-in unfairness here. It is part of the difficulty of life that we may not have what we would like to have to make our life as rich and fulfilling as possible. Some of my most difficult clients have been those who would not or could not accept certain givens in their lives, who raged against their systems, who shouted at me because I had more than they had. "Life is unfair," they cried. Until the day they could stare those givens in the face and acknowledge that "Once we truly know that life is difficult—once we truly understand and accept it—then life is no longer difficult" (Peck, 1978, p. 15), our therapy was in a stuck position. Only as these individuals came to terms with the dreams that would never come true, the hopes that would not be fulfilled, the fact of mortality that wouldn't go away, were they able to pick up the reins of their lives in a more creative fashion.

Eda LeShan has wryly commented that "life is what happens when you have other plans." The exigencies, the crises, the interruptions, the hurts and disappointments of aging are what happen to us when we have other plans. Some of us are going to have it easier than others. Some of us are going to have it harder than others. These are the inequalities of life that have absolutely nothing to do with democratic fairness.

Creative aging means continuing to work with the disappointments and limitations, the "curve balls" that life tosses our way. It means keeping our meanings as alive as possible even as our bodies lose their flexibility and stamina. It also means going beyond ourselves to see that our society and our governmental structures facilitate our freedoms within our limits. It certainly means, too, that we don't ignore the insensitivities of others, the prejudice, the unequal choices and distributions which make life more difficult for older people (and, ultimately, for ourselves).

But What, Exactly, Is Creativity?

Many of us are captured by the questions surrounding creativity: What is it? How does it work? What kinds of people are more likely to live and think creatively? What are the cognitive processes which are involved? And how does all this translate into the concepts and practices of creative aging?

Probably we can say there is no "exactly"—there simply is no such thing as a precise recipe for creativity. Yet, over and over, in the lives of artists, scientists, thinkers, and other creative people, certain processes repeat themselves. Here is a brief summary synthesized in a brochure for the traveling Chevron exhibit, "Creativity: The Human Resource":

1. Challenging assumptions in a "daring to question what most people take as truth."
2. Recognition and creation of patterns by "perceiving significant similarities or differences in ideas, events, or physical phenomena" (Silvano Arieti, 1976, calls this the "catching of similarity").
3. Seeing in new ways that take the commonplace and transform "the familiar to the strange, and the strange to the familiar."

4. Making new and unusual connections in "bringing together seemingly unrelated ideas, objects, or events in a way that leads to a new conception."
5. Taking risks in "daring to try new ways or ideas with no control over the outcome."
6. Seizing the chance to take "advantage of the unexpected."
7. Constructing networks to form "associations between people for an exchange of ideas, perceptions, questions, and encouragement." (Ideas and quotes from the brochure designed by the Burdick Group of San Francisco in 1980)

Here is the "destroying of one Gestalt [or system of making sense of the world] in favor of another" (Taylor, 1988, p. 119). Here is the quality of mind which transforms bits and pieces of knowledge into new patterns of meaning. Here are the transformational experiences of change, development, personal evolution. Here are abilities to go beyond old solutions, to transcend conventions, to step into the uncharted territories of new thought and idea. Certainly, here are demonstrations of human capacities to exploit possibilities—in materials, in situations, in people—with a sensitivity, independence, and personal strength, which enable the person "to deal with the complexity and disorder such sensitivity brings, able to choose, reject, organize" (Tyler, 1978, pp. 191, 194).

Creativity draws together human capabilities that are quite extraordinary. Artificial intelligence is sharpening our appreciations for these capabilities as it seeks to duplicate the processes of our minds. I, for one, find it rather reassuring that this study of mechanical process is leading us into the heart of human creativity. In the words of Henry Mishkoff: "People . . . instinctively do something that has been very difficult to program into a computer: we discover relationships between things, we sense qualities and spot patterns that explain how various items relate to each other" (1985, p. 13). Roger Schank writes that the essence of this creative patterning is found in two basic subprocesses: (1) a search process for an explanation of what is happening as the mind sorts its files—its memory bank of experience and understanding—for some sort of way to make meaning of the experience or the problem; and (2) an alteration process as the mind moves into gear to alter the explanation pattern, to create a new pattern of explanation and understanding.

All these amazing processes and expressions go into the building of our lives—into the product which is our unique creation. So, a life is there to create—in our careers, in our relationships, in our retirements, in our productions, in our buildings of self, in our personal style. The more we can open our minds to possibility, the more we are willing to free our beliefs for active questioning and reframing, the more we are able to play with ideas, the more we can keep a certain gullibility and naivete in opening ourselves to the world (Arieti, 1976), the more we can relax our rhythms to enter into this "sacred moment," the more we can open our eyes to mystery—the more we can incorporate into ourselves a style of living that can be called creative.

PSYCHOLOGY AND CREATIVITY

Increasingly, psychologists are paying more attention to the study of creativity, to the point that the *Annual Review of Psychology* (Barron & Harrington, 1981) included a ten-year review of psychological research into creativity. A fairly consistent, ongoing stream of research was illustrated in the wide range of topics: everything from research into the creativity of women to the kinds of applied creativities I am naming here. Increasingly, creativity is being seen as "central to all of psychology; it is general psychology, and it reaches out to philosophy, the arts and humanities, the natural sciences, and human affairs generally in its ramifications" (Barron, 1988).

In her 1988 presidential address to the American Psychological Society, Bonnie Strickland summarized findings linking states of mind to creative behaviors in living. From her presentation I have collected several research findings that name states of mind that either hinder or enhance creative attitudes and behaviors. These identified states of mind become goals for our creative therapies with older clients.

Strickland reports on Seligman's research into *explanatory styles.* Explanatory styles are the habitual ways in which individuals explain the occurrence of events, their experiences of change and crisis, and their expectations for what lies ahead (I consider the processes of "life review" an opportunity to name one's explanatory styles). Many times these explanatory styles have a strong effect on health outcomes:

A pessimistic explanatory style in early adulthood appears to be a risk factor for poor health in middle and late adulthood and is related to lowered immune function and illness. The explanatory styles of pessimism and, in contrast, optimism also predict good or bad performance in academic, athletic, and work domains. (1989, p. 5)

Hardiness is another state of mind—one which incorporates the human capacity for commitment, control, and response to challenge. Research with executives has shown that a clear sense of values, goals, and capabilities, as well as a firm commitment to one's sense of self, are personal capabilities and attitudes within this state of mind. Executives with this quality of "hardiness" were shown to be actively involved with their environments, holding an "unshakable sense of meaningfulness and internal control" (p. 5).

Another state of mind reflects either *constructive thinking* or *low constructive thinking*. Strickland cites Epstein's belief that each of us is in a continual state of processing information (which is what I call "meaning-making"), and this includes experiential responding at some level below awareness. "This process is a constructive and creative one for those persons who are willing to integrate various aspects of their intellectual and affective states and move beyond stereotypical or conventional responding" (p. 6). (From my perspective this moving beyond often requires a certain cognitive "deconstruction" that opens the mind to new, constructive solutions.)

I have already mentioned Strickland's use of the concept of *mindfulness*. Mindfulness is a state of mind combining emotion and cognition within a "state of alertness and lively awareness." It is a state characterized by and expressed through active information process. It includes an awareness of context and a flexibility of thinking that can "lead a person to the creation of multiple perspectives and new ways of looking at things." It is what Harold Rothbart (1972) describes as the "dynamic experience of learning, as opposed to the passive reception of ideas or other people's work. Creating is doing . . . " (pp. xi–xii).

The state of mindfulness enables the person "to move from the unknown to the known and enhances personal feelings of control"—a significant psychological state that can increase health and well-being. In negative contrast, "mindlessness" is seen in a "state of reduced attention, expressed in behavior that is rigid and rule governed. Mindlessness is inflexibility by default rather than by design" (p. 6). Ellen Langer (1989) adds enormous insight to these statements by Strickland in her book *Mindfulness*. Not only does she bring us a synthesis of research on mindfulness and mindlessness, she shakes our thinking in the way she presents her material. I, for one, found the book delightful reading as well as strong support for my thesis of creative aging. In her words:

Many, if not all, of the qualities that make up a mindful attitude are characteristic of creative people. Those who can free themselves of old mindsets . . . who can open themselves to new information and surprise, play with perspective and context, and focus on process rather than outcome are likely to be creative, whether they are scientists, artists, or cooks. (1989, p. 115)

And whether they are young or old!

Here we have another set of variables, then, to include in our repertoires of creative thinking and process. But our patterns of explanation and understanding, our neat structures of thought and idea, need some sort of applied translation if creative aging is to become more than an abstract vision or a simple exercise in mental juggling. For that reason, I bring us now into the realms of the tangible—to the notion of applied creativity.

APPLIED CREATIVITY

Frank Barron playfully wonders, "Is this a barbarous notion?"

What would an artist say, or a poet? Shall we have *applied* poetry next? And are we not all of us artists at heart, in our lives? Is not creativity a spark of the divine in us? Do we not reduce it, reduce ourselves, in fact, when we subordinate creativity to utility, when we make our creativity serve extrinsic ends? Is not this call, the call to create, nothing less than a call to give ourselves to the sacred in human life? Is it not the master, are we not its servitors? Put creativity to work, indeed! (1988, p. 76)

Then, in a delightful way, Barron answers his question: "With all due respect for that archetypically artistic point of view" we are ready for applications of creativity. Indeed, he emphasizes, as a species, at a confused and turbulent time in hisory, we must harness all of our powers, especially those of creativity, in solving the problems that "evolution has set for us" (Barron, 1988, p. 76).

Put creativity to work! That is certainly the thesis of this book. Learn about it, incorporate it, use it, teach it—whatever will work in helping people to live life as effectively as possible at every stage. We are only now capturing the essence of these ideas in working with children (see Howard Gardner and Teresa Amabile for many fruitful ideas about the expressions of creativity), in developmental wonderings and models (Michael Basseches, David Feldman, and Howard Gruber, among others), and now, in studying the lives of older people to gather understandings of how they have managed the shoals of their own agings (John A.B. McLeish, B.F. Skinner, May Sarton).

By actively teaching the principles of creativity early on in life, and by making people of all ages more creative in their expectations and perceptions of aging, we just might stop the "brain drain" when creativity is neither cultivated nor used; when an individual operates out of the premise "I am simply not creative!"; when creativity is not seen as creativity because it comes from a gray-haired, curve-backed older person.

I think here of a friend whose manuscript was rejected shortly after he retired. Even though this man had published extensively and was highly respected in his field, the new title of "retired person" influenced the judgment of his reviewing editor. Lest you think this is all some "sour grapes" hypothesis, he has the editorial comments that label him as "just another retired teacher wanting to publish a book." (He received these accidentally, by the way.) I don't know whether his book was worthy of publication, but it is the prejudicial linking of age and level of talent that is the serious problem here.

To interrupt brain drains born of age we will frequently have to widen our definitions of therapy. More than just one-to-one dialogues in a private room, more than just single modality approaches reflecting one set of theories, our therapies will need to expand into imaginative interventions of every kind: memory therapy, life review, family therapies, pet therapy, gardening and art therapy, music therapy. All these will help our clients alter their environments, surmount stimulus deprivation, and influence institutional structures which force them in upon themselves. In our therapies we may become teachers and activists as much as reflective, caring listeners. Our work is to interrupt situations of "crazy-making."

What is it like to be a fairly intact person sharing a nursing home room with someone with Alzheimer's disease? Waking up at night to see your roommate struggling with the restraints imposed by the nurses? How does one keep the mind open to the present in such horrifying circumstances? Is it not an act of "health" to retreat into the inner worlds of the mind? I saw all this in the life of a friend whose only reason for being in a nursing home was that her family could not take care of her. Her determination to do the best she could with a most difficult situation was one of the inspirations for this book.

Thus, for the therapist involved in creative aging, therapy may mean acting on our sensitivities by fighting back when we see older people just fading away, eyes dull from lack of stimulation and purpose, losing abilities they once had, simply because these skills are no longer required or requested. It is to be hoped that this therapeutic sensitivity will make us react when someone is rejected because of stereotypes — like the man whose book was rejected for the wrong reasons, like the friend who had been recognized nationally for her design of mechanical aids for the handicapped but whose offer to share her expertise with a rehabilitation program was turned aside because "You are too old."

Part of our applied creativity, then, involves the alteration of environments and attitudes that contribute to mindlessness, a brain drain, or the failure to recognize creative contribution when it is there.

American culture has not always done too well in its attention to the creative. Barron, for one, believes the current American system either militates against creativity or neglects it to the point where it fades away. I quote his summary statements:

- Creative potential is not identified systematically and nurtured responsibly.
- Established organizations in government, industry, and education do not take creativity as a value and consequently do not make provision for creative use of the creative individuals they employ.

- There is at present no national or international recognition that creativity is itself a product.
- There are virtually no "centers for research on creativity" in existence, certainly none at the national level. (Barron, 1988, pp. 96–97)

But there are signs that our culture is paying more attention to the nurture of creative process. Certainly, the Chevron exhibit, "Creativity: The Human Resource," made a contribution as it traveled from city to city in the United States (it is now housed in the Science Center in Seattle, Washington). It also seems that more books are being written that emphasize approaches to creative thinking—for example, James Adams' *Conceptual Blockbusting* (1979), Robert W. Olson's *The Art of Creative Thinking* (1980), and Roger Von Oech's *A Whack on the Side of the Head* (1983). I also observe new programs in applied creativity in schools of business and engineering (which just might suggest that we're having a slight shift of values from the "bottom line").

Where a fairly specialized M.B.A. program was formerly considered essential for success in the business world, new requirements in the humanities are being introduced into business programs across the country. Business is finally recognizing that if you are to work with persons you had better take time to know them. Engineering programs are also broadening their technological focus to include studies in creative thinking. A notable example of this is seen in the teaching and writing of James Adams at Stanford University. An engineer who decided he didn't like engineering very much and turned to art, he eventually returned to his professional work in engineering to introduce ideas and exercises to interrupt the linear thinking of his engineering students.

Thus, in the teaching and application of "applied creativity," our culture seems more attuned to the meanings and values of creativity. Hopefully that appreciation will sift into the preparations for aging as people become more alert to those qualities that are indeed creative.

CREATIVITY AND AGING

And now, a few thoughts which link creativity as a process, as a learning, and as an application, to the beings and becomings of aging. Here I like to think of the life of the person as a most incredible *product*, which will remain in production until the individual dies. The more effectively the production is maintained, the more interesting and complete the product will be.

John A.B. McLeish has turned his creative attentions to the lives of older people, doing a remarkable piece of research in drawing together

stories of people whom he calls "Ulyssean Adults"—people who continue an active creative adventure until they die. In fact, he started a
"Ulyssean Society" for those people who want to actively "maintain and
extend their powers to learn, produce, and create" in their middle and
later years.

Out of his considerable research he has assembled some qualities
that he sees in the creative, older person. I summarized these in *Meaning-Making* and repeat that summary here:

He describes these creative "Ulysseans" as adults incorporating a sense of control of personal standards, of going someplace to the end of life. With openness
and flexibility they savor the complex as well as the simple, often coupling the
primitive with the sophisticated in a willingness to be open to what life brings
them. They carry the ability to see and to respond, to be puzzled by ideas and
happenings, to let go and to flow with the abandon of a child, to savor momen-
tary chaos while ordering the disorderly. They are people who demonstrate
dialectical thinking as they maintain a capacity to hold two contradictory ideas
at the same time, developing what the poet Keats called the "negative capability" without retreating into dogma, stereotype, or a quick search for the facts.
(Carlsen, 1988, p. 231)

To stimulate these outlooks, attitudes, and process skills, is a central
task for a therapy of creative aging. I find important suggestions for
these ongoing stimulations from some of the programs of The Ulyssean
Society that was founded in December, 1977 by a group of former
students from John McLeish's seminars on creativity and aging at the
School of Continuing Studies, University of Toronto. When a person
becomes a member of this group he or she is called a "Companion" and
commits to the principles of the "Creed of the Society" that emphasize
that "men and women in the middle and later years can, if they choose
to do so, richly maintain the powers to produce, to learn, and to create,
until the very end of the life journey" (McLeish, 1983, 207-209).

In the Ulyssean Society people are encouraged to be deeply involved in activities that stimulate them in a variety of ways but even
more particularly in habits of the imagination and the creative use of
the mind. Their creed (or "Benediction," as they call it) calls upon the
person to maintain a "zest for learning," a continually "renewing power
of seeking," the "healing joy of laughter," the "redeeming power of serving," a "devotion to passionate causes," and the "transforming actions of
love" (1983, pp. 208-209).

Members are urged to take part in discussion groups that provide
connections with others as well as a joy of learning and serving. I quote
three descriptions that are illustrative:

• *The Cosmic Trails Group:* provides a little forum for discussion of some of
  the religious and philosophophical concepts outside the great conventional
  religions.

- *The Music Appreciation Group:* makes available the opportunity to listen to fine classical and other recordings on stereo.
- *The Playreading Group:* offers the opportunity for any Companion to join in reading plays by Chekov, Shaw, Ibsen, Williams, Maughan, Wilde, Sheridan, and others. (McLeish, 1983, 209–210)

Even more, participants are encourged to enhance sensual sensitivity by stimulating and responding to each of the five physical senses. This means interrupting old routines that tend to dominate doing, thinking, reading, and speaking by "opening up the whole being to fresh, invigorating experiences."

In my applications of creative thinking and purpose to therapeutic process I use many of these ideas as mini-goals or mini-purposes. And I see therapy as a chance to "deconstruct" rigid thoughts and beliefs, to undo the mythologies that clutter expectations of age. Here, certainly, is the opportunity to utilize the creative power of narrative process and life review. Through such activities, such reworkings of personal mythologies and memories, we may be able to reframe some of the debilitating emotional reactions and interpretations from our past. This frees our minds and spirits for experiencing the "now" of life. Through such processes perhaps we become more accepting of a more relaxed pace, of the opening of our creative explorations to times of waiting, of growing, and of developing which are born of rhythms more in tune with the ages and less in tune with the frenetic pace of contemporary life. Leopold Rosenmayr (1985) has influenced my thinking in this, as he emphasizes that personal creativity may be something quite different from "mechanical and prefabricated innovation. The capacity to wait, 'to let grow,' and to develop may then be valued more highly. Such a change may have positive effects on the status of older people in society" (p. 192).

There is a shift in rhythm, then, and an honoring of that shift. I find a fresh outlook on this in these words of Margaret Saunders Ott, a piano teacher and concert artist who continues to influence many students, and whose life is a model of the joyous and the imaginative. I find her words unusual in their imagery:

Life is an improvisation. . . . What if there's a mistake? You just go on . . . rhythm is the thing. Stop the piece — or a life — to correct a wrong note, and it's ruined. Rhythm — always rhythm. What's a mistake? The word should be removed from the English language. You make the best decision you can at the moment, and if it proves wrong, you simply make a new decision. It's all rhythm.

Most of the things we do in our culture are some kind of fast thing — you push a button and something happens fast — zip, zip, zip — that's not the way — that's not the way wheat grows; wheat grows slowly — months, days and hours. Nature takes longer—and art is part of nature. There's no such thing as an instant artist. Art is an organic thing. It is not a mechanical thing—and there is no way to hurry it. (Ott, 1982)

There is no such thing as an instant person or an instant wisdom. Maybe, just maybe, we will come to honor older people as those individuals who can model the organic processes of creative ripenings.

We can never bathe twice in the same stream, for it is ever-
changing—and so, it must be added, are we. To those who
want to rest, this changefulness is a burden, to those who can
embrace change, a challenge, and a pleasure.

—Howard Gruber, 1984, p. xii

Any span of the cycle lived without vigorous meaning, at the
beginning, in the middle, or at the end, endangers the sense
of life and meaning of death in all whose lifestages are intertwined.

—Erik Erikson, 1961, p. 161

At any moment, each man is suspended somewhere between
his own birth and his own death, but also between the birth
and death of the human race, the birth and death of the
world, and more. If we only view him within very narrow limits of time and place, we may dismiss many human struggles
as trivial or neurotic which may appear in a different light if
we consider a wider context and a longer journey.

—Miller Mair, 1976, p. 168

CHAPTER 3

Developmental Models for Aging

T O TRACK THE ETYMOLOGY of the word "development" is to find a
root metaphor of the *seed* which is opening and evolving out of its
protective cover. It is more than the shedding of a skin or a shell,
moreover; it is the process by which the seed moves through its intended forms. In the words of the *Oxford English Dictionary*, it is a growing
"into a fuller, higher, or maturer, condition" (which must assume that
there is such a state as a "more mature condition"). Thus, this developmental unfolding is not just cumulative—it is *transformational*.

But the seed can be deformed or stunted in its development because it does not receive enough water, light, or nourishment. It may
wither, it may shrivel, it may remain in its protective shell, it may never
trans-form.

Without pushing this metaphor too far I couch human development in similar epigenetic terms as I examine the conditions that either
encourage or inhibit its growth. Thus, I search developmental models
for more than road maps. I sort the end points, the qualities, the

personal, cognitive expansions for what they suggest for mature, healthful living. In my sortings I also work to shape an image of creative aging that transcends the defeating representations of age so tightly linked to what happens to the body—like Shakespeare's "sans teeth, sans eyes, sans everything," for example. In doing this I hope to interrupt too easy generalizations of aging as a biological problem and of old age as a disease.

DEVELOPMENTAL MODELS FOR AGING

Each developmental framework is a point of departure for examining life—a mapping of passages of thought and emotion, of self and other, of work and love, of meaning and meaning-making. In these structurings are estimations of human potential, theoretical descriptions of an "apex of life," constructions of what Robert Kegan (1982) calls "norms for growth." He writes that these norms for growth come from more than science or social science—they come from a developmental framework which is at once psychological, biological, and philosophical. These norms certainly form a tacit dimension for therapy, raising the danger of imposition on the client of a particular set of values. Kegan writes thoughtfully about this, stating his case in a manner congruent with my own:

The therapist's regard for the integrity and individuality of each person's made meaning in the world leads to the conviction that one way of making meaning is no better than another, and there is no justification for imposing on another one's own conception of the direction toward which personal change should tend. I want to suggest that while there is much to admire in this position, and that its refusal to impose values on another is a great discovery which must never be lost sight of, it remains a position with very grave problems. (Kegan, 1982, pp. 291–292)

Thus Kegan questions adamant refusals to incorporate values into the therapeutic experience. First, he believes, it creates a confusion between our judgments of the person and our judgments of therapeutic process and therapeutic goals. It is indeed essential that we respect the meaning systems of our client and enter them with care. But that does not mean we throw away those guiding theory systems and guiding values that shape the therapeutic experience.

Kegan calls the conviction that "there are no nonarbitrary bases upon which to consider one state of meaning-making as better than another" a philosophical confusion and a psychological confusion. In seeking some sort of clarification of this complex dialectic, Kegan asks a key question: "How do I confirm the integrity of the person's attempts to make the world cohere [in other words, to create a personal system of meaning], without appearing to be confirming or disconfirming the validity of the way he makes the world cohere?" His question suggests answers: To join a young woman caught in the impulsive promiscuity of delayed adolescence is to confirm her as a person, but not to validate her lack of developmental resolution towards a more mature concept of love and intimacy. To join an older man who is unwilling to face his own denial of the processes of aging is not to reject where he is as a person, but to seek to open his thinking to a more constructive, creative approach to later life. What is offered here, therefore, is what I have called a "better way" for living and aging.

I have named these before but I name them again — those developmental goals that seem to transform limiting patterns of thought and relationship. In my therapeutic work with clients of all ages I seek to stimulate:

- wisdom and integrity over stupidity, ignorance, and despair;
- generativity and care over self-aggrandizement and narcissistic preoccupation;
- open-mindedness over rigid, closed thinking;
- a willingness to entertain new ideas over opinionated self-righteousness;
- transcendent relationship over the extremes of either self or other. (Carlsen, 1988, p. 228)

Even as I name such a "better way" I acknowledge the dangers in adhering too rigidly to any one model or in treating stages as some sort of fixed sequence of developmental process. Quoting Kegan once again:

The stages, even at their very best, are only indicators of development. To orient around the indicators of development is to risk losing the *person developing*, a risk at no time more unacceptable than when we are accompanying persons in transition, persons who may themselves feel they are losing the person developing. (1982, p. 277)

From my perspective, genuine developmental transformation moves the person through increasingly inclusive and complex cyclings and recyclings of meaning and personal construction. Within each recycling there is renewed opportunity to rework previous challenges in the service of the new. Though some of his critics miss this point, Erikson emphasized this as early as 1961 when he wrote that the "idea of a resolution of crises without any leftover of loose ends fits modern man's idea of a perfect adjustment, as if developmental crises were so many efficiency tests applied to an organism with accidental flaws in design and production." Herant A. Katchadourian's interpretation enlarges on this perspective:

At each phase, components from each of the eight major tasks are present simultaneously as "precursors," "derivates," and as the decisive "crisis" itself. Thus, childhood does not end nor adulthood begin with adolescence. Rather, the adult is anticipated in the child and the child persists in the adult. This is the thread that gives continuity to Erikson's developmental scheme. (in Erikson, 1978, p. 51)

And, in truth, we do not yet know the developmental capabilities of the human being—most developmental models simply do not take us into the last third of life. More frequently they cut us off in midlife, leaving us dangling without clear images of the kinds of growths that can still be ours. Freud's model is notable for ignoring the opportunities for growth in adulthood. Indeed, "Freud was inclined to regard adult-hood primarily as a scene in which the early unconscious conflicts were re-enacted, rather than as a time of further development" (Levinson, 1978, p. 4).

Roger Gould, Daniel Levinson, and George Vaillant are among those who have dealt with developmental process, but much of their material was gathered when little empirical knowledge of late adult-hood was available. Levinson is appreciative of this, writing in 1978 that it "is obviously an oversimplification to regard the entire span of years after age 60 or 65 as a single era. Given the lack of research data, we can only speculate about this concluding segment of the life cycle" (p. 38). But then, after speculating that a new era of late late adulthood begins around age 80, he asks:

What does development mean at the very end of the life cycle? It means that a man is coming to terms with the process of dying and preparing for his own death. . . . To be able to involve himself in living he must make his peace with dying. . . . He must come finally to terms with the self—knowing it and loving it reasonably well, and being ready to give it up. (1978, pp. 38–39)

Levinson's statement serves as an effective summary of what this business of development is about—and an appropriate introduction to this next discussion of those theoretical models that are more specific in naming the issues of the last half of life.

AN INTRODUCTORY OVERVIEW

I start with a set of "demands" named by task theorist Robert Havighurst. Although Havighurst has linked these formally with chron-ological age stages, I reframe them as thought questions quite separate from any designated age classification. I also suggest them as sequences of challenge which can harness the creative problem-solving of the person.

Robert Peck's framing of a set of midlife/latelife alternatives prepares the way for a consideration of Erikson's concepts of the "virtues" of age. This framing of alternatives is an expansion and refinement of Erikson's eighth stage — the "integrity vs. despair" stage of adult development. Peck has called that stage a representation in a "global, nonspecific way all of the psychological crises and crisis-solutions of the last forty or fifty years of life." Because he saw Erikson's model this way (take note of my alternative conceptualization below), Peck found it useful to divide this global description of the second half of life into a "Middle Age" period and an "Old Age" period, and then to describe tasks specific to these periods but not tightly bound by chronology.

Erikson's eight stages of life development as viewed through the language of the "virtues" is the subject of my next discussion. In his genius, Erikson has given us a developmental model that keeps adapting itself to expanding conceptions and interpretations, and which I choose to identify not only as a psychosocial stage theory but as a transformational, cognitive-developmental theory. From this constructivist perspective, Erikson, in naming eight successive alternative frames of outlook and relationship, has both named stages and transcended them. To introduce hope, or love, or caring, into one's life is to transform one's images of life and self. And to counterbalance the psychological, emotional dilemmas of integrity and despair is to deal with a central dialectic of life (perhaps *the* central dialectic?). Thus, unlike McLeish (1976, p. 81) who interprets Erikson as somehow assigning people to one or the other of two states of being — integrity or despair — I see Erikson pointing us to the paradoxical juxtapositions of these processings in *every* individual's life.

My final theorist in this sequence of frameworks is philosopher/historian Huston Smith. His work does not usually keep company with those named above, for his ideas take us into the developmental realms of the philosophical and the spiritual. In so doing, Smith offers a counterbalance to our more objective, empirical traditions. What he suggests is a series of meaning-making systems that can lead us to an allowing and an appreciating of the incredible mystery of life. It is to face ultimately that which is unexplainable.

Following are more detailed examinations of each of the theorists named above.

ROBERT HAVIGHURST

Stimulated by the Committee on the Dynamics of Family Interaction at the 1948 National Conference on Family Life, Robert Havighurst joined others like Reuben Hill and Evelyn Duvall to name tasks from birth to old age. He then went beyond those task formulations to name a sequence of "demands" for successive periods of life —

demands that challenge the person to address a series of salient concerns that are keyed to the evolution of time and chronology:

- Age 0–10: Coming into independent existence
- Age 10–20: Becoming a person in one's own mind
- Age 20–30: Focusing one's life
- Age 30–40: Collecting one's energies
- Age 40–50: Exerting and asserting oneself
- Age 50–60: Maintaining position and changing roles
- Age 60–70: Deciding whether to disengage and how
- Age 70–80: Making the most of disengagement

I reframe these demands as thought questions for aging, and I accept Morton Puner's suggestion that, though these demands may sound simple, they actually represent profound insights into the kinds of concerns we face at different stages of life. Puner respects Havighurst's insights because they grew from hundreds of studies in aging, work that began in 1945, "a long time ago in the short history of gerontology" (Puner, 1974, p. 47). Underscoring this accomplishment, Puner reports a moment of insight which came to Havighurst when he was addressing a Gerontological Society meeting:

[He began his address as follows:] "One of the principal unanswered questions about the human life cycle is: How do people structure their lives after about age 65? Under what conditions do they achieve satisfaction?" He stopped himself suddenly struck by the realization of how far gerontology had traveled. When he first started out, he explained, he would not have thought, in talking about people over 65, of using so active a term as "structure their lives." The idea that a person growing old could be taking any such initiative would simply not occur. (Puner, 1974, p. 47)

What Puner has acknowledged in Havighurst's insight is the "widespread and . . . superficial view of aging held in the 1940s [which] saw it as a period of declines, losses, and stresses, with society outside the family doing little to help an older person make a satisfactory adjustment." What is also highlighted for all of us is the dramatic shifting of roles within the processes of aging—for society and for the old themselves—which is a sure sign that Havighurst and all the rest of us are taking part in "the quiet revolution of our times" (Puner, 1974, p. 47).

Honoring Havighurst's contribution, I take his demands, break them loose from chronology, and suggest them as a sequence of thought questions to be used in any time of transition: a career change, a move to a new area of the country, bereavement, the entrance into a new marriage, whatever. In case you wonder about this, remember that the entrance into a retirement community, for example, calls upon a new form of dependence/independence relationship, a new conception of one's role as a person, a new facing of ways to exert and assert oneself. So consider carefully these themes:

- Coming into a new independent existence
- Shifting gears on being a person in one's own mind
- Focusing and refocusing the activities of life
- Collecting, sustaining, and nurturing one's energies
- Continuing some form of exerting and asserting oneself
- Exploring and implementing new life styles
- Deciding how much to *engage* or *disengage*: where, how much, in what way
- Making the most of one's choices

I have found it a helpful exercise to contrast the words "engage" and "disengage." Indeed, one of the tasks of the later years is not just determining how or when or whether to disengage, but to continue to creatively decide how much and in what way to *continue to engage*. It is not a global decision—it is a set of decisions—ongoing, active, and involved in the current events of daily living; the continuing challenge for the aging person to evaluate personal limitations within the light of what is possible—or, turning this around, to evaluate possibility within the acknowledgment of personal limitation.

And here, in the last decade of the 20th century, we are seeing people in their 70s and 80s and 90s (and 100s!) who are definitely not disengaging from life. I think of Neva Waggoner who in 1989 has just published her own book at the age of 85; I think of the 83-year-old oil painter who hands out business cards with his winter address on one side and his home address on the other. Despite having only recently begun to paint, he is active as an artist and already selling his work.

I think, too, of Professor Giovanni Costigan who continued his creative research and teaching well beyond his retirement to the time of his death in 1990. I shall always remember this remarkable historian and teacher riding his bicycle onto campus and wandering with great absorption through the stacks of the university library. In tribute to his scholarly contribution and to his remarkable modeling of the involvements possible in later aging, the "University Week," the weekly newsletter of the University of Washington, offered the following commentary:

Giovanni Costigan was one of the most prominent members of a generation of great teachers on campus. After his retirement he continued to serve the entire community as a scholar and very popular lecturer. His voice, never silent on issues of human rights and human dignity, will be sorely missed. (April 5, 1990, p. 1)

Wise scholars, speaking from their own aging, *do* remind us of the tasks and challenges of mature adulthood. These words from Senator Fulbright are a strong example of what I mean:

Adulthood means the acceptance of permanent responsibilities, of continuing tasks, of enterprises that advance imperceptibly toward fruition with neither climax nor completion. It means ambiguity when we would prefer precision, tedious labor when we would prefer dramatic action, infinite patience when we would prefer immediate rewards. Above all, maturity requires a final accommodation between our aspirations and our limitations. (Date unknown)

Acceptance of tasks and responsibilies, yes. But more than that, an acceptance of the reality that climax or completion may not be the reward of all our efforts. Even more, Fulbright has suggested that ambiguity, imprecision, tedious labor, and a need for infinite patience may well be a part of the program of adulthood. Above all, "maturity requires a final accommodation between our aspirations and our limitations." That accommodation seems to be very much a part of the suggestions I have gathered here—an ongoing dialogue between that which is possible and that which will have to be set aside.

A SERIES OF DIALECTICAL DILEMMAS

Robert Peck (1956) breaks the last half of life into two major periods, midlife and old age, and suggests a schema of alternatives for each period. Not placed into closely defined slots of chronological age, these alternatives constitute life questions which take on unique form according to the needs and circumstances of each individual person.

Midlife Alternatives:
- Valuing wisdom vs. valuing physical powers
- Socializing vs. sexualizing in human relationships
- Cathectic flexibility vs. cathectic impoverishment
- Mental flexibility vs. mental rigidity

Alternatives in Later Aging:
- Ego differentiation vs. work-role preoccupation
- Body transcendence vs. body preoccupation
- Ego transcendence vs. ego preoccupation (Peck, 1956)

(I might choose to reframe Peck's challenges as a dialectic by using the words "vis-à-vis." In that manner we might more easily see the fluctuating, intertwining, point/counterpoint dynamics of the challenges.)

Valuing wisdom vs. valuing physical powers: I think of my midlife client, a triathalon participant, who begins to wonder about his almost obsessive physical activity. Though he savors the rush that comes in meeting this intense physical challenge, he also begins to wonder if he really wants to spend his extra time working out in the gym. He is also questioning the price he pays in time away from family and in the aches and pains which grow more intruding as he gets older. But it is not a rejection he is considering. It is a reworking of his goals and time schedules to introduce other new experiences into his life. Being a bit of a philosopher, he wants time to deal with the matters of life meaning at the same time as he keeps his body alive.

Peck describes "successful" agers as those who *do* "calmly invert their previous value hierarchy, now putting the use of their 'heads' above the use of their 'hands', both as their standard for self-evaluation and as their chief resource for solving life problems." And further, "For people to whom pleasure and comfort mean predominantly physical well-being, this may be the gravest, most mortal of insults. There are many such people whose elder years seem to move in a decreasing spiral, centered around their growing preoccupation with the state of their bodies" (1966, p. 163).

Socializing vs. sexualizing in human relationships: I certainly don't like to think of this as an either-or. Isn't it a mix—a rebalancing of the tensions and dynamics of social/sexual energy as the person hopefully faces, accepts, and works constructively with the slowing of the processes of the body? With a positive approach to resolving these dilemmas we can continue to enjoy the pleasures and excitements of interpersonal intimacy and sensuality, even as we adjust to whatever shifting of sexual energy and capability might come with age.

But take heart! Alex Comfort, a rather noted advocate for the excitements and innovations of sexual experience, takes time in *A Good Age* (1976) to address the concerns related to sexuality in aging. He assures us that "in the absence of two disabilities—actual disease and the belief that 'the old' are or should be asexual—sexual requirement and sexual capacity are lifelong" (p. 192). But he also suggests that if actual intercourse becomes impaired by physical problems in aging, "other sexual needs persist, including closeness, sensuality and being valued as a man or as a woman."

The cultivation and honoring of these experiences are sometimes at odds with the kinds of ageism that all too frequently intrude to paint images of "dirty old men" (and women?). These images distort sexual expectations and sexual opportunity. With a pungence of language, Comfort writes: "Nursing homes appear to be run by people with sexual problems—otherwise it would be difficult to explain the attempt to run them as mixed-sex nunneries; a few even refuse to permit married people to share a room" (p. 197). So, amen and amen! Here's to the stimulation of sexual enjoyment and to the cultivation and appreciation of every possible means for "closeness, sensuality, and being valued as a man or as a woman" (p. 192). (I call your attention to Carl Eisdorfer and Donna Cohen's poignant discussion of sexuality and the Alzheimer's patient in *The Loss of Self*, 1984, pp. 173–179.)

Cathectic flexibility vs cathectic impoverishment: By "cathectic flexibility," Peck means an emotional flexibility that can shift attachments and investments from one person to another, and from one activity to another. He feels this is important because the years from midlife into old age are the times when parents die, when children grow up and leave home, when a spouse may die, and when circles of friends and relatives of similar age begin to be broken by death (p. 161). The wisdom here? To develop a flexibility of contact, a variety of interactions with people of differing ages, a tapping and enriching of the contacts developed through the years.

Mental flexibility vs. mental rigidity: Peck contrasts two kinds of people: (1) those who learn to master experiences at the same time they are able to achieve a kind of detached perspective on them—a perspective that enables them to use this learned experience to provide "provisional guides" to the solution of new issues; and (2) those who seem dominated by their experiences: "They take the patterns of events and actions which they happen to have encountered, as a set of fixed inflexible rules which almost automatically govern their subsequent behavior" (162). These contrasts are particularly significant in the cognitive developmental psychology that shapes my writing here. In Chapters 5 and 6 I will address the kinds of thinking processes that all too easily reinforce mental rigidity.

The following alternatives are more representative of the challenges of later adulthood: (1) ego differentiation vs. work-role preoccupation, (2) body transcendence vs. body preoccupation, and (3) ego transcendence vs. ego preoccupation (pp. 162–164). Although Peck resists age categories in assigning these sets of choices, most of the people dealing with these life questions will no doubt be in their 70s or 80s or older. These choices are expansions of earlier decisions and take on their own intensities with shifts in work investment, in the condition of the body, and in one's increasing closeness to death.

The person will need to find new determinations for self-identity and meaning that are not linked so closely to work roles, to the health of the body, and to narcissistic preoccupation with the self. This is the time when investments in others—family, friends, causes—can help the person to transcend the self; when spiritual and philosophical wonderings may take the person past the physical into a transcendence which is "meta-physical." That word has gotten bad press because it is linked with extremes of spiritual experiment and with a wide number of experiences not easily researched or analyzed. By taking the word apart, however, we are enabled to see the "meta" position that is required if we are to transcend many of the dilemmas of later aging. And it is certainly the metaphysical that Jung was referring to when he described spiritual questions as central to the last half of life.

The questions of "ego transcendence vs. ego preoccupation" are not easily defined; furthermore, they bring us face to face with the certain prospects of our own deaths. Peck suggests an attitude for handling these prospects:

To live so generously and unselfishly that the prospect of personal death—the night of the ego, it might be called—looks and feels less important than the secure knowledge that one has built for a broader, longer future than any one ego ever could encompass. Through children, through contributions to the culture, through friendships—these are ways in which human beings can achieve enduring significance for their actions which goes beyond the limit of their own skins and their own lives. It may, indeed, be the only *knowable* kind of self-perpetuation after death.

That is quite a remarkable ideal! Only a very few, I would imagine, ever reach that state of mind.

What I emphasize in my own thinking is that when a mind becomes preoccupied with what is lost rather than with what can yet be— preoccupied with the losses of personal independence, with the insults to the body—then this is a mind that will lose its capacity to break loose, to step back, to transcend some of the difficulties of age. And this is a hard task: The threats of invasive medical techniques, of financial devastation, of the loss of personal independence, are so serious that one wonders how anyone can *not* be preoccupied.

I recently (1990) talked to Gilbert Wrenn about this issue. He comments that when older people live in a retirement community where there is a terminal care facility they often spend considerable time volunteering with peers who are fragile and may require full-time care. In that environment of continuing care these volunteers and friends are constantly exposed to the frightening extremes of illness and dependency. It then becomes all the harder to return to their own residences without dwelling on the sad states which they have just witnessed. It constitutes a real mental discipline to turn the mind to other matters, to engage in new learning, to converse with a friend, to meditate. Some accomplish this but some do not.

In a sense all developmental theory is about "tasks" or challenges or demands arising within successive stages of life experience. But if we are to remain true to the cognitive developmental position, it is important to see development as a *movement through forms,* a series of expansions of personal paradigms, openings and reopenings of systems of thought, relationship, and outlook (see Basseches, 1984). What is described is more than a set of linear stages—it is a cycling and recycling of developmental questions and interactions, of systems of thinking, doing, and relating which gather, break, and reform within larger and more encompassing systems of personal being. This is what genuine development is about.

ERIKSONIAN THEORY AND CONTRIBUTIONS

At a 1982 conference devoted to developmental issues involving the infant and the young child, Erikson took an interesting tack in describing the important links between the experiences of the elderly and the growth and development of the infant. In reporting on this in the *APA Monitor*, Martha Cliffe observed that "Erikson stood his well-known theory of human development on its end, reexamining it from the perspective of old age."

[According to Erikson] old age should be seen not as a "new childishness" but rather as the stage which has the potential to fulfill the promises of childhood. Rather than viewing the last stage as "pervaded by a regressive connection to earlier stages,"... old age should be understood as "an attempt to recapitulate developmental potentials." (1982, p. 7)

This process of developmental recapitulation was affirmed when Erik Erikson, Joan Erikson, and Helen Kivnick gathered and synthesized developmental stories for their book *Vital Involvement in Old Age* (1986). Their subjects, the parents of the 50 children who were followed in the longitudinal "Guidance Study" sponsored by the University of California, Berkeley, ranged in age from 75 to 95 years of age. These older people shared many intimate thoughts, feelings, and experiences which did indeed confirm Erikson's premise that "old age should be understood as an attempt to recapitulate developmental potentials"— that the eight stages are not rigid in their evolution, that they are not fully completed when movement is made into a new stage, that they are ever evolving, ever synthesizing, ever reforming within and around each other. These findings give pause to any simplistic rendition of Erikson's model and add new flavor to the meanings of the stages.

A theme that is emphasized in the reporting of these three researchers is that the person needs to maintain a vital investment in life. It is that "vital investment" that is weighed against the backdrops of the struggles of integrity vs. despair, generativity vs. stagnation. Because these last two stages represent the leap from midlife into old age, I focus on them to the exclusion of the other stages in Erikson's schemata. But since those other stages are *within* these two stages I suggest that you examine the summaries in Tables 3.1, 3.2, and 3.3.

Psychosocial Crises

		1	2	3	4	5	6	7	8
Old Age	VIII								Integrity vs. Despair, disgust. WISDOM
Adulthood	VII							Generativity vs. Stagnation. CARE	
Young Adulthood	VI						Intimacy vs. Isolation. LOVE		
Adolescence	V					Identity vs. Identity Confusion. FIDELITY			
School Age	IV				Industry vs. Inferiority. COMPETENCE				
Play Age	III			Initiative vs. Guilt. PURPOSE					
Early Childhood	II		Autonomy vs. Shame, Doubt. WILL						
Infancy	I	Basic Trust vs. Basic Mistrust. HOPE							

From *The Life Cycle Completed* by Erik H. Erikson by permission of W. W. Norton & Co., Inc Copyright 1982 by Rikan Enterprises Ltd.

TABLE 3.2 Erikson Concept: Generativity vs. Stagnation

STAGNATION	GENERATIVITY
Boredom	Energy, motivation
Mental decline	Mental growth
Self-absorbed	Other-absorbed
Obsessive pseudo-intimacy	The establishment of the next
Narcissistic self-indulgence	generation through the production and care of offspring, or through other altruistic and creative acts

RELATIONSHIPS

1. Deteriorating	1. Growing
2. Selfish	2. Selfless
3. Taking	3. Giving
	4. Involved in community, children, others

MIND

1. Closed	1. Open
2. Rigid	2. Flexible
3. Stuck	3. Growing
	4. Creative

PHYSICAL

1. Unrealistic body image	1. Realistic body image
2. Imbalance	2. Balance

VOCATION

1. Disillusionment	1. Sense of being needed
2. Boredom	2. Ongoing exploration, discovery
3. No sense of contribution to others	3. Contribution to society, children
4. Stagnation	4. Generativity

from Carlsen (1988), p. 242

CARE: GENERATIVITY VIS-À-VIS STAGNATION

Erikson has used the language of the "virtues" in his developmental naming of the evolving systems of *hope, will, purpose, competence, fidelity, love, care, and wisdom* that provide an overall vision of what mature humanness is about. In choosing this language of the virtues Erikson has acknowledged its less objective, less explicit quality. Indeed, in his 1961 writing he agrees it is a language with countless connotations—

TABLE 3.3 Erikson Concept: Integrity vs. Despair

DESPAIR	INTEGRITY
Arousal/anxiety/blocking	Serenity
Pulling in from life	Continuity, openness to life
Decline of perceptual acuity	Growth or maintenance of perceptual acuity

RELATIONSHIPS
FAMILY

1. Loneliness	1. Ability to be alone
2. Excessive dependency	2. Solution of problems presented by others: aging parents, children, spouse
3. No support system	3. Maintenance of support systems

MIND

1. Decline in mental functioning	1. Continuing study: adult education
2. Boredom	2. Artistic expressions
3. Self-absorbed	3. Service to others

PHYSICAL

1. Repression of fears of physical decline	1. Realistic evaluation and acceptance of losses
2. Rejection of aging peers	2. Acceptance of aging peers
3. Development of invalid role	3. Perceptual awareness
4. Preoccupation with illness	4. Satisfactory resolution of illness experience

VOCATION/MEANING

1. Disillusionment	1. A sense of being needed
2. Boredom	2. Continuing shaping of personal meaning
3. Stimulus deprivation	3. Effort to find novelty
4. No investment of meaning	4. Something to be committed to
5. Negative outcome	5. Use of personal abilities in interesting, challenging activity

from Carlsen (1988), p. 243

optimists will make the virtues sound like "gay and easy accomplishments," and pessimists will see them as "idealistic pretences" (p. 151). Nevertheless, in shaping his theoretical language, Erikson continued to use these words because he believed that the "everyday words of living languages, ripened in the usage of generations, will serve best as means of discourse" (p. 151).

I adopt Erikson's language here. I also incorporate Erikson's wisdom into my outlook on the adult capacity to care:

From the point of view of development, I would say: In youth you find out what you *care to do* and who you *care to be* — even in changing roles. In young adulthood you learn whom you *care to be with* — at work and in private life, not only exchanging intimacies, but sharing intimacy. In adulthood, however, you learn to know what and whom you can *take care of*. (1974, p. 124)

Erikson has firmly stated his belief that such caring is an integral part of the only happiness that is lasting: "To increase by whatever is yours to give, the good will and the higher order in your sector of the world. That, to me, can be the only adult meaning of that strange word *happiness* as a political principle" (1974, p. 124).

Kivnick and the Eriksons found that this was a principle that was lived out by many of their research subjects who found meaningful involvements and participations in their relationships with their children and their grandchildren (1986, p. 326). There was a pride and deep gratification in seeing their contribution to the development of these young people, and in seeing the arrival of new generations that will continue the family name and family tradition. These researchers label this response a natural enthusiasm. "Before we were, there were ancestors — when we leave, there will be descendants and/or memorable deeds and accomplishments" (p. 326). These are the rewards coming from invested, caring generativities.

As I write about this I wonder about the maladaptive responses that may result from contemporary shifts in family systems and family investment. What about the huge divorce rate? What about the high rate of abuse and violence within the domestic environment? What about the displaced homemakers, the uncommitted single people, the victims of abandonment and separation? How will these people be drawn into the caring investments that seem to correlate highly with increased satisfaction as one grows older? These are important questions for those of us who accept Erikson's model. I, for one, wonder what special effort it will take to interrupt maladaptive responses to the challenges of generativity, to interrupt the kinds of alienated self-absorptions, the varieties of silent, bitter resignations that the Erikson and Kivnick research team found among those who have never invested in others.

Other negatives that tilt the scale towards stagnation include a "truly obstinate refusal to accept obvious symptoms of deterioration" (Erikson, Erikson, & Kivnick, 1986, p. 330). The woman, for example, who is too proud to use a wheelchair and whose stubborn refusals to be helped make it difficult for family and friends to support her reengagement with life. And those other negatives: surliness and persistent self-pity, an unwillingness to accept the help of others, a "pompous pretension to wisdom or integrity," a withdrawal into a "mistrusting despair," and the failure to "press for ever-renewed integration in the face of disintegration." All these negatives, of course, interrupt the maturation process as they prevent the joys of mutuality and the rewards of invested caring.

WISDOM: INTEGRITY VIS-À-VIS DESPAIR

Erikson has written that *integrity* is the ability of some old people to "envisage human problems in their entirety" and "to represent to the coming generation a living example of the 'closure' of a style of life. Only such integrity can balance the despair of a limited life coming to a conscious conclusion" (1961, p. 161). It is the finding of a continuity and consistency of self even as the person is pointed towards a transcendence of self, a wisdom which is a "detached concern with life itself, in the face of death" (Erikson, Erikson, & Kivnick, 1986, p. 37).

Integrity further is defined as a "sense of coherence and wholeness." This integrity is at "supreme risk under such terminal conditions as include a loss of linkages in somatic, psychic, and social organization. What is demanded here could be simply called *integrality*, a readiness to keep things together" [italics added].

Integrity seems to come with the considered feeling that one played the roles and met the challenges of each of the eras of the life cycle. It does not mean perfection; it does not mean the absence of regrets. It does mean having found a way to make one's life count in caring for — and hopefully enhancing — the ongoing flow of life. From the experiences one gathers, from the suffering and the gladness, one accrues the virtue Erikson calls wisdom. (Fowler, 1984, p. 26)

Thus does Erikson juxtapose integrity with despair in a dialectic that honors the losses of age at the same time it gives opportunity for the integrities of age. This word *despair* is a powerful one. Rollo May emphasizes this power when he writes: "*Authentic despair is that emotion which forces one to come to terms with one's destiny. It is a demand to face the reality of one's life. The 'letting go'* . . . *of false hopes, of pretended loves, of infantalizing dependency, of empty conformism which serves only to make one behave like sheep huddling in a flock because they fear the wolves outside the circle*" (1981, p. 235). He describes despair as a necessary preparation for freedom. I would describe despair as a necessary preparation for wisdom — which is, no doubt, its own freedom.

When we do hit bottom, when we do face our "dark night of the soul," we are thrown into the necessary work of the crisis experience.

With our illusions blasted to bits, our false hopes seen for what they are, our desperate struggles to avoid facing harsh realities turned about, we have a choice of settling into the darkness or working our way through to a new perspective on life. May calls this the dynamic in all authentic "conversions." It is the turning around of a cognitive system, a way of making meaning of experience, a set of expectations for life. It is similar to Erikson's idea of "radical change in perspective" (1968, p. 6).

Despair is often essential to a client's discovery of unique personal capabilities and assets, an opportunity to interrupt simplistic, stereotyped perspectives, to interrupt experiential patterns that are defeating rather than helpful. This may be the central challenge for any therapy. In harnessing the energy of conflict we may have to sidestep therapeutic tendencies to teach our clients to deny despair—by premature reassurance, by too ready administrations of drugs, by running away from the dialogical conflicts that can thrust the client into major life questions. With a more direct confrontation of all facets of the crisis experience we gain an important opportunity to stimulate our client's belief that he or she *does* have the capacity to survive even when faced with the serious threat of hopelessness and despair.

Wisdom is the "virtue" that Erikson names as a culminating synthesis, a psychosocial achievement gained by working through the developmental tasks of life. Wisdom is the successful integration of integrity and despair, and arrival at what Erikson calls a "truly involved disinvolvement" (1986, p. 51). Transcending the ego seems to be Erikson's point here—a getting past limited perspectives on the self and its purposes to recognize a little piece of how one fits into the order of things, to see purposes and connections larger than the self—all at the same time one maintains a vital involvement in life. Here, again, is the paradox of wisdom seen as a state of "truly involved disinvolvement."

To close this discussion I share Peck's interpretation of wisdom as an "end-of-life state of mind whose vision shapes and colors all the actions of an older person" (1966, p. 158). With such an alteration of perspective:

... then might not the human end-point be this: to achieve the ability to live so fully, so generously, so unselfishly that the prospect of personal death looks and feels less important than the secure knowledge that one has built for a broader future, for one's children and one's society, than one ego could ever encompass. (1966, p. 158)

HUSTON SMITH: FIVE SYSTEMS OF MEANING-MAKING

In naming and suggesting passages of human development that can be useful both to the professional and to the lay person, I have been struck by some ideas not ordinarily found in the writings of psychology and psychotherapy. These come from historian-philosopher Huston Smith whose book, *Condemned to Meaning* (1965), evolved out of his writing for the John Dewey Lecture Series, "For the Study of Education of Culture." In this short, pointed work, Smith faces the problems of a society devoid of meaning and takes his text from the French phenomenologist Maurice Merleau-Ponty: "Because we are present to a world, we are condemned to meaning." This book becomes his portrayal of five categories of meaning which the person "exercises to structure his billions of life-impressions which would otherwise remain random and pointless" (1965, p. 47).

Smith's commentator, Arthur Wirth, challenges education and psychology to allow for this topic of life-meaning in their research studies — not to negate the scientific, analytic standards of their disciplines, but to allow for the comprehensive investigation into what is human. He asks if the intellectual community can "remain responsible while avoiding the hazardous questions of value and meaning," while avoiding those "ventures beyond the boundaries where scientific techniques are readily available."

Tools of analysis can play their important role in forcing clarity, without making man timid of exploring questions that extend beyond their scope. To act otherwise makes a man a victim instead of a master of the tools. (Smith, 1965, pp. 10–11)

Smith postulates five meaning-making systems: *trouble, hope, endeavor, trust, and mystery.* Although the poetic language of his five stages does not have analytical precision, these stages are important because they offer another way to open our thinking to the issues and challenges of life process. I use Smith's descriptors to provide a structure for my interpretations.

TROUBLE: Whether it comes as foulness that sucks like mire or as time's slow contractions on the hopeful heart, man is born to trouble as the sparks fly upward. The human heart is star-crossed; its tensions will never completely go. (p. 47)

Within the presenting problems that my clients bring me I see much evidence that *trouble* can indeed be a shaping force in personal identity and meaning-making. Within grieving, for example, the person shapes personal reality through the windows of loss, deprivation, disability, and disillusionment, as if that is all there is. We all face trouble as a force in our lives. That is not the issue here. But when trouble becomes the only shaping force, the only organizing perception that we maintain, then we are doomed to pessimism. To make trouble our only framework for interpreting our day-to-day experience is to be grounded in despair.

HOPE: In their loneliness, in their lack of love and craving for it, the troubled are ever in danger of drifting to meaning's edge. But a reverse motion usually occurs. Short of having lost its fire completely, the human spirit rises like a spark from trouble's anvil, flying upward and outward toward hope. (p. 48)

Hope is the stirring of the human spirit from its capture by trouble and despair. It is the manifestation of the human gift and capability for imagination with which we can anticipate what might happen next. With this imagination we plant the seeds of hope. I saw this transitional shift with a widow who, after months of grieving, began to feel that life could be different. This woman came to see that she needed an identity that went beyond that of "widow"; she began to liberate her sense of self from the tendrils of her husband's influence. Yet, in a quite wonderful way, she was enabled paradoxically to name, honor, and incorporate his influence. (And how strange it often was that those around this woman sometimes made it hard for her to change.)

ENDEAVOR: Once we have put our problems and troubles in perspective within the meanings of hope we approach the meaning of work where we put our goals in operation. (p. 49)

I see the shiftings of meaning towards endeavor in my career development work. People who have lost a job or a career purpose are often enmeshed in their troubles and feel extremely hopeless. But gradually, as they name themselves in a variety of ways, they gain new perspectives which incorporate elements of hopefulness. Moving outside negative images of themselves they are enabled to search actively for a job and eventually find one.

TRUST: This is the sense of "being supported by the scheme of things, the feeling that one receives from life at least as much as one gives . . . endeavor can itself succeed only within a matrix that supports and sustains it, and man's basic matrix is not self-made or even man-made." (p. 50)

Out of endeavor can emerge a growing belief in an ordering of life that can sustain one's life—an ordering that establishes a sense of personal order and trust. From within trust can come the creative attitudes and creative happenings that point the person in the direction of risk taking, novelty, adventure, the putting together of the "some-things under the sun" in new and interesting combinations. But because it takes trust to open oneself to risk, undergoing therapy is sometimes a requirement for launching the program. It is the undoing of those outlooks that prevent outlook. It is the stimulation of the mind to new cognitive venturing and synthesis. And it may well be a kind of cognitive/emotional liberation that frees the person for the next step.

As trust grows, a person is better able to move towards the less easily named realms of mystery.

MYSTERY: A genuine mystery is received through a state of mind that contradicts ordinary awareness. . . . In this form of mystery information will not exorcise the mystery. . . . Less and less does our knowledge resemble floodlights progressively illumining reality's stage; a more appropriate image is that of nebulae separated by immense expanses of darkness." (pp. 53–55)

The reference point for mystery is a kind of "radical ignorance," says Smith, "that which we not only *do* not know but *can* not know through normal modes of cognition" (p. 52). Understanding of this is enhanced by knowing the word's etymology. "Mystery" is derived from *muein*, meaning "closing the eyes" or "closing the mouth." These definitions warn that "mysteries cannot be stated in ordinary language because their meanings transcend the purposes and perspective within which language was devised" (p. 52). In this manner a mystery is quite different from a problem or a secret, and is really very different from the kind of puzzle found in a "murder mystery."

A sense of the mysterious, an allowing for the mysterious, would seem to be an important way of shaping meaning as one approaches death. It means that we face an ignorance that we can ponder and estimate but which we can never fully resolve. And it would also seem that in mystery is born a sense of wonder—that quality of the person that is receptive to excited curiosity, to spontaneous response, to an allowing for the unfolding processes of life. In mystery, writes Smith, we are carried out beyond ourselves to find ourselves. I think I like that definition the most of all of these. It is the essence of the spiritual search and, I would say, a vital preparation for the processes of death.

The achievement of a personal harmony comes in the delicate balancing of these fives forms of meaning-making and not through the denial of any one of them. Even as we move into trust we will still need to acknowledge trouble if we don't want to be simplistically optimistic. If we enter the realms of mystery we need the anchorings of endeavor to avoid mystical preoccupations. And so it is, each one balancing off another in a profound mix of outlooks. And here, ultimately, are our dialogues between the growing ascendency of mind and spirit over the increasing degenerations of the body; between the positives and negatives of aging; between the hopes and fears that are part and parcel of our living experience.

Smith says it best:

If spirit stalls on the first category, trouble, without complementing it with hope, it stays in despair. If it moves on to hope, but refuses to acknowledge the labor needed to make hope real, it idles in fantasy and wishful thinking. If it accepts endeavor, but not trust, it is proud and brittle, stalking the world as a stage while melodramatically stressing the self-world dichotomy that it may boast of its unconquerable soul. If it trusts, but sees no mystery, it is shallow, unendowed with the awe Goethe named as man's best feature. In addition to being balanced, the categories must be complete. If their syndrome is deficient on either count it falls short of the human requirement." (pp. 56–57)

It is in our progressive, evolving, wondering, mysterious, creative meaning-makings that our lives take on a form, that we keep alive to the moment, that we continue to grow even unto death.

Indeed, finally, I propose no solutions. It is a question of becoming familiar with the various roads and the regions into which they lead us. I deny that the North road is absolutely and for all purposes better than the South; but this is by no means to assert that each is always as good as the other. We need to devise maps showing how each road leads in a genuinely different and interesting direction.

—Herbert Fingarette, 1962, p. 89

In the traditional parable, each of the blind men "owns" his element of the elephant. This leads to an embedded belief that his elephant, the snake, the tree trunk, the wall, is the only true elephant. Until we have generated far more information than now exists, and until our view of aging as a process and the older persons who undergo that process is far advanced from its present state, we must eschew such close identity with any narrow model lest we become wedded to it, worse still own it, or, disastrously, become owned by it.

—Carl Eisdorfer, 1983, p. 202

CHAPTER 4

A Therapy of Meaning-Making

IN MY THERAPY I meet a young man in his 20s, a high school dropout, who has just started wandering down the aisles of libraries to browse and explore. Stimulated by the discovery of learning possibility, he is becoming cognitively alive as he grasps new ideas. His eyes sparkle as he asks questions never asked before. Yet, he is troubled because he is trying to make sense of it all, trying to mesh who he was previously with the person he is only beginning to become. He wants answers and he wants them now.

Then there is Lisa, a young woman at crisis point finding her "voice" in her mid-30s, daring to explore new thoughts and ideas, to open books never attempted before, and to challenge the paternalism of her husband (who is actually delighted that she is beginning to grow).

And Leonard who, at 57, is overwhelmed by a crisis of meaning—a crisis that is bringing the realization that he has been locked into a closed mind, judging friends and experiences too quickly and dogmatically. This challenge to identity, to habit patterns, to ways of structuring his personal reality, is frightening and confusing. Yet, this man continues to move forward in a creativity of thought born of his identity crisis.

In sad contrast, I meet Elaine, a woman of 68, who has never learned to step outside herself to face the difficult questions that life can and does bring. It is very hard for her to accept the reality of physical decline, the reality that the aging process is beginning to affect her with subtleties not yet named or faced. Although her doctor has assured her that she does not have any serious disease, her imagination is running rampant. As a result, she is unable to work with her aches and pains, to come to terms with her anxiety, or to step out of her severe depression.

These various clients, coming at different stages of life, illustrate the kinds of transformational challenge, cognitive awakening, and confrontation of developmental blocks and stagnations, that are subject matter for a therapy of meaning-making. They reinforce my belief that this therapy can be used at any time of life because its sightings and its processes are geared to the evolving meaning-makings of developmental experience. And they further demonstrate for me the very real need for people to learn about themselves *early on*, to get in training *early on* as they name and practice ways to live creatively and constructively.

From this perspective, therefore, therapeutic process can move along a continuum from the continuous to the discontinuous; from that which works for all ages to that which is particularly attuned to the concerns of later life; from that which can be called a "core therapy" for life to an eclectic repertoire of "therapies" that are chosen according to particular need. What is named here is a "systemic eclecticism" within the systems-designing, systems-ordering concepts of meaning-making (see Allport, 1968, pp. 3–27).

In this manner the therapeutic experience can shift its focus from the global to the specific, from the abstract to the concrete and practical, from those therapies more properly called "counseling" (when advice-giving or teaching is the dominant modality), to that which is called "psychotherapy" as the therapist and client work together on a more in-depth transformational process. With a flexibility that moves back and forth along such a continuum, the therapist is better able to avoid the trap described by Carl Eisdorfer (1983): a close identity with a narrow therapeutic model, an identity that can cause us to become "wedded to it, worse still own it, or, disastrously, become owned by it." The therapist is also better able to increase familiarity with "the various roads and the regions into which they lead us" (Fingarette, 1962). In fact, I think this is a central challenge in working with the concerns of lifelong, creative development.

With these thoughts as introduction, let me take you into my therapeutic approach with its orientation to a cognitive, developmental point of view. First, I describe the global therapy called "meaning-making" as I share premises, goals, and tasks for the therapist. Narrowing my focus and emphasis, I then devote my discussions to therapeutic work with older people. Although I will allude to "therapies" within this overarching discussion, I will save their specifics for a later section of this book. What I offer here is my constructivist program of psychotherapy, the assumptions and biases that shape that program, and thoughts and suggestions regarding the particular challenges of creative aging.

A MEANING-MAKING THERAPY

From earliest childhood we have been drawing together the jigsaw pieces of experience in some very particular ways—ways tied to learnings both negative and positive, shaped by emotional reactions and interactions linked to many influences: family ideologies and tendencies, peer relationships, crisis experiences, cultural contexts, and environmental inputs. Here, certainly, are the inner images, emotional reactions, and cognitive systems that are so much a part of us that we often do not know their influential power. But it is this very experience, this body of our personal tacit dimensions that serves as raw material for this developmental therapy. In the uncovering and naming of this subceptual knowledge[1] and experience therapist and client work together to unravel that which is not helpful from that which can motivate and stimulate the person to the novel, the enlightened, and the enjoyable.

The reworking of our systems of meaning may come in a time of crisis, that time for "raising the possibility of making relative what [has been] taken for ultimate" (Kegan, 1982), a "crucial period of increased vulnerability and heightened potential," when one has an opportunity for "marshalling resources of growth, recovery, and further differentiation" (Erikson, 1968). The poetic juxtapositions of Chinese calligraphy say it well: crisis is "danger and opportunity" even as the person is faced with a "threat to basic psycho-social supplies where normal and available adaptive resources are exceeded for a time"—a time, therefore, when typical coping or problem-solving skills do not handle the resultant stress or tension (Caplan, 1964). These are "episodes of disorder that reflect discrepancies between environmental challenges and the individual's present capacities" (Mahoney & Gabriel, 1987)—a defini-

---

[1]Huston Smith has used this terminology in *Condemned to Meaning* (1965), building on the ideas in Lazarus and McCleary (1949), who coined the term "subcept" (as contrasted with "concept"), to refer to those things that we know but that we don't know that we know. Subceptual knowledge and meanings influence us on every level of our lives.

tion that makes this therapy's outlook particularly supportive of the dilemmas of the older person.

A major task of the therapist, then, is to work closely with the client in resolving crisis dilemmas in the service of new growth. By treating the emotional turmoil of transitional times as manifestations of developmental challenge, the therapist is frequently able to ease the fears of those clients who are certain that they are "going crazy." I have had a number of clients look at me in grateful surprise when I have quietly commented, "It sounds to me like you are going through a major life transition." In that reframing is a normalization which gives relief and reassurance.

In this therapy attention is paid not only to the cognitive but to the emotional. Indeed, I consider emotions "barometers of meaning" reflecting the meaning states and cognitive processes of the individual. Nico H. Frijda of the University of Amsterdam couches my intuition in these terms: "Emotions arise in response to the meaning structures of given situations. . . . Events that satisfy the individual's goals, or promise to do so, yield positive emotions; events that harm or threaten the individual's concerns lead to negative emotions." And further, "Emotions form the prime material in the exploration of an individual's concerns" (1988, pp. 349–358).

Another closely related concept is that of *hot cognition*. In the words of Lazarus and Folkman:

When information is appraised as having significance for our well-being, it becomes what we have called "hot information," or information that is laden with emotion. Subsequent processing takes place with this hot information, which means that the stuff of processing is no longer cold, meaningless bits. . . . We are saying that it is not only possible, but in the context of most stressful events highly probable that emotion and information (and therefore cognition) are conjoined for large portions of the evaluative appraisal process. (1984, pp. 276–277)

Thus, emotion and emotional memory both influence and reveal our meaning-makings, offering windows into personal significance and orientation. By sorting these we may come to understand more fully the negative and positive influences in our lives and to recognize the powerful two-way dynamic between our meanings and our emotions. Even as we experience, temper, and utilize the pain of crisis awakenings, we can allow for their integration into current understanding and outlook.

Which is to say: Meaning-making is not just a detached, analytical, intellectual enterprise; it involves our excitements, our griefs, our passions, as well. And certainly, for the older person experiencing progressive losses, and sometimes frightening and anxiety-producing changes, the emotions are pain responses to the "hot burners" of such personal upheaval. It is important that gerontology and a psychology of aging pay careful attention to the emotional life of the person—that we listen carefully rather than too quickly diagnosing, judging, or medicating. In our respectful listening comes new understanding of what aging is about.

THERAPEUTIC PREMISES

In harmony with other constructivist positions (see Mahoney & Gabriel, 1987, for example), this therapy is *less externally directive* as it honors and stimulates the self-organizing processes of the individual. Those processes are allowed to influence the course of therapy in order that problem resolution and personal development emerge from the mutuality of the therapeutic dialogue rather than from arbitrary impositions from the therapist. This requires a particular set of skills on the part of the therapist: pacing, reflective listening as well as active dialogue, a flexibility of style and direction, a dialectical cognitive structuring that sees into the systems of the client at the same time the therapist honors his or her own expertise and his or her place as a detached yet concerned participant in the therapeutic drama. And further, as I will discuss below, it calls upon certain kinds of attitudes and awarenesses sensitive to the needs and uniqueness of each person.

An overarching purpose in this therapy is the *facilitation of the person's sense of identity and life narrative*—a task that challenges the therapist "to facilitate a sense of sameness, continuity, and the 'real me' in creating a life of meaning" (Carlsen, 1988, p. 71). What is helpful to this process is a perspective that sees the person as both a reactive and proactive being, a person shaped by learnings and conditionings yet capable of new awarenesses and insights which can bring about change.

The therapist *approaches the client with a respect that rejects anything that might trivialize the problems of the client or demean the person*. This means that "a treatment that is essentially manipulative, for example 'paradoxical intention' is eschewed if its rationale is not clear to the patient, or if it cannot be applied with the informed consent of the patient" (Bedrosian & Beck, 1980, p. 129). Indeed, if we believe in personal meaning as an individual's organizing construct of the world, then it is arrogant, frightening, and "crazy-making" of a therapist to strategically manipulate a client's meaning system. The task is not to intervene or impose, but to join.

To facilitate this joining, *the therapeutic dialogue is adopted as a central dynamic for change*. The dialogical experience is a time of "genuine, fully receptive meeting" when "the therapist offers his or her presence in the creation of a unique dynamic for recovery, reconciliation, and renewal" (Carlsen, 1988, p. 67). A common uniting dynamic to be found in a variety of therapies (however disparate), is the central power of the relationship between the client and the therapist—a relationship that provides "a healing through meeting," where the client can find confirmations that repair previous disconfirmations (Friedman, 1985b, p. xii).

But it is not just a relationship between equals. The therapeutic dialogue is unique, necessarily one-sided, with client and therapist assuming differing roles.

Indeed, they cannot be equal. The therapist is the listener and the helper, not the one who is being helped or listened to. And with a kind of detached presence the therapist offers the contradictory elements which bring the client to moments of awakening and surprise. . . . It is not just a passive acceptance or a simplistic reinforcement of what is; it is a challenge to the individual client to recreate self by facing oneself, by naming oneself, and by daring oneself. (Carlsen, 1988, pp. 66–67)

From within this constructivist position *the therapist views the person as a flowing, interweaving mixture of the past, the present, and the future,* incorporating a "time-binding" capability which is a remarkable human capacity—what Mahoney calls the "I was, I am, and I will be" of each individual and each process. In this therapy, therefore, the therapist and client recycle and rework the learnings of the past in an interaction with the present—an interaction that uses the merging discoveries and personal creations as a springboard of meaning for the future.

THE SHAPE OF PSYCHOTHERAPY

The sequencing of this therapy is a relatively natural cognitive evolution as the therapist and client first come to know each other, to name the conflict, and then to begin the explorations and patternings that bring resolution to the problem. Out of my experience of this, I have named the following overlapping, recycling stages: (1) the *establishment* stage, when the therapist creates a relationship with the client as they begin to name the problems; (2) the *data gathering* stage, when the therapist and client work together to assemble the historical data that feed into this moment in time; (3) the *patterning* stage, with its active work to find and reshape the patterns of personal experience and knowing; and finally, (4) *closure,* an arrival at those reconciliations and resolutions that free the client to leave the therapist and the therapy room.

To enlarge on this: In the *establishment stage,* the therapist first meets the client and does the important work of inviting the person into the therapy room and setting a tone for therapy. What is desired is an atmosphere of acceptance, respect, and personal safety. As this is established, the tentative, exploratory thrustings of sharing, questioning, and answering are begun as the therapist continues to cultivate a receptive environment. Within this receptivity the roots of trust are planted and nurtured towards growth.

Very typically, some sort of unresolved conflict, identity confusion, or crisis experience brings the person to expose the private self to a stranger. These initiating concerns take therapy into the *data gathering* process. Through the intensities of the therapeutic dialogue, therapist and client work together to bring into awareness the bits and pieces of problem definition, personal statement, and emotional expression. In addition to this dialogue, every type of exploratory technique is used to facilitate this process: testing, autobiographical exercise, selected readings to stimulate thought, role playing, imaging, relaxation and meditation techniques, behavioral assignments — all to open both conscious and unconscious process to the light of naming and understanding. But the therapeutic dialogue remains central, adding its own momentum to data gathering with a mix of statement and response, of question and answer, of feeling and reaction. It is here that the therapist can both confirm and constructively contradict in arousing the energy of exploration.

As the recyclings of establishment and data gathering continue (and remember, there are no neat and tidy stages), the *patternings* of the bits and pieces emerge, develop, and accelerate. Ideally, this is a putting together of the pieces of the puzzle, not in the old way but in a new, more complex emergence of the client's knowledge and sophistication. This is the novice becoming the expert in the matters of self.

Insights do not always collect and transform. Resistances may be activated that fight new patternings. For the client, it is frequently frightening to break loose from old systems of knowing in the creation of the new, to interrupt the foundations of personal identity that have already been laid. James Fowler describes the emotional, cognitive power of this transformational interruption and development:

If you follow me in my contention that the stages which I describe are structural wholes, or ways of constructing a world, then you can imagine what it is like to move from one stage to another. In rare instances it is a smooth, gradual, incremental transformation. In most cases stage transition comes with pain. It involves enduring the dissolution of your world. You must be able to endure the falling apart of that which is held together . . . decentering and disintegration . . . are necessary for a new creation. (Fowler & Keen, 1978, p. 138)

Thus, fear, denial, or rigidity of thinking may lead a client to fight back. And if the cognitive patternings of earlier life are fairly well fixed in black/white, either/or constructions, it may be much more difficult to bring about change. Nevertheless, to examine, name, and shake personal reality is the important task of a cognitive, developmental therapy—a therapy that introduces new possibility, teaches and suggests as it models cognitive flexibility and openness (not always accomplished by the therapist, of course), and as it seeks to stimulate clients to arrive at their own insights and resolutions.

From this perspective, insight is seen as a new meaning-making, a cognition that goes *meta* on what was previously known and understood (Mahoney & Gabriel, 1987), a cognition that incorporates the "ha," "aha," and "ha-ha" of a new knowing. David Feldman (1980) calls such insight "transformational power" when a solution "breaks free from the constraints of the original problem, departing from it in a manner which stimulates further thought and reflection" (p. 102).

As insights are created, named, and developed, they need integration into the behaviors, cognitive constructions, and emotional expressions of the person. This integration constitutes a kind of reconciliation of the new with the old, of the present with the past (Loder, 1981). What this means is that new understandings are integrated with the old in an important reforming of the personal system. Not a simple cumulative process but a transformational one, this time of reconciliation and integration is also a time for practicing new behaviors and outlook within the whole business of life. Arieti, in his descriptions of creative process, would call this integrative time the "remembrance and inner replaying of past traumatic conflict" in the service of personal creativity. As one remembers, acknowledges, and integrates former conflicts, they can be seen through new eyes and new cognitive freedoms. Again, it is an ability to "go meta" on the traumas of the past—all this in the service of creative growth (Arieti, 1976, pp. 372–383).

Through the shifting, overlapping, evolving processes of establishment, data gathering, and patterning, therapy moves towards *closure*. Closure is a kind of "revolving door" which honors the reality that developmental process is never ended, that new experiences of living can bring further challenge to the person for therapeutic work. What the therapist seeks to do within this model is teach the client to handle these future transitional experiences with new understandings and new security, so that clients are independent of the therapist and the therapy room. Nevertheless, there are times when clients return for what I whimsically call "tune-ups," when a time of renewed dialogue and therapeutic process can free them once again to move on their way (for a more comprehensive discussion of the closure experience, see Carlsen, 1988, pp. 167–182).

GOALS FOR THERAPY

A listing of therapeutic goals is implicit within the overarching patternings of therapy that I have described above:

- To join each client wherever he or she is.
- To create a genuine therapeutic dialogue.
- To fully explore the feelings within the crisis experience.
- To face and use crisis experience as the energy for constructive change.
- To help the individual face basic "existential fears" without building neurotic defenses.
- To teach, facilitate, and reinforce creative thinking processes.
- To model, stimulate, and encourage dialectical thinking patterns.
- To facilitate creative aging.
- To foster meaning-making.
- To facilitate a sense of sameness, continuity, and the "real me" in creating a life that is meaningful. (Carlsen, 1988, p. 129)

This first set of goals is subsumed within a second, which speaks more directly to the problems and dilemmas of a therapy for later aging:

- To see both the negatives and positives of aging.
- To come to terms with stereotype and bias.
- To appreciate the challenges and losses inherent in the aging process.
- To explore and facilitate second careers in reframing retirement as possibility rather than withdrawal.
- To identify and teach models for creative aging.
- To facilitate the fulfillment of personal needs.
- To encourage and develop dialectical thinking, intergenerational love and care, and a transcendence of the dichotomies of self and other, of the communal and the autonomous.
- To support exploration and review of personal history in order to create a narrative of life. (Carlsen, 1988, p. 248)

Many of these goals are cognitive tasks for the therapist rather than just a set of interventions. They reflect my perspective that a developmental psychotherapy has more to do with attitude, awareness, acknowledgment, and a content of knowledge, than with a set of techniques and interventions to use with a client. They certainly reflect my further belief that to stimulate the creativity of the client requires creativity on the part of the therapist—in imagining new questions, exercises, experiences, challenges, practical solutions, possible referrals

for personal adventure and support. Within these goals is the conviction that the therapist for later aging is ready and able to step outside
the therapy room for active, innovative involvements with the environments of the person, ready and able to use practical, behavioral solutions as well as affective and cognitive ones. (I incorporate these dimensions of therapy into Chapter 7.)

In a creative manner, then, the therapist widens his or her tasks into
the practical as well as the abstract—all this while working to avoid
prejudice and simplistic categorization in working with older people.
And, at the same time that the therapist works to avoid false segrega-
tions, he or she must also avoid another extreme—that of ignoring very
real differences and needs when they are there. This constitutes another goal: *To maintain a sense of the diversities of aging at the same time
the common themes and difficulties are identified.*

One of the nicer reminders of our tendencies to paint simplistic
portraits of aging comes in this letter to the editor of *Modern Maturity*:

My siblings and I are tired of the bouncing, hyperactive "seniors" pictured in
your pages. *Seniors,* my fat foot! Life is not all that blissful when you hit the
mid-70s. Engines knock and wheels wobble. . . . Me, I'd like some practical
exchanges about ways of dealing with those wobbly wheels and knocking engines. "Golden Years"? Phooey! Not inspiring—irritating! Give us a magazine
about the realities of old age! (June–July 1989, p. 7)

But then, another "senior" writes for the same issue protesting: "If I
had joined AARP at age 50, when I was quite alive and hopeful, and
had begun receiving this magazine, I would probably have had suicidal
thoughts from just glancing through it. . . . What ever happened to
LIFE—real, throbbing life? You have me practically buried and I'm not
dead yet."

Whom do we believe? Both, of course—the two sides of aging which
defy simplistic definition but remind us to keep checking our conclusions, point-counterpoint in a dialectical approach to aging. So let's
take a moment to go into Bryan Kemp's thoughtful reminders that
there are certain dynamics in the lives of many older people that need
to be carefully considered in adapting a therapeutic program to the
unique kinds of concerns that may multiply in later aging. These can
include losses of income, peer relationships, physical vigor, and, all too
frequently, a status in life. These losses interact with other possible
issues: "impaired self-confidence, helplessness, and lack of purpose,"
the impact of stress upon bodily symptoms, and the lessening of constructive motivations and achievement-orientations (Kemp, 1985, p.
660). The therapist and client need to examine and work with these
issues against the backdrop of each individual's unique development,
personality, and current context of experience, but a central point re-

mains to be emphasized: Later aging does bring challenges and difficulties unique to its own period of life.

Writing from within the later years of his own life, Gilbert Wrenn (1989) echoes these ideas with his own: "It is generally accepted that when persons enter an older person age category they do not become different persons but are 'more of the same persons they have been.' This generalization omits the effects of a *marked loss of life roles* that have dominated earlier years" — roles that can include the following:

- establishing and rearing a family (children are now on their own and sometimes do not appreciate a carry-over of parental attitudes);
- establishing oneself vocationally (that has been done and is no longer a motivating factor);
- establishing financial security for later years (the later years are here, security is or isn't established); — accumulating things; acquiring property (for many people the limits have been reached, there is little motivation for getting more);
- competing with others for status, money, or recognition. (Most older folks have arrived at whatever peak they will reach — competition is a small factor in life.) (p. 13)

This alerts me to another goal: *To break the mythologies and negative expectations* all too frequently planted by some of the early research efforts of gerontology and psychology. In a 1985 *APA Monitor* report, Kathleen Fisher quotes Robert Kahn who cautions, "It still remains for researchers on aging to test and correct its dominant myths." He calls for therapists to design constructive interventions for the losses that occur with age; he also asks us to expand our knowledge of positive changes and to replace societal values and measures that are biased against age (Fisher, 1985, p. 12).

This alerts us to the reality that gerontology's strong emphasis on aging as a biomedical problem has all too often equated old age with illness and "has encouraged society to think about aging as pathological or abnormal" (Estes & Binney, 1989, p. 588). It is no wonder that we so easily incorporate the negative stereotypes of age, a forming of prejudice which is against ourselves as much as it is against our clients.

To break the negative equations of age, to promote the goals of a therapy for creative aging, the therapist needs a *broad base of knowledge* of the psychological, social, physical dimensions of aging — not from just one perspective but across interdisplinary lines. This includes understanding historical and cultural contexts which both shape and interact with the experiences of the person. The more inclusive is our knowledge the more effectively do we enter worlds of client meaning.

Even as I link this therapy with the concerns and challenges of successful aging, I name another goal: Accepting Carl Eisdorfer's definition, it is our task to *"optimize or maximize the adaptive capacity of the individual* by providing assistance and support where necessary, and gradually and appropriately withdrawing those supports in order to help the person retain control over his or her own life to the greatest extent possible" (Pfeiffer, 1974, p. 60).

I would emphasize the qualities of *informed sensitivity and empathy* if the therapist is to join the meaning-makings of the older person. As I have already noted, there is simply no way that we can fully understand and appreciate the demands on the older person in terms of life shifts, inner stress, interruptions of personal meaning, physical pain, and unique disorder.

For example, although investigations into achievement motivation show a lessening of achievement activity in the lives of older people, the researchers caution that *the externals do not tell the whole story.* Much that constitutes achievement may be taking place in the *inner life of the older person* as he or she struggles with all the losses and adaptations that are a part of late life disruptions of work, home, and relationships. The psychological, emotional, and social challenges of old age in an insensitive world can keep an inner pot brewing far more than is apparent on the surface of things. Frequently, the pride and autonomy of these older people are not going to let us into their inner worlds without a reason why, without a genuine trust for our motivations.

For the therapist to enter the world of the older client requires the same attitude of respect and appreciation that one has for any client, an attitude that honors the courage that it takes to grow old with dignity. It means an attitude of listening, of gentle probing, of active honoring of the integrity of the person. To come in with a set of interventions, a stereotyped set of assumptions about what this "old person" requires, is going to destroy the therapeutic relationship and do more harm than good. Such technical procedures can reduce the person to a degenerating machine instead of an expanding human being and raise the question suggested by Viktor Frankl (1969, p. 16): "Are we preserving the humanness of our clients within our therapies?"

In his preface to Jane Myers' book on gerontological counseling (1989), Gilbert Wrenn makes specific suggestions for "preserving the humanness" of older clients. An overarching theme in all his premises is the maintenance of respect for the older person and regard for his or her pride, independence, and personal dignity. Two suggestions are illustrative:

If counselors can make "counseling" a two-way street, by asking to learn from the older client as well, their mutual independence is affirmed.

Always respect the private space of the older person. If you see them having difficulty walking ask if they want help, don't assume they want help. . . . offer your arm, don't *take* theirs. (pp. 9–15)

In other words, *sensitive awareness* is another goal for the therapist who wishes to work effectively with older people — an awareness that is sophisticated and attuned to the variety of problems which come with later life; of the paradoxical juxtapositions of the unique and the universal (see Feldman, 1980, for a discussion of these themes); of the many practical dilemmas that join with those more abstract and spiritual; of the types of physical degeneration that can take place. This awareness pays attention to a wide variety of themes — themes named in the following manner by contemporary social psychologists:

- life satisfaction
- interpersonal processes
- stereotyping
- heterogeneity
- concerns of women
- health issues
- problems of financial security
- personal control issues
- problems of the physical environment
- matters of public policy (adapted from Spacapan & Oskamp, 1989)

All of which makes us agree with Robert Butler that "realistic and appropriate treatment is greatly facilitated by a fairly sophisticated understanding of social, psychological, and medical phenomena" (Butler & Lewis, 1982, p. 4).

A *constructive awareness* is heightened by heeding researchers who tell us that the "real story" in aging is "not in the average curves of maturation and decline, but in individual differences that cannot be attributed entirely to genetic functioning" (Hansson, 1989, pp. 29–30). Some of the differentiating variables that are being examined are exercise regimens, cardiac status, autonomy, personal control, lack of stimulation, lack of social support — all to see how these interact with and influence the genetic processes. To these searches can be added those linked to creativity, to lifelong learning, to volunteering and social activism, to caring for one's neighbors, to fulfilling a need to be needed — meaning-making explorations which may prove as significant as the more physically oriented interventions named above.

I am emphasizing a therapeutic awareness that is informed by emerging knowledge bases, that keeps itself up-to-date. By doing this we interrupt the promulgation of negative stereotypes and misinformation. I also emphasize a therapeutic need to open reductionist perspectives to the less understood and more mysterious processes of creativity and spiritual development. In this manner we are better able to join our clients in individualized journeys into meaning-making. We will be less likely to judge and label and dissect the processes in advance.

This further calls us to heed the research findings of Kahn (1975), who shows us how important it is to follow the principle of "minimum intervention" in the kinds of care and interventions that are offered. Particularly pertinent to institutional settings, these words of advice are also important for medical, therapeutic interventions. I become very concerned when clients are "treated" rather than "empowered," when they are medicated rather than facilitated. Again, Kahn's words are important: "too much care can lead to a self-fulfilling prophecy, result-ing in decreased coping, diminished self-concept, and premature decre-ments in cognitive and functional performance" (pp. 24–31). These are words that support Eisdorfer's admonition that an important role of the therapist is to join clients in their problems and then quietly withdraw as the person regains his or her own power.

One of my former clients returned to bring her mother for consultation. This woman had lost her husband a year before and had moved miles from her longtime home to be with her daughter. Alone in a new apartment, far from her close friends, separated from her husband by his death, she was very deeply depressed. Currently she was hospitalized and her doctors wanted to use electroshock therapy. Terrified by that prospect, she simply did not know what to do or where to turn for advice and understanding.

I tried to break through to her grief, but her heavy medication and her depression made it very difficult to accomplish anything. I also felt that she needed counseling with someone who shared her religious beliefs. I worked out a referral, but as I watched these two women leave my office I felt deep concern that this woman would not have an opportunity to work through her losses in a supportive, understanding atmosphere. I also wrestled the questions of medical intervention vis-à-vis the woman's rights and her needs to make meaning of her husband's death.

The postscript to this story is that this woman did not have electroshock, she did return to her home in the east, and she did eventually take her own life. Which raises many questions for each of us to ponder.

The therapist of aging faces many difficult questions, then, as unique personalities and backgrounds interact with the universals of aging. Even as the older person grows more dissimilar to a neighbor, he or she is thrust into the great leveling experiences of aging: the living in neighborhoods where people are all similar in age; the emerging similarities of appearance as graying hair and sagging features mute distinctive appearance; the losing of work distinctiveness and meaning just as other losses occur.

I have seen these juxtapositions in retirement communities and RV resorts where people are thrust into close proximity even as they bring dissimilarities of knowledge and outlook: the liberal next door to the conservative; a Ph.D. looking for conversational connection with a man who has never gone beyond high school; a spiritual person wondering what to do in a community of golf enthusiasts. The new juxtapositions (as one RV resident commented, "We all live in tin houses, don't we?") bring a challenge to "cathectic flexibility" as we build new bases for connection. It is here that the developmental ideals that I have named take on a new salience—when skills and attitudes of caring and giving are more helpful than self-absorbed bitterness.

In the leveling experience of old age people face a common enemy—the superordinate foe, as it were. But it isn't death that is the foe—it is the intermediate steps to dying that concern them. People are afraid of these steps because they are uncertain, unclear, unpredictable, and threaten loss of control. Even though they sign living wills and powers of attorney, a pull of the emergency cord in the night can send them flying into the arms of the medical system, whisked off by ambulance to a hospital emergency room not of their choosing, a place where the personnel have no knowledge of the neatly prepared pieces of paper that can protect the older person from lingering death. Even though a cache of pills lies hidden under a pillow, a stroke or heart attack can make it impossible to devour those pills. (Here I am not addressing the ethical concerns of such choices, simply reporting what older people share with me.) One man I talked to says he considers this the most serious problem older people face. They worry, he says, they are afraid to pull the emergency cord in their room, they live with a fear that their control will be swept away. "If you could come up with a solution for that, aging would be much easier for all of us."

This frightening dilemma for the old illustrates one of the unpredictables in old age. Bodies are less predictable. People can plan exercise programs and take charge in that way, but the unforeseen illness can strike, destroying the program. Economics are less predictable—one major illness can destroy savings and neatly laid-out plans for a comfortable retirement. And the reactions of one's culture, one's younger neighbors, are also less predictable—sometimes less easily understood or recognized in advance of being old.

Emotional reactions can hit without warning as older people face losses and disruptions not understood in advance. A doctor in Mesa, Arizona, reports that many of the older people he meets lead frenetic lives as they keep as active as possible to avoid facing the concerns of age (and I really don't find much wrong with that approach). A psychologist in the same area reports the depression born of leaving community and children behind; the panic attacks that signal deep worry that one's newly chosen life-style is beyond one's means; the marital tensions born of too much togetherness. These are the hidden stories of aging which people are reluctant to share.

[Think of the names given to retirement communities — Leisure Time Village, Carefree Acres, for example. Methinks thou doth protest too much!]

The erosion of self-concept may be an insidious invasion not expected in advance. Desire for independence may run headlong into the need for connection and forms of dependence. The glorious plan for unending leisure, for a place in the sun, may or may not be what the person hopes it will be. Unending golf games may lose their appeal, especially after one's neighbor has a heart attack on the golf course.

I make it sound so negative. It is not so negative. There is much that is good and rewarding in life-styles designed for later years — but it does take a creative, courageous spirit to tackle these major adjustments head-on and to make them work. *This is where societal preparation for creative aging can help all of us to know the pitfalls and to prepare more fully for the tasks which are to come. This is where the therapist can come in with information and methods to aid the aging person. This is where the therapist needs to understand and know the needs of people in general and, in this case, the needs of the older person specifically.*

HUMAN NEEDS IN LIFE AND IN AGE

I found a strong statement of basic human needs in my dissertation study of a group of mature women, 35 years and older, who returned to undergraduate study at the University of Washington (Carlsen, 1973). In response to my survey they noted how very important it was for them to contribute, achieve, partake, earn, challenge, exert, compete, explore, prove, and succeed. Additionally, they wanted opportunity to:

- give
- be an active part of life
- view the world with a widening perspective
- complete difficult goals
- build a balance between creative learning and creative vocation
- find monetary success in a world that honors money
- find a feeling of self-identity

The body of needs articulated by these older women gives clues as to the kinds of meaning-makings that call out to all of us, regardless of age. We have needs to develop a sense of self, a continuity in how we make meaning of ourselves. In the development of this uniqueness, this dependable sense of self, we need to have our needs mirrored by others and to see that our meanings make sense; we need freedom and respect for unique creative expression; and we need to be seen and accepted for who and what we are.

Not only do we have needs tightly entwined with the sense of self, but we also have needs to be participating in the business of life — in the order of things. Is not the dilemma of every minority group the dilemma of not being allowed "into the order of things"? What a denial for older people, then, when they are removed from their channels of order and influence! No wonder some older people buy RVs and head out. They are creating a new order of things that is their own — that they can control. I think of colleagues who say their RV enables them to *go* to their children rather than always sitting back and being at the mercy of their children's timetables. Isn't "control" a question of the order of things — to have an order that one has created? A meaning, therefore, of one's own choosing?

So, what if some of the basic therapeutic questions in working with aging folks include the following: "How can we keep on finding uniqueness, a sense of participation in the order of things, and a place and time for intimacy and partnership? How do we handle the losses of our need fulfillments? How do we prepare ourselves early on for these losses as we find other needs to fulfill and other orders to maintain?"

These questions reflect human needs to shape continuities of identity and patterns of significance. These continuities and meaningful patterns are just as essential for our sense of well-being as life participations, neededness, and interpersonal connections. Indeed, our drive to live meaningful lives is at the heart of all our needs. We need to pay attention to this drive and to realize that anxiety, depression, or despair are frequently signs that our ways of making meaning are no longer functioning effectively. These emotional signals may be telling us that it is time again to refresh and order the purposes for our lives.

A final need: People need to be mirrored in the reactions and dialogues with others. A strong statement of this comes from physician Arnold Beisser (1989) who faced the horror of almost total helplessness as the result of a polio attack. He observed, from his isolation in his iron lung, many of the dilemmas of meaning-making between his caregivers and himself. They were in their worlds and he was in his and often these two worlds did not meet in the mutuality of understanding and dialogue. But there were the exceptions — those who could and were willing to enter his reality for a time. At those moments his sense of self was somehow redeemed and he was once again able to give back to those around him.

The responsiveness of these compassionate helpers made me feel human again, and brought forth the qualities in me that made it possible to be a support to others. With them I felt returned from exile. The pariah was forgiven for his crime, and felt restored to life. (p. 38)

In the next two chapters I describe those prejudicial attitudes that just might keep us from forgiving the pariah for his crime or from making him feel human again.

SECTION II

Cognitive Interruptions in Creative Aging

... every careful observer can see that great numbers of adults in their later years do little or nothing to keep alive the fires of mental alertness and learning capacity. They confront rich potentiality only with passiveness, which is indeed a form of resistance. Or they have organized their lives as a flight from the occasional discomforts and real delights of systematically breaking into new fields. It is a truism of the adult learning world that performance is transformed by an active rather than passive mind-set, and by a life filled with the thrust for learning. Passivity and a turning-away from the challenges to learn are not part of the aging process per se; they are self-induced or peer-induced attitudes about the roles and purposes of older adults.

—John A.B. McLeish, 1983, p. 102

CHAPTER 5

Patterns That Interrupt

THUS FAR I HAVE presented a number of dilemmas which can interrupt the process of creative aging: tendencies of all of us to divide humanity into categories of "them" and "us" according to age; the muting of individuality within the "leveling" experiences of old age; the fears and worries engendered by unpredictabilities of economics, personal health, and control (the pullcord on the wall that can catapult a person into the arms of medical technology, for example); and all the demographic changes that are interacting with resources, allocations, and generational relationships.

Then there are others: the greed of a "bottom line" society; the dilemmas of technology vs. quality of life, personal choice vs. legislative decree; the costs of health care eroding one's carefully hoarded resources; disease orientations denying the older person's capacity for healing; heavy-duty pharmacology regimens muting the aging mind. There are the problems of loneliness and drug addiction. Even more, there are the problems of caregiving that challenge family and friends to handle physical, economic, and emotional demands while caring for their older loved ones—and all too often these caregivers are older adults themselves, with limited resources of energy and financial support to meet the stress and requirements of their role.

The list is long, pointing to those interruptions of creative aging that come very frequently from outside ourselves. But there are other kinds of interruptions to be considered—interruptions that result from limited perspectives and restricted ways of thinking, either our own or those of others around us. Here are cognitive rigidities, black/white processings of experience, simplistic generalizations, stereotypes—all processes that distort and narrow perceptual possibility even as they contribute to separatism, anxiety, depression, loneliness, and overreaction. These are not the interruptions of mental retardation or dementia, those born of genetic limitation or physical derailment—these are the limited, negative thinking patterns that place tight restrictions on the kinds of information that are processed and that seriously distort our meaning-makings.

This chapter constitutes a brief overview of some of the cognitive interruptions to creative aging. In describing these I am preparing the way for my discussion of ageism in the next chapter.

STEREOTYPING AND PREJUDICE

The term *stereotype*, first coined in 1798 by the French printer Didot, was originally used in the printing and newspaper industry to refer to a one-piece metal sheet cast from a mold that had been taken from a printing surface. Approximately a century later, psychiatrists began to use the related term *stereotypy* to designate a particular kind of repetitive, unchanging manner of expression. Although stereotypy is different from a stereotype, its meanings and the "related notions of 'fixed,' 'unchanging,' and 'persistent' point to one of the major themes, usually referred to as 'rigidity,' in stereotype research and theory" (Ashmore & Del Boca, 1981, pp. 1–2). A third stage in the application of the terminology occurred in 1922, when sociologist Walter Lippman took the term as a metaphor to refer to the "pictures in our heads" of various racial, national, religious, or ethnic groups. Lippman's basic thesis was that human beings do not respond directly to their external realities but to a "representation of the environment which is in lesser or greater degree made by man himself" (1922, p. 10).

In 1933, Katz and Braly conducted a classic empirical study of stereotypes and later linked their findings about stereotype to attitudes and prejudice. Gordon Allport (1935) also linked prejudice and stereotype and articulated his point of view that stereotypes are bad. Adorno, Frenkel-Brunswik, Levinson, and Sanford brought many of these ideas together into their monumental, two-volume work, *The Authoritarian Personality* (1950). Throughout much of the research generated by this work, the link between prejudice and stereotype has been reinforced with a logic that prejudice is a social problem; it is bad to be prejudiced; therefore it is bad to hold stereotypes (Ashmore & Del Boca, 1981, pp. 6–10).

But this automatic labeling of the cognitive processings of stereotype as "bad" was not inherent in the thinking of Lippman. He actually took an equivocal stand on this question, even as he acknowledged the possible consequences of stereotyping: "The abandonment of all stereotypes for a wholly innocent approach to experience would impoverish human life. What matters is the character of the stereotypes and the gullibility with which we employ them" (1922, p. 90). Thus, according to Arthur Miller (1982), Lippman actually made a sharp distinction between the process and the product of stereotyping, "an insight that would often be rediscovered by later scholars" (p. 6).

The reason I emphasize these contrasts is to encourage appreciation of the value of stereotyping as a cognitive process at the same time that I emphasize how easily stereotyped thinking can lead us into prejudice. I find this definition from the *Harper Dictionary of Modern Thought* to be a helpful clarification:

An over-simplified mental image of (usually) some category of person, institution, or event which is shared, in essential features, by large numbers of people. The categories may be broad (Jews, gentiles, white men, black men) or narrow (women's libbers, Daughters of the American Revolution), and a category may be the subject of two or more quite different stereotypes. Stereotypes are commonly, but not necessarily, accompanied by prejudice, i.e. by a favourable or unfavourable predisposition towards any member of the category in question. (Bullock & Stallybrass, 1977, p. 601)

What is to be remembered is that the word stereotype has received bad press because "to stereotype" has often been equated with "to be prejudiced" and "to discriminate." But again, the act of stereotyping is not inherently bad. In fact, it is a very important cognitive means for handling the mass of input into our perceptual systems. Stereotypes help us to bring order out of chaos by organizing our observations of human behavior. They represent convenient packaged models for interpreting complex events and interactions.

Stereotyping is negative when we respond in a fixed, unconscious way to some person solely in terms of the person's classification. In doing so we lose the person as an individual. Although stereotypes allow us to complete incomplete pictures and are often born of legitimate observations, they may also lead us to assuming without question that anyone possessing a particular key trait (femaleness, for example, or being "a gray-haired man who owns an RV") automatically possesses a whole range of related traits such as docility, emotionalism, and lack of managerial skills in the first example, or being retired, getting old, leaving children behind in the other (many RV adventurers have definitely not retired!). Such assumptions block us from seeing uniqueness or from creating new combinations of traits. When we stereotype our judgment may be not only premature but also faulty (Wortmann, Loftus, & Marshall, 1981).

Stereotyping was sharply illustrated when I was traveling to another country with my husband and his colleague, an attractive black woman professor.

We stopped for the border check where the guard leaned through the window to ask who we were and what business we had in his country. My husband described himself and then, pointing to his colleague in the back seat, said:

"This is Dr. Jones, a professor from the University."

"What is his business in our country?" the guard asked.

"She is presenting a paper," my husband replied.

"Where does he come from?"

"She comes from Seattle."

This strange dialogue continued without our interrogator ever acknowledging that the person in the back seat of our car was a woman. We puzzled over this later, finally coming to the conclusion that the border guard simply could not fit "black woman, professor" into his cognitive processing. We theorized that his sexist and racist stereotypes were colliding in a way that prevented him from really seeing.

How are stereotypes maintained even when we receive evidence to the contrary? Part of the answer lies in the way human memory works. We filter new information through screens of existing knowledge and beliefs. Anything that doesn't fit our preconceived notions is ignored or reshaped. And anything that does conform to our expectations is likely to make a strong impression on us. As a result, "we are often victims of illusory correlations: we think that certain stereotyped associations are far more frequent than they actually are" (Wortman, Loftus, & Marshall, 1981, p. 569).

To support our assumptions and our illusory correlations we dismiss conflicting evidence with "yes-but" reasoning. For example, "He's a gentle, thoughtful man, but he is an exception." "Claude Pepper was an outstanding leader right up to the time of his death, but he was an exception." "Florida Scott-Maxwell was vital in her thinking, still writing in her eighties, but she was an exception." And so it is—our lenses of gender, of race, of age, leading to overgeneralization of what is true for the individuals who populate these categories.

The problem for human liberation of every kind is that stereotypes can exclude people from opportunity. A further problem is that science, operating with its own stereotypical lenses, may actually create more. Thus, in ageism, we begin to treat aging as a disease process, older people as rapidly losing their capabilities, and thus we frequently arrive at the kinds of prejudice that negate the creativities and personal capacities of the old. Here is the "New Ageism" which Richard A. Kalish describes:

The message of the New Ageism seems to be that "we" understand how badly you are being treated, that "we" have the tools to improve your treatment, and that if you adhere to our program, "we" will make your life considerably better. You are poor, lonely, weak, incompetent, ineffectual, and no longer terribly bright. You are sick, in need of better housing and transportation and nutrition, and we—the nonelderly and those elderly who align themselves with us and work with us—are finally going to turn our attention to you, the deserving elderly, and relieve your suffering from ageism. (1979, p. 398)

Such prejudices lead to the angry protest of Maggie Kuhn, who decries the "playpens" for the old:

Take, for instance, the so-called Golden Age Clubs which I call glorified playpens. It is assumed that old people are like children and that what we really need, in order to feel contented and cared for, is a place to play. And of course, like children, we must be protected from physical danger. We are thus isolated from the mainstream of life, not only by playing instead of working and producing and contributing, but by the fact that we are not given even a shred of choice of "games." (Kuhn, 1974)

But lest we only point the finger elsewhere, this chapter is about us as well as others—about the patterns we all use and misuse and not just in the matters of age.

INTERPRETIVE PARSIMONY

Another form of cognitive processing which may contribute to narrowed perspectives is what C.G. Prado (1986) has named "interpretive parsimony." In the manner of stereotyping, "the parsimonious get that way by succeeding at what parsimony is all about, the ordering of experience" (p. 51). Thus, a teacher may learn to anticipate the types of questions students ask in the course of their study. This experiential understanding helps the teacher to field the questions that arise and to maintain the status of expert. This is helpful, of course, but if the teacher closes off innovative questions to protect this position, or if the teacher is afraid to say "I don't know," the very ordering of material, this very parsimony, can impede effectiveness rather than facilitating it. This is true because parsimony "conditions perception and reinforces the practices in question" (Prado, 1986, p. 51).

It is the conditoning and reinforcement that can shut the eyes and ears of therapists when dealing with their clients, for example. Or of doctors who listen to their patients through the ears of theory and diagnosis. Indeed, I can't help thinking of some of my colleagues who describe their cases in the jargon of the trade, so that unique individuals become "borderline," "manic-depressive," "obsessive." Although its orderings are important, diagnosis can be the kind of parsimony that limits new insights into the problems of the person, that does not pay attention to all the other dilemmas at hand.

The dilemma in interpretive parsimony is that the ordering is helpful in the organization of our inputs, but the capability can carry us too far. A strength carried too far can become weakness: To carry justice too far is to lose compassion; to stereotype too far is to build prejudice; to organize life too definitively and too parsimoniously is to lose cognitive openness and the playfulness of imagination. To repeat, the "parsimonious get that way by succeeding at what parsimony is all about, the ordering of experience."

It is the very reality that successful responses lead to their own reward and reinforcement that may lead us down blind alleys into a simplistic reliance on "too few and too familiar ways of construing situations or ordering experience. Every time a familiar response proves satisfactory, there is selection against new construals and therefore against new responses" (Prado, 1986, p. 52). If we continue to practice these habits as we grow older we may very well become the narrow-minded, rigid older folks who fit into stereotypes of aging. But as Prado cogently notes, it is not aging *per se* that makes us that way, it is all the many practicings of these cognitive processings in the name of perceptual efficiency that lead us into restricted outlooks as we grow older.

Such parsimony of thinking can keep us locked into mythologies that shape our lives and expectations. These "infrastructures" of belief and actions may well lay down simplistic rules of what is right and proper in "old age," or influence a statement such as "This is the way I've always done it and I am not willing to change." Such parsimony can lead to the negative patternings typical of depression—to the selectivity of cognitive response which reinforces a sense of failure, of low self-esteem, of hopelessness:

[In working with the patient to review life history and to identify major patterns which influence the emergence of depression.] It is generally possible to demonstrate to him that he responds *selectively* to certain types of experiences; i.e., he does not overreact to *every* type of difficult or unpleasant situation, but has a predilection to react excessively to *certain* events. (Beck, 1967, p. 319)

To interrupt such simple assignment and response is the task of any therapy, but it is a particular focus of the psychotherapies of cognitive behaviorists like Aaron Beck and his colleagues. All of us in the field of aging have much to learn from their suggestions and framings of therapeutic intervention.

COGNITIVE/EMOTIONAL BLOCKS

An engineer, artist, administrator, and teacher of creative thinking to engineering students at Stanford University, James Adams has used his research skills and creative imagination to identify selective patterns of thought which can all too easily interrupt the flexibility and openness to experience that is characteristic of creative thinking. He summarized his ideas in *Conceptual Blockbusting* (1979), which he opens in this manner:

Few people like problems. Hence the natural tendency in problem-solving is to pick the first solution that comes to mind and run with it. The disadvantage of this approach is that you may run either off a cliff or into a worse problem than you started with. A better strategy in solving problems is to select the most attractive path from many ideas, or concepts. (p. xi)

Adams describes conceptual blocks as "mental walls that block the problem-solver from correctly perceiving a problem or conceiving its solution" (p. 11). He says we all have these blocks but are frequently unaware of their extent and their influence on our thinking. But as we become more aware of different kinds of blocks, as we increasingly identify our particular version of these blocks, and as we consciously interrupt these limiting thinking patterns, we can begin to open our minds to new possibilities for problem solution. Such awareness can help not only our own perceptual awareness and openness, but that of our clients as well. This is important remedial and preparatory work for creative aging.

One conceptual block is stereotyping: *Seeing what you expect to see.* When a person processes information primarily through stereotype it is difficult to see something without being controlled by preconception (Adams, p. 13). Which brings us back to the problems of ageism when we process people according to a prototype, a category of traits and qualities that are supposed to be true of old people in general. It also brings us back to the problems of simplistic diagnostic category at any age. If we are specialists in borderlines we may begin to see everyone as a "borderline"; if we are phenomenological therapists we may forget the biological in the name of the cosmic; if we are gerontologists we may inadvertently create separatisms in the name of aging.

Difficulty in isolating the problem. Adams believes that problems can be obscured by either inadequate clues or misleading information. "If the problem is not properly isolated, it will not be properly solved"

(p. 22). In fact, the beginning of solution is found in the naming of the problem as we clear the debris of inadequate clues and misleading information, as we sift and sort the body of concerns to be addressed. But there is an interesting problem to be found if we move to the next conceptual block which Adams names.

A *tendency to delimit the problem area too closely*. In general, Adams writes, "the more broadly the problem can be stated, the more room is available for conceptualization. . . . A problem statement which is too limited inhibits creative ability" (p. 21). Thus, as the therapist and client work together to find the *essence* of the problem, they may, paradoxically, have to *spread* the problem. Kegan (1982) has addressed this issue, suggesting that therapy offers the potential for "spreading out" the problem as the therapist helps the client to step outside of the problem to perceive it in entirely new ways. I do this with my clients by shaking open the meanings of the problem with various kinds of questions: "What do you mean by this?" "Are there other ways you can express this problem?" "What are some of the words that come to mind when you think about this problem?" Even further, I help the client "spread the problem" by seeing how it interacts with other areas of life, with personal relationships, with history.

In some areas of life, then, problem definition needs to be done quite directly, but in other areas of life, problem definition may require the willingness to wander down a number of pathways before the clutter of influence is cleared away. Perhaps the wisdom of the therapist and the wisdom of the client are what are cultivated here—the ability to know the difference in the kinds of problem-solving required.

Inability to see the problem from various viewpoints. In many cases, no solution is possible until each person involved can gain a feeling for the viewpoint of the other. This is a reminder of the capacity for dialectical thinking which Michael Basseches has named—the dialectical capacity that enables us to look into the systems of meaning of the other person without losing a sense of our own. Limited capacity for this kind of understanding is a serious factor in breakdowns of communication, whether they be between therapist and client or husband and wife. Certainly, one of the major tasks of marital therapy is to first identify the unique perceptions, history, and concerns of each partner. This starts movement towards greater understanding, appreciation, and, one hopes, acceptance of marital differences.

Saturation is another form of cognitive block:

Saturation takes place with all sensory modes. If the mind recorded all inputs so that they were all consciously accessible, our conscious mind would be very full indeed. Many extremely familiar inputs are not recorded in a way that allows their simple recall. (p. 34)

Thus, in a manner similar to stereotyping and parsimony, saturation is an important mechanism in cognitive processing, essential if we are to simplify our worlds, to bring sense out of the bombardments of stimuli which come from our environments. Because this is so we need to examine our saturations, to shake loose periodically, to freshen our perspectives. I think of art of every kind as a kind of "freshening," an awakening to new experience within the familiar. To examine the diversities of aging, to separate the particular person from the mass, is certainly one way of breaking free our saturations within our day-to-day processings.

A failure to utilize all sensory inputs. This raises a point for the therapist: If we fail to utilize a variety of sensory inputs we may be limiting the creativities of our client and of ourselves. And we may be neglecting a way to interrupt the saturations described above. Or we may be neglecting opportunities to help our older clients to sharpen sensory awareness in whatever way possible—for example, substituting new kinds of stimulus which will bring renewed sensual enjoyment (like introducing a new taste experience or experimenting with touch and smell).

Emotional blocks. Adams describes a number of emotional blocks which can interfere with creative process. These include a fear of taking a risk, no appetite for chaos, a tendency to judge rather than to generate ideas, the inability to incubate, either a lack of challenge or an excessive zeal, and a lack of access to areas of imagination. Because these blocks touch areas of feeling not always articulated by seniors reared in more stoical culture, working through them with clients may take some sensitive work on the part of the therapist.

Then there are the *cultural* and *environmental blocks* which reflect a variety of belief systems:

a. Fantasy and reflection are a waste of time, lazy, even crazy
b. Playfulness is for children only
c. Problem-solving is a serious business and humor is out of place
d. Reason, logic, numbers, utility, practicality are *good*; feeling, intuition, qualitative judgments, pleasure are *bad*
e. Tradition is preferable to change. (Adams, 1979, p. 33)

And then there are all the taboos which enter one's thinking and feeling about what is OK and what is not OK: It is not OK to be too loud; it is not OK to show anger; it is not OK not to go to church; it is important that family secrets never be shared; in this family we do not talk about sex or tell sex jokes. Each one of us probably knows a few of these which guide us in ways we may not even know.

Intellectual and expressive blocks. These may result from "an inefficient choice of mental tactics or a shortage of intellectual ammunition" on the one hand, and the inhibition of the "vital ability to communicate ideas—not only to others, but to yourself as well" (p. 72). Adams refines these further, giving us a listing which could well serve as a set of challenges for therapy:

1. Solving the problem using an incorrect language (verbal, mathematical, visual) . . .
2. Inflexible or inadequate use of intellectual problem-solving strategies
3. Lack of, or incorrect, information
4. Inadequate language skill to express and record ideas (verbally, musically, visually, etc.). (p. 71)

As I close Adams' discussion I alert you to Roger von Oech's *A Whack on the Side of the Head* (1983), which is geared to business but helpful to therapeutic work as well—at least my clients enjoy reading his books and are often shaken into examining their thinking habits with a more open perception.

ARNOLD LAZARUS

The ideas from Adams complement those of Arnold Lazarus, who wrote his *Behavior Therapy and Beyond* (1971) as a kind of revisionary treatise on his evolution from strict behaviorist to cognitive behavioral theorist and therapist. He asks, "Why do so many psychotherapists who view themselves as 'scientists' behave with the same defensive fervor that we ordinarily associate with religious fanaticism?" (p. 24).

I like Lazarus' question and I like his modeling. He is courageous in naming his changes in perspective, in illustrating a "dis-ordering" of theory to make room for a more flexible, open position. In the process he suggests some very helpful approaches to therapy as well as a summary of cognitive blocks similar to and/or overlapping with those named by Adams. He also gives us a "multimodal" therapy, which he calls a "technical eclecticism," asking us to widen our repertoires for therapy. "Our primary assumption is that the more people learn in therapy, the broader their coping responses become, the less likely are they to relapse" (1976, p. 4). This is also a way to break the cognitive parsimony of some therapeutic approaches:

As soon as one identifies with a particular theory or subscribes to a definite school of thought, one develops vested interests in strengthening and confirming that system's basic theoretical underpinnings. Almost inevitably, one's selectivity of perception comes into play, so that pet theories become blessed with all sorts of confirming "data" and substantiating "evidence." (1976, p. 3)

Within a multimodal, trans-theoretical framework, the therapist is freed to sample therapeutic work with (1) behavior, (2) affect, (3) sensation, (4) imagery, (5) cognition, (6) interpersonal relationship, and (7) drug therapy, if needed. These varying approaches can be particularly helpful if therapy becomes "stuck" in its own adaptations and stagnations. For both the therapist and the client, these differing techniques suggest ways to shake loose, to interrupt limiting cognitive patterning of the type that Lazarus has identified:

Dichotomous reasoning: This is black/white, either/or thinking which doesn't allow much room for the exploration of the gray areas of ideas, or a third alternative in decision making. This kind of thinking also leads to success/failure, perfect/imperfect models of personal action, models that sometimes make people surrender a project or an idea because they are so afraid to fail or to be imperfect. Much therapeutic time is spent in efforts to interrupt these patterns.

Belief and disbelief are a part of this. When people are frightened or insecure they may close their minds to alternative belief systems and to any information that might crack the systems of their tightly organized beliefs. Defending these tightly held beliefs can contribute to tension and defensiveness. To facilitate the opening of rigid categories of belief, Lazarus has found it very helpful to "assign to some of my patients the task of discovering some facts and accurate information about their very strong disbelief systems. When they become more open minded, it is often impressive to observe the ensuing reduction in their overall tension and anxiety" (1971, p. 168).

Overgeneralization. This cognitive patterning is similar to stereotyping and to the problems of dichotomous reasoning. Here are the tendencies to see the work of a homemaker as just the opposite of a career woman, or the writing capabilities of an old woman as very different from the skills of a woman in midlife. In overgeneralization is the tendency to assign a body of traits to an individual. In Lazarus' words, "The person who overgeneralizes see *all* women drivers as dangerous, *all* salesmen as crooks, *all* politicians as corrupt, and *all* insurance companies as unreliable" (1971, p. 169). And here certainly, is the person who sees all seniors as incompetent drivers, all frail elderly people as mentally incompetent, all RV travelers as "white, Anglo-Saxon, Protestant" Americans.

To interrupt patterns of dichotomization, of overgeneralization, I am ever alert for the languages of "always," "totally," "never," which I challenge with new definitions. I also have my clients draw a continuum from success to failure, or from young to old, and ask them to indicate the moment of truth when definition slips from one to another. In viewing the continuum, clients see a graphic representation of the reality that the either/or is very difficult to interpret or assign. We also work at definition: "What is success? What is failure? Is there another way of looking at this? Another way to ask our questions or interpret the results of our efforts?" Many clients have had what I call a "cognitive flip," when their thinking leaps towards a more dialectical perspective that can name and weigh alternative cognitive processings.

Another block to creative thinking and living is *excessive reliance on other people's judgment.* Here is the "should" and the "ought," not born of self-definition and determination but passively accepted from the edicts of others. Here is the confusion of reports like "I am a housewife" with judgments such as "I am only a housewife." It is the therapeutic task to awaken client thinking to these habits and tendencies, and to help each person to sort and challenge each judgmental conclusion. (I do have to remind some clients, however, that evaluation is okay. These individuals feel elitist and judgmental if they name something as being good or not so good, worthy or not so worthy. This dynamic is a different pattern of thinking and feeling.)

And, finally, *enculturation and oversocialization* can be blocks. Lazarus believes that personal, emotional "suffering is often a consequence of cultural enslavement. Many people regard cultural values as absolutes and have never paused to consider their relativity. They are entirely molded by the culture and assimilate all its contradictions" (p. 171). When unhappiness is clearly the outcome of passivity and an uncritical yielding to cultural shaping, the therapist's task is to facilitate the client's ability to be more objective, more detached from the system, more independent in thought and action.

This has been a brief summary of a few habits which all too easily shape and reinforce cognitive rigidity. By thus stepping outside our own habits to think about thinking—in other words, to go "meta" on our own systems—perhaps we can become more alert to tendencies in ourselves and in others to block creative, imaginative thinking, or to reinforce limited perspectives on aging. Perhaps, at the same time, we can help shatter the ageist "pictures in the head" which are the curse of ageism.

White racists do not suddenly wake up to find themselves
black; male sexists cannot turn into women; but ageists are
prejudiced against a minority group that they all one day will
join. Thus, individuals who have grown up in our age-denying
culture will grow old in an environment that fills them with
self-loathing when they reach the magic age of sixty-five.

—Robin Marantz Henig, 1985, p. 6

"Agism" is a new word in the lexicon of fashionable evils. Like
. . . sexism and racism, it seeks to express an old evil in a new
way—in this case prejudice in thought and deed against the
old.

—*Oxford English Dictionary*, 1989

CHAPTER 6

Ageism

AFTER BEING INTRODUCED by Robert Butler in 1969, the word
"ageism" stands alongside sexism and racism in contemporary vocabularies of prejudice and stereotype. And like these others it represents
patterns of thinking and perceiving which are part of our normal human processing but which have become locked into "pictures in our
head," our mental templates, our categorizing of a group of people
according to some significant set of characteristics.

This chapter is the story of ageism, of the prejudice and stereotype
which places the elderly in the category of "them." Here is Jennie
Keith's "exotic breed," outside the pale of ordinary human perception.
Here are those people called geezers and crocks, those people who
become the "invisible generation" as they are pushed to the edge of
cultural experience. Here are people seen first as old, people who have
many of their unique qualities and assets negated, demeaned, or ignored through the sightings of age. When ageism operates older people
are simplistically categorized in a manner Art Linkletter effectively
describes:

Although I can be included in the category commonly referred to as old, I'd rather think that when someone describes me, that's the last thing that comes to mind. It has nothing to do with who I am, what I am, or how I live my life. My age now, like my age 20 years ago, marks the year in which I was born. That's all. (*Mature Outlook*, July/Agust 1988, p. 75)

Ageism includes subtleties named by two retired professors:

I think, too, that the current emphasis on "gerontology" puts retired people into a special category that isolates us from those who are still working. Caring for the elderly may be a form of compassion, but I wish it were not becoming such a growth industry.

The present pattern [of retirement] is rather strange. Before retirement a professional person is much admired and sought for his contributions, but as soon as he retires he is forgotten as though he is a changed person. (Milletti, 1984, p. 83)

Indeed, writes Neugarten (1982, p. 27), "Policies and programs aimed at 'the old,' while they have been intended to compensate for inequity and disadvantage, may have the unintended effect of adding to age segregation, of reinforcing the misperception of 'the old' as a problem group, and of stigmatizing rather than liberating older people from the negative effects of the label, 'old.'"

Stereotyped perception can contribute to strange dynamics and conversations like the following:

We were at a convention party in preparation for one of the improvisational mystery theaters suddenly popular at convention dinners. I was to play the part of the mother-in-law and, appropriately garbed in a long shawl, I was chatting with a counselor friend who had also been drafted to perform. Catching the spirit of my role, my psychology colleague told the following joke: "It's true. Just like wine older women ripen with age. But, unlike old wine, they are best left in a dark cellar."

Ageist perception contributes to an experience like that of a professional colleague, a leader in the field of aging. She was a guest on a local afternoon talk show where she was answering questions about her professional work. As she offered ideas and suggestions for helping older people, the young announcer abruptly plunged in to ask, "Why should I be paying attention to you? You're just an 'old bag.'"

These experiences join the many others that illustrate the restricted visions and limited cognitive processings of ageist stereotype and prejudice which eliminate large portions of the qualities of the individual. They are manifestations of distorted attitudes towards and interpretations of the aged, old age, and the aging process. They breed discriminatory practices and foster institutional practices and policies "which often without malice, perpetuate stereotypic beliefs about the elderly, reduce their opportunities for a satisfactory life and undermine their personal dignity" (Butler, 1980, p. 8).

A stereotype is a cognitive prototype of what a category of persons is all about. These prototypes come from many sources, some so subtle and longstanding in the psychology of our culture that they are difficult to distinguish. Bianchi (1982) is one of those students of aging who has traced some of these influences. He describes both Chaucer and Montaigne as writers who portrayed repulsive moral traits in the old, often interlinking bodily and moral decline. Montaigne named envy, greed, injustice, and malice as somehow part of the promise of old age; and Chaucer saw little significance left for the elderly because "For oldsters, save for dotage, there's no more" (*Canterbury Tales*, Chapter One).

Literary depictions of what aging is about resonate in our mythologies and imagery, no doubt influencing us in far greater ways than we realize:

These depictions of elderhood mold collective, inherited attitudes that manifest the curious interplay of psychological projection and ageism. Surely some old people display many of the traits cited by Chaucer and Montaigne. But the common, almost socially acceptable, ways of attributing reprehensible qualities to the old awaken the suspicion that mental projection is at work. The obvious physical decline of aging persons becomes an occasion for projecting onto them moral flaws. The observed physical infirmities of the old become convenient excuses for ascribing moral weakness to them. (Bianchi, 1982, p. 171)

Bianchi calls ageism a "grim preface against which we shape our personal lives in elderhood." To interrupt its prejudicial influence, he believes, we must first identify the stereotyping and then resist its insidious intrusion by changing the images of age within ourselves as well as in the public domain. By naming the enemy, by understanding more clearly how "ageist attitudes have been deeply seared into our civilization for centuries," by acknowledging that we live and die in a relatively ageist society, we can continue to find understanding of the processes, manifestations, and solutions to the problems of this continuing prejudice in our time.

Just how important this is not only for the "elderly" but for younger generations is emphasized in an informative booklet, "Truth About Aging," published by the American Association for Retired Persons:

Biases against aging are often so deeply ingrained in our culture that they are difficult to identify. They unintentionally creep into our writing, films, and conversation. Only through a conscious effort on the part of publishers, producers, advertisers, writers, and other communicators can ageism be eliminated. But the benefits are well worth the effort. First, communications will be more accurate, thus realistic. Second, they may enjoy a larger audience. And third, in a broader sense, such efforts may help individuals — older and younger alike — realize their potential, thereby enhancing the well-being of our society. (AARP, 1986, p. 3)

All this is central to creative aging. If we live life with a negative, fearful approach to later aging we will defeat many of those processes that can lead to creative aging. The AARP booklet says it well: "The pernicious effects of ageism . . . are not limited to older persons. Their impact on youngsters is particularly sad. Studies show that when young people develop a negative view of aging and of older persons, they may lower their goals for achievement in later life" (p. 2).

And from Eric Pfeiffer:

We pay a very high price for our single-minded and simple-minded stereotypes of growing old. Growing old comes in many different flavors and we misperceive the situation badly when we think or treat all older persons as though they are alike. (1974, p. 7)

To interrupt ageism a variety of tasks are ours: (1) Name the manifestations of ageist prejudice present in contemporary American society, (2) describe and define the kinds of cognitive process that influence such manifestations, (3) identify how these cognitive processes spread into decision-makings about the elderly, and (4) offer possible solutions which we can all — therapists, helping professionals, younger and older persons — begin to incorporate into our thinking, feeling, speaking, and doing.

And I here acknowledge my own prejudice. Just as I discovered my prejudices against women in my earlier work in gender discrimination, I have found many of my ageist perspectives in my researching of this book. This writing is a genuine effort to break free from those automatic emotional and cognitive reactions. Even as I acknowledge my own ageist images and attitudes I state how ageist it is to go in the other direction to classify all of the elderly as happy, healthy, and satisfied — to portray the senior as living in the so-called "Golden Years," the "prime time" of life.

Richard Freedman (1978) dares us to remember that the "greatest literature . . . frequently reveals with unblinking truth the very negative attitudes to the elderly which, if we were honest, most of us would admit we feel" (p. 49). And he asks us to realize that improving the material plight of the elderly requires us to discard our pretense that "old age is any happier a condition than in fact it is" — that we must face the worst that has been thought and written about it in order to rise "superior to our negative feelings which this literature so forcefully expresses" (p. 51). This means, certainly, to face directly our varieties of reaction in working with those older or more disabled than ourselves, to face and name our possible "gerontophobias," our possible fears and hatreds of old age which parade in a variety of disguises, presumptions, and assumptions about what it means to grow old (Freedman, 1978, p. 61).

NAMING A FEW INFLUENCES

Susan Tamke (1978) identifies three models from Victorian literature which contribute to ageist "pictures in the head." First she cites the model of "wise, moral old people who are essentially passive":

... when they function actively they do so largely through or for other people, primarily children. They teach wisdom and good behavior to children or if they are wealthy, they can function as gift-givers. Their good behavior is rewarded by admiration, by promises of salvation of their souls in the next world, or, if they are poor, as many are, by charity. These old people are staple characters in evangelical, moralistic tracts. (p. 64)

Then Tamke goes on to describe "foolish or malevolent old people" manifesting behaviors unacceptable and inappropriate for the kinds of roles they were supposed to assume within Victorian society. They are the people who disregard social conventions by "remaining active and self-directed." These older characters are to be found in nursery rhymes where they become the objects of laughter, or in more serious literature designed to teach. There their conduct "is punished harshly by ridicule, by threat of social ostracism, or even by threat of damnation."

Finally, Tamke portrays a third collection of those older people *"who exhibit no behavior and, therefore, are neither good nor bad but simply old."* In the literature of the Victorian era they are rarely treated kindly. They are punished and laughed at simply because they are old; they are denied the rewards that are normally given to the young. (Aren't these last images the most damning of all?)

Compare these Victorian models of aging with a few that are present in today's television programming. Part of a rise in sexual explicitness in the '70s and '80s was a trend in giving sexual identities to older women. (But what strange identities they are!) A summary of this is given in a brief editorial citation in *Psychology Today* (Vol. 22, #10):

The character Blanche on The Golden Girls sleeps with an inordinate number of men and brags about her sexual prowess. Another character, Sophia, is in her 80s but watches porn videos vociferously and scans the obituaries to identify bereft husbands who might be future partners.... "The consistent portrayal of 'elderly tramps,'" the researchers say, "may reveal television writers' and producers' discomfort with 'sexual grandmothers.' [Perhaps] the only way to make these women palatable is to portray them as extreme characters."

One question I ponder: Do the images of meddling older women, as portrayed on TV in the characterizations of Agatha Christie's "Miss

Marple" and Angela Lansbury's "Jessica Fletcher" in "Murder She Wrote," help or hinder the breaking of stereotypes? Fortunately, both female characters are portrayed as highly intelligent, independent, assertive women, who eventually bring the recalcitrant detectives and skeptical bystanders to their side. It seems to boil down to how simplistically we generalize our data from such characterizations.

On the other hand, we see sensitive portrayals of older people in movies like Cocoon, Driving Miss Daisy, The Whales of August *— portrayals that go deeply into the meaning of these unique individuals and their lives. The aging of performers no doubt brings new openness — but as our current older performers die off will they be replaced in the minds and eyes of the public? It will be interesting to see.*

Stereotyping is manifest not only in these portrayals in literature and the media but in the kinds of cognitive statements and vocabularies that people use in referring not only to older people but to their collective outlooks and their generalized capabilities.

An example of this discrimination comes from Dorothy Sennett's report of what happened when she tried to sell her book, *Full Measure: Modern Short Stories on Aging* (1988). Not only did she find it difficult to interest prospective publishers, but she also found some peculiar kinds of reactions. For example, "Older people are only interested in promoting their own causes" was the response of a New York editor, a response she found quite typical of the publishing industry. But the book did come out — to raves from reviewers and gerontologists. "It's not sweet," warns Sennett. "These storytellers make us feel the last years of life as funny, pathetic, painful, tragic (often all at once), and, above all, as complex" (cited by the editor of the "Upfront Column" in *Modern Maturity*, Dec. 1988–Jan 1989, p. 9).

By this time you have no doubt observed the number of quotes I take from the AARP magazine, Modern Maturity. *I do this because I respect their writing and reporting — it is carefully done, well written, and representative of a broad base of input and opinion. For any student of contemporary aging this magazine and its counterparts — Prime Time, New Choices, Mature Outlook — offer remarkable insight into what is actually going on in the lives of many Americans.*

In another report from *Modern Maturity*, the editor of the "Upfront" column heads one of his reports with "Some ageist myths never die" and then reports some myths mentioned at the 1987 American Academy of Neurology's Annual Meeting. These myths are followed by some pointed rebuttals:

Old age takes all the fun out of life. "When [people] complain like that, the fault is one of character, not of years. Old [people] who exercise self-discipline, who are not peevish or insensitive, find old age quite bearable."

Old age causes your memory to fail. "No doubt it does, if you don't keep in trim or if you're born a trifle dull. I'm not worried by the saying 'Read tombstones and lose your memory.' It's by reading those stones that I refresh my memory of the dead."

Old age means death is near. "What could be more in accord with the Law of Nature than for the old to die? Fruits, if they are green, must be forcefully pulled from the bough, but if they are ripe and mellow, they drop off."

And who offered the rebuttals to these myths of age? The Roman philosopher Cicero in 45–44 B.C. (Cicero, 1909)[1] So is there really anything new under the sun?

Stereotypes are born of literary image, of media presentation, of advertising copy, of myths old and new, of the extremes of making aging too good or making it too bad — the examples are all around us if we will just take time to see and name them. But I go further here to name selectively those ageisms that actively engage the older person in serious, sometimes life-threatening dilemmas. At the very least these ageisms have the potential to demean and defeat the dignity of the older person.

AGEISM IN THE MEDICAL PROFESSIONS

In *The Myth of Senility* (1985), Robin Henig challenges the ageist prejudice that has festered around notions of "senility," prejudice that is all too often internalized and promulgated by the medical profession and that is all too easily accepted and disseminated by family members, mental health professionals, and by older persons themselves. Indeed, according to Margaret Gatz and Cynthia Pearson of the University of Southern California, Alzheimer's disease may be the new ageism. "The media focus on it, the public overestimates its prevalence, and clinicians overdiagnose it" (Gatz & Pearson, 1988, p. 188). The reason this prejudice is so serious is that incorrect, generalized expectations can lead us to misinterpret and exaggerate normal mental changes, ignore those that are abnormal, and treat victims of senile dementia as more dependent than they really are. To interrupt these expectations, overestimations, generalizations, exaggerations, is a task that everyone of us faces, not only for the sake of our clients and patients, but for the sake of ourselves as we grow older. How important it is that we undo the

---

[1]The 1909 Shuckburgh translation that I cite is slightly different from these quotes from the neurological society's presentation. That particular translation has not been available to me.

myths and stereotypes that equate aging with senility, with the loss of memory, wit, and mind. And yet, Henig reminds us, we must also learn "not to be optimistic to the point of blindness to the mental and physical changes that do occur over time" (1985, p. 6).

To break loose from simplistic categorizations of individual capability and dependency in Alzheimer's disease is the highlight of an important article by Tom Kitwood (1990). He challenges the determinisms of medical models asking us to consider the "dialectical interplay between neurological and social-psychological factors, with special emphasis on aspects of the latter which deprive a neurologically impaired individual of his or her personhood" (p. 191). Exploring his thesis that the social, psychological, and neurological dynamics of each unique situation must be carefully analyzed and utilized, Kitwood writes that much of the current negative prognosis and pessimism is simply not justified. Although neurological impairment cannot be reversed (at least at the current time), there is possibility for creative change by using an enlightened social psychology to work with both the patient and those who are serving caring, supportive roles. The work of Carl Eisdorfer and Donna Cohen (1984) affirms some of Kitwood's ideas as they also offer some hope within the normally hopeless view of the Alzheimer's patient.

BUTLER STUDIES

Henig reports a 1977 interview with Robert Butler in which he described findings from a National Institute of Mental Health research study that revealed that (1) those who are weakest and most vulnerable are the ones hardest hit by stereotype, (and 2) those individuals who are victims of stereotype frequently adopt the characteristics that they are supposed to have. Such people may collaborate with their ostracizers (in the manner of concentration camp survivors) as they "seem actually to choose to lose hold of their mental powers—just as some choose to let their bodies turn to fat—rather than fight to stay sharp and active. Either consciously or subconsciously, some old people will bend to the subtle social pressure to become crotchety, withdrawn, asexual, passive, dependent, depressed" (Henig, 1985, p. 7). It is all too easy to bow to societal expectation because it is somehow expected and because it is just too difficult to resist the subtle (not so subtle?) pressures of society.

In the NIMH study, aged volunteers were given tests that compared them with prisoners of war in Korea. The results showed "that the volunteers who accepted all the stereotypes about age—that you're washed up, you're senile, you're not able to be physically active—reacted to those tests in the same way as those prisoners who had collaborated with the Communists. . . . And those people who disagreed with what society expected from the aged followed the patterns shown by the prisoners who resisted collaboration." (pp. 7–8). In this manner those who are stereotyped may well internalize and act on the ageist stereotype without realizing they are doing so.

THE DANGERS OF MISDIAGNOSIS

In her survey of the literature on senility, Henig shows that the stereotype of the decline of intelligence in old age developed out of a series of studies conducted in the first half of this century, studies that may have been carefully designed but were, in her opinion, "wrongheaded" (p. 71). The seriousness of "wrongheadedness" is manifest when physicians too quickly diagnose confused elderly patients as caught in the inevitable decline of aging. This misdiagnosis not only can be an example of prejudice and mistaken generalization, but can actually be a sentence of death. All too easily such an error can prevent proper treatment, cause delay, and "turn a reversible condition into a permanent one" (p. 109). The tragedy that Henig names is that once a person is labeled as "senile," he or she may be relegated to the isolated outskirts of medical care and societal interaction, deprived of needed stimulations and normal human response in a manner that actually fosters further decline.

In her chapter on "pseudosenility" Henig tracks the various dead ends of diagnostic stereotype and diagnostic error. As she does this she warns that current medical training actually contributes to the misdiagnosis of cognitive/emotional disorders, often creating the condition that one gerontologist has called "pseudosenility." What is often seriously confused is the reality that states of agitation or disorientation may well be the results of treatable diseases or drug reaction. The tragedy for those who suffer these conditions is that their symptoms may be tossed into the scrapbag called "senility." And because senility is the "Great Imitator," because the dominant symptom of almost every physical disease of old age is confusion, it is essential that physicians learn a refined differential diagnostic for their older patients.

DRUGS AND THE ELDERLY

At a 1989 press briefing in preparation for the APA Convention, a variety of specialists in geriatrics, pharmacology, drug abuse, and psychology shared some appalling conclusions. Peggy Eastman (1989) has synthesized some of these:

The problem of over-medication and mis-medication is so widespread that some people are calling this the nation's other drug problem. (Quoting Bryant Welch)

Some nursing homes administer the wrong kind of drugs, speakers said. In a study of one nursing home it was found that only 36 of the 221 residents receiving drugs to treat psychosis . . . actually had a diagnosis of psychosis. (p. 3)

Doctors may . . . misdiagnose drug-induced confusion or depression as symptom of "old age," and prescribe yet another drug to treat a problem *caused* by drugs. (Quote of Jerry Gurwitz, p. 3)

It was the consensus of these presenters that the overdrugging problem is a frequent result of stereotypes about aging—stereotypes that encourage drug treatments rather than nondrug therapy (think back to my earlier discussion of Antonovsky's contrasts between the "salutogenic" and "pathogenic" perspectives). Lacking understanding of the creative potential available to older people, and caught in the stereotypes of age, general-care physicians and even the elderly themselves think of psychological problems as "natural" or "expected"—just part of getting old.

These geriatric specialists pointed to another dilemma for the older person—the excessive use of tranquilizers and antipsychotic drugs in nursing homes, a practice that demands more attention if older people are to find an increased quality of life while living in these institutional settings.

Many of us who have dealt with aging parents in nursing homes can tell horror stories about over-medication. I, for one, think of my mother-in-law, who was given Mellaril to the point where she sat mummified in her wheelchair, her mouth sagging and twitching due to the drug's side effects. Finally, we were able to move her into an enlightened nursing home where she was withdrawn from her major tranquilizer, given physical therapy to strengthen her arms and provide greater independence of movement. We saw her regain strengths that had been held in abeyance during her long months in the other home.

These personal thoughts are reminders of significant roles in working with the mental health concerns of older people. They call upon us to keep our knowledge of psychotropic drugs current. Indeed, according to a 1989 flyer from the American Psychological Association, we need to be aware that although elderly Americans constitute about 12% of the U.S. population, they purchase 35 to 40% of sedative-hypnotic drugs. In addition, persons over age 60 account for 39% of all hospitalizations from adverse drug reactions. The elderly are more susceptible to adverse drug reactions because their bodies do not respond to drugs in the same way as younger patients, and because they tend to take multiple prescription and over-the-counter drugs (quoted in the *Washington Psychologist*, June 1989, pp. 1, 22, 23).

The prejudice inherent in medical advertising is another serious matter in the "overdrugging" of the elderly. According to Arluke and Levin (1984), prescription drug ads often portray older people "as having personality and moods typically characteristic of children; they may even be dressed in children's clothing or may be pictured as having the physical problems of children" (p. 76). This tendency to view older people as living out a "second childhood" is closely intertwined with tendencies to drug older adults rather than to engage them in the processes of psychotherapy. It is also intertwined with our tendencies to protect older people, to make their decisions for them, to reduce them to pawns within the dubious protections born of ageism.

DUBIOUS PROTECTIONS BORN OF AGEISM

Senior Americans have the right to independence, privacy, and choice of persons with whom they live and associate; they also have the right not to fear abridgement of those rights because of advancing age. (Linkletter, 1988, pp. 49–50)

Dubious protections are frequently offered to senior adults in the name of "helping." But what is done in the name of "helping" sometimes ends up taking away their rights and independence as individuals — something we say we don't allow in the United States but that is not unusual in the lives of older people. Documenting one example of this, Barbara Coleman (1988) tells the story of Marguerite Van Etten, a victim of a serious automobile accident. Left in a coma with serious head and body injuries, she was temporarily unable to manage her business affairs. While she was thus incapacitated her daughter petitioned a local court to declare her mother incompetent in order that she could assume guardianship for her mother's affairs. All that was done here seems appropriate under the difficult circumstances of this woman's injury and her daughter's caregiving dilemma.

But it is what happened afterwards that injects a note of fear into the minds of older people who contemplate a similar situation. Once Mrs. Van Etten had recovered, she found she was still under the legal care of her daughter, deprived of the rights all of us take for granted: She could not own a house, marry, divorce, drive a car, or handle her own money. Even more frightening, she discovered how difficult it is to end a guardianship once it is established. According to Coleman's review of the situation:

Critics say judges rarely review a case to see whether guardianship is appropriate. . . . Even when guardians argue for ending the arrangement, judges are often reluctant to reverse themselves. But for wards, terminating guardianship can be almost impossible, particularly if their guardian does not agree. (Coleman, 1988, p. 2)

Highlighting the seriousness of this type of dilemma, the late Claude Pepper told his congressional colleagues that "Even a convicted felon is guaranteed more rights than innocent elderly and disabled Americans who are the subjects of guardianship proceedings." All it takes is an equating of old age with disablement or temporary incapacitation to be sentenced "the incompetent." These negative legal evaluations can leave the older person helpless in the name of the law, a situation that is unfortunately all too prevalent. Penelope Hommell (1989, p. 1) cited an Associated Press study that showed that 500,000 Americans had been denied the right to exercise control over their own affairs because a court decision had named them "incompetent" or "incapacitated."

Something is being done about this particular problem as advocates work to protect vulnerable older persons. Recently a set of national *model guardianship standards* have been presented in a report by the House Select Committee on Aging's Subcommittee on Housing and Consumer Interests. Called "Surrogate Decisionmaking for Adults: Model Standards to Ensure Quality Guardianship and Representative Payee Service," these standards are designed to protect those least able to protest on their own behalf. (As of this writing I do not know the status of these standards but cite these efforts as an encouraging move in supporting older adults in their efforts for autonomy and self-respect.)

A different kind of "dubious protection" is that imposed by well-meaning children who take over the decision-making powers of their aging parents. In a 1966 article that remains pertinent today, Dr. Walter E. O'Donnell raised thoughtful questions for the practitioner and his aging patient to address.

... some of the unhappiest older parents a doctor sees have the most loyal and devoted children. These sons and daughters allow their sense of duty, love, and obligation to make their parents' life miserable.... There are innumerable ways to do this, but three of the commonest are to make parents feel useless and unneeded ... to treat them like children ... and not to allow them to do anything for themselves. (O'Donnell, 1966)

Thus, in the name of loving concern children will deprive their parents of the kinds of stimulation that keep all of us involved in the challenges and tasks of everyday living. In doing this they make a mistake reflective of our society's emphasis on reducing stress, on denying many difficult realities, and in believing older people become less capable of handling difficult problems. Families as well as therapists can make these mistakes as they mistakenly assume that all stress is negative. This is a common assumption which both Hans Selye and Aaron Antonovsky have challenged. There is an important "good stress," which Selye calls "eustress" (1978), that is needed to keep life interesting and stimulating to mind, body, and spirit. We need to go beyond the simple quantitative listings of stress factors to the meanings inherent in the stress and to the kinds of stress that are actually beneficial. As Selye so nicely put it:

Sitting in a dentist's chair is stressful, but so is exchanging a passionate kiss with a lover—after all, your pulse races, your breathing quickens and your heartbeat soars. And yet, who in the world would forego such a pleasurable pastime simply because of the stress involved? (1978)

And I quote a little piece I wrote several years ago:

We are complex, noisy, nosey creatures who need stimulation. Our activities, exercise, hobbies—and, yes, our involved carings—all contribute to our psychological well-being and add spice to our everyday activities. In fact, the stress of our unexpected creative surprises draw us again and again to savor the challenge of creative experience. We need our arousals to motivate us, inspire us, teach us and give us pleasure. (Carlsen, unpublished material)

Jules Willing addresses this concern in his thoughtful book, *The Reality of Retirement* (1981). He asks us to realize that "older people need the freedom to worry—to be challenged and involved in the conflicts and tasks of everyday life—it is part of their needed stimulation" (p. 161). Thoughts for us to consider, then: Older persons do have the capacity to share in family problems, to add their wisdom, to put up with aches and pains in order to help (let *them* make the choice!). Interested, caring older adults ask for this opportunity—and they ask for our listening without negative evaluation when they come to us to state their case. To negate their ability to argue, to confront, to question, is to deprive seniors of their personhood, their need to be needed. It is to demean their ability for analysis and decision-making and possibly to push them into silence. (No wonder older people climb aboard RV's and drive off into the sunset! No wonder they become depressed when no one will listen to them! Do we ever analyze depression from the standpoint of negation or psychic abuse? It's about time, I think.)

O'Donnell suggests we strike a balance between sharing our lives and family with older persons and setting them free to live their own lives. How? By trying a few of the following:

- Help them to enjoy their later years by relieving them of onerous duties or worries, but don't make them feel expendable or surplus.
- Watch your attitudes. Often it is not what you do but the way that you do it that defeats you. If your parents are somewhat a burden to you, and your attitude conveys this to them, it matters little what you do or say.
- Give up trying to reform them. . . . [Don't] count on changing an ingrained character trait that has been well over a half a century building.
- Listen to them. This is the key to good relations with older people.
- Remember that one day you will be in their shoes. (O'Donnell, 1966, pp. 66, 89, 92).

Let the therapist heed these words. Too often we parent our clients, turning them into people who are less than competent, less than adequate. Here is where we must examine our underlying attitudes, our bodies of prejudice, in applying those pieces of advice to our roles. Here is where we must become facilitators and supportive advocates for our clients as we guide them, their families, and their caretakers into more enlightened solutions to these problems.

ANTIDOTES FOR AGEISM

Educating psychologists about normal aging, minimizing hyperbole, and attending to factors beyond "professional ageism" that affect service provision are reasonable antidotes to over-emphasis and should improve psychologists' ability to help. (Gatz & Pearson, 1988, p. 188)

How do we implement these antidotes for ageism suggested by Gatz and Pearson? Certainly, by examining carefully the models named in this book. Certainly, by continuing research into the dis-ease/health continuum as suggested by Antonovsky. Certainly, by attending to the models for creativity that reframe age as a dialectical point/counterpoint of growth and development vis-à-vis the realities of physical decline. Another way is to give increased attention to how we use language to describe the states and disabilities of age, an attention that alerts us to our shortcut labels, our simplistic linguistic summaries, as we focus our efforts to interrupt imprecisions of thought and language.

Hadley and Brodwin (1988) tell us that all too ofen professional helpers use imprecise language in referring to patients and clients who have disabilities. One place this happens is within high stress hospital situations where students and physicians use black humor to survive. Unfortunately, they often become flip, and this flippancy can easily turn into casual, nasty assignments of terms to patients — *and the words available for the old patients are the nastiest*:

The elderly are called crocks, geezers, fogies, snags, neuropaths, rounders, shoppers, crud, and crap. A term recently applied is "gomer," an acronym for "Get Out of My Emergency Room," reserved for the disoriented old persons who seem to show up from nearby nursing homes in the middle of the night. The sad reality that Henig describes is illuminated even further by these words from *The House of God*, a novel about a year's internship: Gomers are not just dear old people. . . . Gomers are human beings who have lost what goes into being human beings. They want to die and we will not let them. We're cruel to the gomers, by saving them, and they're cruel to us us, by fighting tooth and nail against our trying to save them. (Shem, 1978, p. 38)

No easy antidotes here! To bring about change the perpetrators of such putdowns would need to be aware that they are engaged in prejudicial, demeaning practices, and then they would need to *want* to bring about change. That requires an attitude and outlook quite different from the insensitive cognitive processings that contribute to stereotype and discrimination. Let us heighten our awareness that more than 22 million old people lead independent lives that are productive and fully human (Butler, in Henig, 1985, p. 226). Indeed, that is one of the major purposes of this book. Now, it is time to pay attention to the ways that we can open and alter our languages in ways that interrupt ageism.

ALTERING OUR LANGUAGES

In *Metaphor and Meaning* (1966), Weller Embler writes that "mostly we conduct our affairs on the fringe of thought" (p. 30) and that "words often use *us*, instead of our using *them*" (p. 143). He suggests that our figurative languages, our metaphors, frequently contain deeply entrenched and unexamined beliefs and mental attitudes (p. 43). These structures of unexamined knowledge resonate through our cognitive systems to shape our labeling and our prejudicial language. Haig A. Bosmajian summarizes some of these manifestations in *The Language of Oppression* (1983, p. 5), as he pays attention to the "power which comes from names and naming."

The power which comes from names and naming is related directly to the power to define others—individuals, races, sexes, ethnic groups. Our identities, who and what we are, how others see us, are greatly affected by the names we are called and the words with which we are labelled. The names, labels, and phrases employed to "identify" a people may in the end determine their survival. The word "define" comes from the Latin *definire*, meaning to limit. *Through definition we restrict, we set boundaries, we name* [italics added].

An antidote for ageism, therefore, is the reworking of our languages, our namings, our metaphorical usages which in their very vagueness, may carry a message that we have never acknowledged. Hadley and Brodwin (1988) have taken time to address these issues as they challenge professionals to take a hard look at the languages they use when dealing with disabled people.

To both alert and guide the professional, they suggest that professional language should be characterized by four qualities: First, *precision*—a precision that conveys "a speaker's or writer's intended meanings exactly and unambiguously." Second, the language should be *objective* as it avoids (a) implicit biases or unwanted surplus meanings, or (b) the equating of opinions, interpretations, or impressions with facts. Third, *perspective* needs to be carefully considered: Whenever we describe a patient or client we should choose language that emphasizes the uniqueness of the person and places any disability or limitation within the context of the whole person. After all, disability may be totally irrelevant to many of the person's qualities and activities; it may be omitted as a descriptor if it is not pertinent to the issues at hand. Finally, Hadley and Brodwin emphasis that *portrayal* needs to be carefully examined: "People with disabilities should be portrayed as actively going about the business of living as other people do, not as passive victims, tragic figures, or super-heroes" (1988, p. 147). Let us go further in discussing these four categories.

Precise language is exact rather than approximate, literal rather than figurative, and quite "exclusive" in the sense that other meanings are screened out to give focus to the intended language. What Hadley and Brodwin are describing is at variance with the use of metaphors and calls attention to those metaphors that sneak into our thinking and speaking—metaphors which do not really say what we mean. For example, to describe someone as "wheelchair-bound" is to see him or her as somehow a prisoner of a vehicle, unable to live life outside it. This idea leads to the ambiguities around the words "disability" and "handicap."

The words disability and handicap have been discussed extensively. Some writers use these terms interchangeably. Others define a disability as a condition of the person, and a handicap as the interaction between disability and either the environment or an activity the person wants to do. For example, a blind person always has a disability; it is handicapping with respect to some activities, but not with respect to others such as speaking or thinking. (Hadley & Brodwin, 1988, p. 147)

Objectivity: When a writer practices objective writing, he or she is careful to acknowledge contrasts between impressions, interpretations, opinions, and recommendations and documented facts. By maintaining a clear differentiation between facts and subjective opinions, objective writing has greater clarity and is less likely to carry hidden innuendoes, biases, and subtle stereotypes. The objective writer is aware that dichotomous terminologies or generalized evaluations ("good versus bad, strong versus weak, fast versus slow") can confuse specifics of meaning and inadvertently introduce negative description about the disabled person. For example, the "wheelchair-bound" person is somehow devalued, subtly described as somehow less valuable, less potent, and less active.

The guidelines for *perspective* are very important in matters of stereotyped interpretation. I remember a friend, a former English professor, gifted in his field and known for his ability to convey ideas in innovative and imaginative ways. This man had a partial leg, but he certainly was not handicapped except perhaps in his maneuverability on icy streets. Otherwise, he moved quickly and fairly easily from task to task. But, he rather somberly noted, if people see him first as a cripple, "they have already lost a part of me." And so it has been with women and Blacks—with any group that has particular qualities that make them highly visible and exceptional.

And so it is with aging. To call older persons "elderly" is to place them in an arbitrary category where they are portrayed in particular ways. The language is imprecise, certainly not linked to objective definition. A chronological number does not make a person elderly—in fact, I don't really know what the word means. This brings to mind a newspaper photo of a vigorous 66-year-old man which carried a caption describing him as "elderly." I did a double take, asking myself, "Where is the turning point into elderly?"

Portrayal may get into trouble within the languages of metaphor. Certainly, metaphors are vital and useful because they shake our thinking and open new avenues of thought. In fact, Lakoff and Johnson, who believe most of our language and thinking is metaphorical, have written a book which argues this thesis (1980). Nevertheless, in matters of stereotype, we must examine our word portraits for their hidden messages and vague allusions. Our goal again is precision, objectivity, and a perspective from which we see the person in his or her wholeness rather than with simplistic attention to one particular trait or characteristic. "Usually, portrayal will take care of itself if the principles of precision, objectivity, and perspective are observed. A person with a disability will not seem to be a victim, tragic figure, or super-hero in a description that (a) is exact, literal, and unambigious; (b) is free from bias; and (c) treats the disability in an appropriate perspective among the person's other characteristics."

The caution I take from these ideas is that we need to normalize the person's condition within the repertoire of available life activities; we need to properly name the person's condition in a manner that puts it in a proper perspective vis-à-vis everyday activities of normal, daily living. In this manner we can normalize aging and weave it more fully into the seamless fabric of life.

One final set of guidelines before I close this chapter. These are pertinent to media presentation and are suggested in the newsletter of the Office of Disease Prevention and Health Promotion of the Public Health Service, U.S. Department of Health and Human Services. They write: "To insure that your materials and publicity appeal to all older people:"

- Include older women and minorities.
- Present a balanced view of strengths and abilities.
- Show older people participating actively; for example, walking, bicycling, swimming, and gardening.
- Show older people in different living arrangements: at home alone or with family, in a group home, or in a nursing home.
- Portray all economic levels or images that do not categorize economic levels.
- Depict the older worker.

In the words of Bosmajian, "This then is our task—to identify the decadence in our language, the inhumane uses of language, the 'silly words and expressions' which have been used to justify the unjustifiable, to make palatable the unpalatable, to make reasonable the unreasonable, to make decent the indecent" (1983, p. 9).

With those ideas echoing in my thinking, I now shift gears and turn to those portraits and presentations that highlight the hopeful, the vital, and the creative. In these highlights are further antidotes for ageism.

SECTION III

Therapies and the Therapeutic

Have we learned how to join or accompany the meaning-maker when he or she faces a world that is already heated up, already stimulating, even to the point of being meaning-threatening?

—Robert Kegan, 1982, pp. 276–277

. . . it is all too easy to focus on technique to the neglect of the person. But we need technique—that "mechanical or formal part of an art"—in order to join discipline and practical detail to the more intuitive processes of therapy.

—Mary Baird Carlsen, 1988, p. 110

CHAPTER 7

Therapies and the Therapeutic

PSYCHOTHERAPY IS MANY THINGS: a theory, a dialogue, a relationship, a set of concepts, a body of attentions, a language, a collection of techniques—all tapped and shaped according to therapeutic bias and therapeutic need. The applied specifics take shape in response to the unique requirements of individuals, their environments, and their relationships. These statements apply to therapies for clients at any stage of life, but they require even further definition as the therapist faces the complex permutations brought with age. And because the "finer and finer distinctions in old age" are only now being delineated, the possible therapies with senior adults are only now becoming apparent.

As recently as 1973 M. Powell Lawton wrote:

The fact is that there is no clinical psychology of old age. The psychologist carrying his tool kit of the Wechsler, Rorschach, and Thematic Apperception Tests never got to the over-65s, and now that period in psychological history seems to have passed. Nor did the psychologist concern himself with the psychotherapy of older people. Thus, the development of personality theory in

117

gerontology was never stimulated by the demands of practicing clinicians in the same way that it was stimulated in the case of children and younger adults. Freud himself rejected the elderly as a class. . . . (p. 339)

Although psychological services for older adults were largely absent prior to 1950 (Maddox, 1987), the decade of the 1980s saw increasing attention to the needs for sophisticated training programs for work with these clients (the 1981 "Older" Boulder Conference, for example, provided important impetus). Though some debate the value of traditional therapies with seniors and argue for brief therapies over long-term therapies, current thinking is tilted towards treating older individuals as being fully capable of participating in the full spectrum of available therapies: "psychotherapy, psychoanalysis, group psychotherapy, drug therapy, occupational, physical and recreational therapies, behavioral modification therapies, family and marital counseling, and last, but by all means not least, sex counseling and therapy" (Butler, 1975, pp. 228–229).

In "Psychological Interventions with Older Adults," Gatz, Popkin, Pino, and VandenBos (1985) name three general, but not mutually exclusive, categories of problems of elderly individuals: "organic brain syndromes (the dementias and deliriums), lifelong patterns (including chronic schizophrenia, neuroses, and character disorders), and special issues of later life (including both situational stresses and existential issues)" (p. 756). All these categories deserve our careful attention as they overlap within the complex interactions of the human being—but we will still have to choose that specific attention that fits our interest, temperament, and expertise. With my own emphasis on creative aging I will continue to pay primary attention to the meaning-making, situational, and existential concerns of older people; I believe that such emphasis puts the meaning-making process back in their individual courts and honors unique potentials to work through to independent choices and solution.

Even as we examine and specify our therapies, even as we name our own unique capabilities and possible investments of care, we need also to assess our attitudes towards our clients. Do we genuinely believe that these older clients are capable of using our services? Are we willing to listen to them from within the perspective of their meaning-makings? *Do we like older people* and respect them and consider them contributing partners and participants in the dynamics of therapy? If a fruitful therapeutic alliance is to be established we do well to answer in the affirmative even as we consider these suggestions from Gilbert Wrenn:

A counselor [for older adults] must like older people and must respect them for whatever achievements they have had. The counselor must be willing to accept and learn as well as to give. The self-respect of the older one, meaning anyone from age 60 through 85 (the "last third of life" begins at age 57–58!) must be protected. (1983, p. 325)

The willingness to accept, learn, and give as well as to listen and to respect is the attitude to be fostered in the therapies that I now suggest. All these varying approaches and techniques fit within the broader system of the meaning-making therapy I described in Chapter 4. They are chosen to facilitate and enhance the resolution of special individualized issues of later life. They are also chosen to stimulate and encourage creativity within the practical and the existential, to open individual eyes to the possible enlightenments, rewards, and growths which can be a part of growing older. (For excellent interview discussions that are rich with complementary ideas, listen to the Connie Goldman tape, "Late Bloomer" (1988), and her two sets of tapes, "I'm too busy to talk now" (1985, 1987), spirited, interesting dialogues with a selection of creative older people—Rollo May, May Sarton, Studs Terkel, to name only three.) These therapies emphasize the creative even as they pay particular attention to the uniqueness of individual feelings, beliefs, and desires. These shape the interior life of the person. Only if we ask will we really know how best to administer treatment or facilitate therapy, whether through reassurance, behavior therapy, occupational therapy, or group activity (Lawton, 1973, p. 342).

My purpose in naming a meaning-making therapy and in gathering a set of *therapies* under its systemic umbrella is to emphasize such a constructive "psychodiagnostic." But it is more than that. Although I tap drug therapies as needed, although I pay attention to the physical and do respect the values of medical technology and diagnostic procedure, I simply and frequently choose to go beyond those to that which is cognitively and existentially enlightening, enabling, and empowering for the individual client. And, in tune with therapists like Carl Eisdorfer, this therapy's purpose is not to psychologize or pathologize but to teach, stimulate, and encourage the individual client until he or she learns skills and new perspectives that make it possible for the therapist to withdraw quietly (see Eisdorfer, 1974, p. 69).

TANGIBLE GOALS FOR
CREATIVE THERAPIES

All the therapies that I name here are chosen because they stimulate and reinforce creative thinking and behavior and point towards the kinds of healthful patterns of living suggested by Seibert, McLeish, Antonovsky and the developmental psychologists cited in Chapter 3. Now I add another set of goals for fitness of mind, body, and spirit.

In a series of 16 research studies with 1,000 healthy subjects, aged

75 and older, Robert J. Samp, M.D., of the University of Wisconsin, discovered that good genes, nutritious foods, stress avoidance, and "saintly living" *are not* the significant ingredients in long, healthful life. The key seems to be moderation. But this is a *moderation of a special sort*—welcoming change and variety and turning the inevitable stresses of life to one's advantage—a moderation that shapes an individual lifestyle that neither burns the candle at both ends nor drifts with the stream (Overholser & Randolph, 1976).

Dr. Samp also found that *flexibility* is important—a flexibility that includes a lack of rigid habits and a growing ability to accommodate to change. This flexibility joins with further moderations *in diet, in activity, in routines* which keep people moving as much and as long as possible—getting out of the house daily, for example, and introducing novelties which keep the routines from stagnating. This flexibility of life and attitude also included *an ability to accept and face challenge*. Not a naive negation of overwhelming odds, this ability included a willingness and a capability to weigh and measure that which is possible against that which is not.

Then, these subjects *looked ahead*. With an optimistic attitude towards the future, they planned for the future, they did things each day that pointed towards the future. In addition, these healthy older folks kept in touch with people and enjoyed them. They were open to sharing their problems as well as listening to those of others.

Finally, this group of subjects demonstrated that *if you want to live long you have to get used to growing old*. I find that statement especially important. It represents an adoption of a particular frame of mind which faces the concerns of aging, does not retreat from them, but learns about them, and then works to maintain the habits of good living named above. In future chapters these qualities will be illustrated in discussions of midlife choices, practices of narrative process, preparations for death, recoveries from grief, creative modelings for aging, and some shared wisdoms of age.

STIMULATING THE CREATIVE

Silvano Arieti has named what he calls "attitudes and conditions" for fostering creativity (1976, pp. 372–383). I have reviewed these in depth in *Meaning-Making*, but I repeat some of that material here because the attitudes and conditions take on a new coloring within the contexts and concerns of progressive aging.

Arieti writes that *aloneness* constitutes a first condition for creativity—an aloneness not to be confused with "protracted or painful loneliness imposed by others, or by one's psychological difficulties. Nor should it be confused with withdrawal from others, persistent shyness, or constant solitude" (Arieti, 1976, pp. 372–383). Rather, this aloneness is the ability to sit quietly with one's own thoughts and feelings to allow the creative to take its own form and direction. The form and direction are shaped not only by inactivity and constructive daydreaming, but by allowing free thinking and gullibility. "What Arieti calls 'free thinking' is not free association but a 'state of abandon,' of 'freedom from inhibition.' He believes that if the mind is open and nonjudging in its processing of information, awareness of similarities (that is, analogies) between perceptions, apperceptions, concepts, and even systems and abstractions will tend to occur repeatedly as the mind creates new patterns and connections" (Carlsen, 1988, p. 112).

Does this seem too demanding a process for the aging mind? Certainly, there are those people who have never been educated in the use of their minds or in the capacity to step outside of themselves. And, yes, for many, the mind does lose its capacity to make such cognitive leaps and connections. Yes, there are many individuals who have shut down the attitudes of free thinking and the kinds of "gullibility" that supply a "willingness to explore everything: to be open, innocent, and naive." Yes, those minds may not be able to do what we are describing. But all we have to do is turn around to read the contributions not only of writers and poets, theorists and scientists, but of those older folks who keep seizing moments and who keep their wonderings alive. To study them is to know that such synthesis is possible.

Read Catherine Chapman Pacheco's Breaking Patterns: Redesigning Your Later Years *(1989). The review by the* Time *critic on her book jacket says it best: "It may be that America is finding a new way to grow old. Far from fading away, the elderly seem to be brightening on the horizons of the mind, the family, the workplace, the community. Everywhere their role and presence are changing."*

In stimulating creativity, then, the therapist will keep his or her mind open to possibility as the attitudes and conditions for creativity are taught, fostered, and encouraged. This means working with the person on the *how* and *what* of aging: to harness mental activities, to stimulate constructive remembrance; to plant seeds of new ideas and imagination to replace a ruminating that can too easily dominate the person's thinking and feeling; to learn the kinds of meditation skills that enable the older person to take greater charge of the thinking process. John A. B. McLeish writes:

What is needed is a new *set*: the "set" which demands that you put a quota on the destructive indulgence of tired drifting of thoughts, or of nostalgic sorrow for the dead days beyond recall, and of resigned refuge in the routine. (1983, p. 198)

With people who have never stimulated their thinking processes the therapist may need to move from the cognitive to the active; from therapies of talk to therapies of doing and seeing and touching. Music, art, and drama, for instance, or the creativities suggested in Nickerson and O'Laughlin's *Helping Through Action: Action-Oriented Therapies* (1982). To read their table of contents is to gain ideas: "Free Writing as Therapy," "Introduction to Music Therapy," "Images: The Use of Photographs in Personal Counseling, " "Puppetry as a Tool in Child Psychotherapy." So why not "Puppetry as a Tool in Life Review" or "Puppetry as a Facilitation of Aging Creativity"? Certainly, puppetry, art, music, imaging are all tools which can be used for constructing a more meaningful portrait of oneself and one's life. Groups can be inspired to share their stories in playacting, dancing, or musical expression. Though this kind of activity may be occasionally threatening or embarrassing to some, patience and gentle urging may convince reluctant participants to give it a try.

As free thinking and openness to ideas stimulate the response of the person, he is guided into the *remembrance and inner replaying of past traumatic conflict*. Certainly this is a goal of many therapies, but here Arieti's emphasis is on harnessing creative techniques to bring into awareness and meaning bits and pieces of personal history so those bits and pieces can be reworked into the fabric of creative process. This can be done in a number of ways: using the "early recollections" technique of Adler (which I describe in the next section), telling stories, joining support groups, and actively engaging in the ordering of personal history. These techniques are the substance of Chapter 9 where I write of narrative process.

Then, writes Arieti, there is the fostering of *alertness* and *discipline*, a necessary next state if creativity is to move beyond wonderings, flights of fantasy, imagination, and insight and if creativities of thought and emotion are to become channeled into life. It is here that therapy can continue to teach, stimulate, and encourage creative exploration at the same time its processes help the client to come to terms with whatever problems are there to be faced. "If you want to live long you have to get used to growing old" remains a guiding wisdom; each of us can resist abdicating to ageist expectations even as we come to terms with the realities of *our* particular process of growing older. That is the constructive, ongoing dialectic of aging.

A VARIETY OF TECHNIQUES

Early recollections. According to Alfred Adler (1958, 1969), who developed this technique, an "early recollection" is one that can be visualized, that is a single incident, and that is a prototype of an attitude.

What one remembers is very much linked to a significance or meaning which forms a selective factor in memory. In the words of commentator Harold Mosak, "an *early recollection* occurs in the period before continuous memory and may be inaccurate or a complete fiction. It represents a single event . . . rather than a group of events. . . . Recollections are treated as a projective technique. If one understands the early recollections, one understands the patient's 'Story of My Life,' since people selectively recollect from their past incidents consonant with their life-styles" (1979, p. 67). Thus, these single, isolated events "are usually recollected within the context of self-image and lifestyle, and can offer unique understanding of how the client has cognitively shaped his or her world" (Carlsen, 1988, p. 115).

To gather early recollections, then, is to learn about the person and the way he or she views the world. To sort these and name these is to uncover mythologies and psychologies of the evolving self which form an infrastructure for outlooks, choices, and meaning-makings (see Feinstein & Krippner, 1988).

Thematic Apperception Test. Although Murray's projective test requires considerable time to administer and to interpret, I have usually found the results a helpful stimulus for therapy, especially as I engage my clients in the interpretive process to see what they see in their stories. I also take some liberties with the test adapting and using both its pictures and its concepts in a variety of ways. When I do that I make no pretense at interpretations following strictly Murray's careful presentation. Neugarten and Gutman (1968) are among those who have used Thematic Apperception techniques as a research tool with older subjects. Their reasons for choosing these projective techniques are in tune with my own reasons for applying them in therapy:

At least two considerations prompted the choice of the Thematic Apperception Test technique. The first was that the responses would be relatively uncensored, more closely related to the respondent's personal values and experiences than those he might feel constrained to give in answer to more direct questions. Second, fantasy material, although presenting certain difficulties of analysis as compared with questionnaire data, would have a decided advantage for exploratory research. The richness and unstructured nature of projective data enable the investigator to follow an inductive process; he can follow up clues as they appear in the data rather than check dimensions and hypotheses defined in advance. (p. 58)

With older people, I may modify the test, eliminating pictures I do not consider helpful, shortening the time of administration, and so on. I also see it as a stimulus bridge to other kinds of exercises—like the sharing of family albums or a sequence of pictures from the entire life span. This constitutes a technique useful at any age.

Genograms. Monica McGoldrick and Randy Gerson's book *Geno-*

grams in Family Assessment (1985), is a most helpful presentation of the genogram technique. By graphing the historical structures of the family system one is able to visualize crisis points, patterns of success and failure, stories of vocation, illness, death, and more. So we study genograms to uncover ideologies and mythologies; to understand personal patterns of thought, behavior, and emotion—patterns that may shape and constrain one's life. For the clinician these diagrams constitute a graphic, efficient clinical summary. For the client they offer awakenings and awarenesses of the streams of influence in personal identity and contributions to continuities of the self.

Memory exercises. The therapist may want to investigate behavioral techniques for reinforcing memory. A number of books are on the market which can be introduced into the therapeutic experience either in one-to-one sessions or in informal classes on aging (and there is much room here for the therapist to be a teacher of aging). But these suggestions for memory improvement have to be incorporated into a discipline of memory-making. As Adams (1986, p. 106) puts it, "If they are to do us any good, we must practice them until they become a natural component of our problem solving."

To buttress his point, Adams offers an exercise:

Without looking at one, draw an ordinary non-digital telephone dial, putting the letters and numbers in their proper locations. (1979, p. 35)

If older people discover an inability to do this and think it is a product of age they should heed Adams' commentary: "Very few people can do this exercise successfully, even though they have used phone dials for a large proportion of their lives. However, the mind does not hold onto the locations of all the details of a phone dial, since it does not have to. If the letters and numbers were not marked on the phone, the mind would store the information for easy recall."

This exercise illustrates that unless we practice recalling a particular memory we may not keep it. It is also a reminder that older people can benefit from thinking about memory in new ways and in sharing private thoughts and feelings about the states of their memories. Such sharing may stimulate new creative memory exercises: drawing the floor plan of an early home or plotting the route from a friend's home to one's own. Here creative imaginations of clients can be enlisted in plotting offshoots from the central exercise, all to learn about memory, stimulate memory, and implement creative ways to enhance memory. (And the tasks have to be meaningful and respectful of client sophistication to stimulate their engagement in the process. What researchers have found, to their chagrin, is that some research results are distorted because their subjects did not find their tasks meaningful.)

Visualization. Cognitive behavioral therapists Aaron Beck and

Arnold Lazarus include imagery in their repertoires of technique. Lazarus, for example, sees this technique as especially useful for purposes of desensitization in work with the depressed person—"for mentally rehearsing the depressed individual to take heed of reinforcing events, and for using 'time projection' techniques, with or without hypnosis, where the depressed individual actually pictures himself engaging in future rewarding activities" (1976, p. 100). Lazarus explains his logic for the place of imagery in the personality process:

It must be stressed that image formation is a crucial component of thinking. In other words, cognitive processes involve various levels of construct formation, abstract reasoning, intentions, plans, decisions, expectancies, values, belief systems, internalized rules, and mental imagery—innumerable events, scenes, people, and places drawn from past experience. Any cognitive schema that ignores imagery is bound to be incomplete. (1976, p. 90)

Certainly, active, imaginative imaging fits into work with early recollections, life review, the use of genograms, the preparations for widowhood and death—in other words, for all the scenarios and possibilities of aging.

Transcendental meditation. Reporter Susan Shatkin has summarized some important findings of Charles Alexander and Ellen Langer in an article for the *APA Monitor* (Shatkin, 1986, p. 28). What these researchers discovered in a study of 73 patients in eight Massachusetts homes for the elderly is that transcendental meditation allows two states of mind to coexist during the practice of its techniques: (1) the relaxation of tensions of the mind and a contribution to the reduction of confusion and possible prevention of a heart attack; (2) a pattern of heightened cognitive awareness. To come to this conclusion they studied three groups of subjects whose mean age was 81 and who were randomly assigned to a TM group, a "mindfulness" group which trained participants in active-distinction making, a "low-mindful" relaxation group, and a no-treatment control group.

The results confirmed Alexander's prediction that "Although mindfulness increases relaxation, TM increases both in one state." The mindfulness group came in second on the variety of cognitive performance, health, personality, and self-report measures, but improved more than the TM group on perceived control (which would seem to indicate that using both techniques would be valuable). The relaxation and no-treatment groups improved the least. What was very revealing in this study was that after three years the survival rate for the TM group was 100%, for the mindfulness group 87%, for the no treatment group 77%, and for the relaxation group 65%. Out of the remaining 478 residents of the home who did not receive treatment, 62.5% were still alive after three years.

What TM contributed to the lives of its participants was both deep physiological rest and heightened awareness. What is shown is the power of mindfulness in not only keeping the mind alive but the body as well. In summary, what we learn from Langer and Alexander's studies is:

- A definition of "mindfulness" as "active information processing which the individual is fully engaged in creating categories and drawing distinctions. "Mindlessness," in contrast, is a cognitive state in which the individual relies on categories already formed and distinctions that have already been drawn (see again Chapter 5 for its commentary on "interpretive parsimony").
- The body seems to start turning itself off as the mind ceases to deal with novelty. Thus, mindlessness may produce ill health or premature death.
- These findings challenge the notion that TM is just simple relaxation or dependent on expectation for its results.

The TM approach is a means for the older person to become self-empowering. By handling stress and becoming more relaxed, mentally alert, and healthy, the individual is less likely to become dependent on a nursing home, on children, or on other forms of support. It is empowerment from within, therefore—an important goal for a therapy of aging.

Bibliographic work. For those clients who are active readers there are many resources to be used. Books on middle age, retirement planning, and the experiences of growing older are proliferating as the population of older people increases. Many of the authors are themselves older adults, which makes the writing particularly helpful. These materials can also be useful in family work as stimulus for discussion. I have found the writings of the American Association for Retired Persons particularly helpful and I will cite others as this writing progresses.

In addition to books, there are excellent tapes for relaxation and positive suggestion, for low-key exercise routines, for stimulating personal wellness programs. If the client has a VCR this adds to learning possibilities. If our work takes us into institutional settings we may have the opportunity to do something about scenarios similar to the following.

I was appalled recently to see the caliber of TV programming accepted in a nursing home. People who were sitting in their wheelchairs were at the mercy of whatever whim guided the turn of the dial. In this particular home, two older ladies sat slumped in their chairs, their eyes lifeless, as two wrestlers threw each other to the mat. Why not a carefully selected set of videotapes at various times of the day? Are we to believe that older people, even those suffering from cognitive impairment, might not profit from meaningful programming? And couldn't those more able help select the tapes — another way to practice the kinds of mindfulness and control that Langer and Alexander suggest? Costs of the VCR could be subsidized by family members, library loans could be arranged, and interested friends and relatives could contribute from their own collections.

The *stimulation of sensory experience.* In his writings on creativity, Adams suggests ways to stimulate sensory experience, a very important exercise for elders whose senses of touch, taste, smell, hearing, and sight, may be fading. He asks his group participants to think of images and then rate them as (a) clear, (b) vague, or (c) nothing:

Imagine: The laugh of a friend; the sound of thunder; the sound of a horse walking on a road; the sound of a racing car; the feel of wet grass, the sensation of a long attack of hiccups . . . and on and on, going through the sensory experiences of seeing, hearing, touching, tasting, sensing. . . . (1979, p. 96)

Using such exercises may be a particular challenge in those settings where older people do not have enough stimuli to keep them mentally and physically alive. In addition to the kinds of negative TV programming named above, their food may be bland and colorless, their daily routines stultifying. Institutionalized seniors may have excellent life-support services but have nothing to arouse them from their lethargy. Arthur Schwartz puts it this way:

The issue can be cast into question form: is spending most of one's days staring at a wall or the floor much of a "career" for an older person even if the floor is spotless and the wall decorated with wallpaper? Is there enough incentive to get up in the morning for an elderly person who feels lonely and depressed, facing too much uncommitted time, struggling with feelings of vulnerability, merely to know for certain that his daily diet is nutritionally sound? (1975, pp. 471–472)

Stimulus deprivations can occur in the areas of the sensory, the aesthetic, the familiar, the enjoyable, the stimulating. Or they can occur in the matters of meaning, of autonomy, of self-concept, self-esteem, and self-direction. And often there are no stimulations for personal creativity. "If you want to become more creative as an individual, start spending more time with creative people" (Adams, 1986). A great idea! All well and good. But how does one implement that with older people who are isolated in their homes or captured within the confines of an unenlightened nursing home? (Please note my contrast of "unenlightened" with "enlightened.") The therapist is challenged to enter the environment to create change in whatever way possible. This might mean helping the older person to become involved in groups that offer interesting activity. It might mean working with a retirement community activities director to see about starting art classes or writing classes. For those isolated in their homes, it might mean arranging car pools to help people of like mind and like interest get together more easily. (How often I have listened to bright, articulate, older people lamenting the lack of compatible, stimulating companionship!)

Another creative technique, suggests Adams, is "plain old-fashioned cheerleading." That makes good sense. So often, in the initial stages of a new exploration, it is easy to become discouraged. It takes the stimulus of creative "cheerleading" to keep the effort going until the new experience becomes more natural. Teachers know this and therapists, as well, although we may sometimes forget that role. To dare a client to take a class, or to make a new friend, or to try on a new career for size — all this takes the stimulation of courage and a cognitive openness to experience. In my career development therapy work I have found how really difficult, frustrating, and delicate it can be to encourage the fearful, depressed, reticent client into the thinking and action of personal change. The cheers can't be too loud or invasive. It is the therapist's challenge to both gently nudge and accommodate by joining the client's willingness and pace. For, indeed, to change can be very frightening and shifts in activity and outlook may run counter to all the habits — physical, cognitive, and affective — that have been shaped and set by years of practice.

The task is to create constructive interruptions and challenges. Here I return to McLeish for ideas. He describes the power of a "small enclave of men and women, meeting to stimulate one another's creative zest and skills." There can be genuine and exciting pleasure in sharing the stimulations of creative exercises like the following (don't write these off as being too simple — they definitely are not!):

List all the unusual uses you can think of for empty cardboard boxes. (Resist the temptation to simply keep filling the box!)

Your college-age son, interested in the occult, has persuaded you to provide housing for a few delegates to the witches' convention. How do you explain their presence to your son's no-nonsense, fabulously wealthy Presbyterian great-aunt who has simultaneously decided to honor you with her presence on the same weekend?

How do you estimate another person's creativity? Write down your criteria. (McLeish, 1983, pp. 199–200)

Wellness therapies. I have already written of Robert Schmidt's program in San Francisco and the work of the National Resource Center on Health Promotion and Aging in Washington, DC. But there are other programs springing up around the country, often building on the pioneering work of Gay Luce, Ken Dychtwald, Eugenia Gerard, and others in the Berkeley, California, SAGE program for senior adults. More recently, Molly Mettler and Donald W. Kemper have been working with colleagues to build and publicize their Healthwise programs in Boise, Idaho. Billed as adventures in physical and mental wellness, the workshop programs assist older adults "to directly confront the myths of aging and overcome them with a more positive, wisdom-based view of the future" (Mettler & Kemper, 1986). The ways the program developed reflect the suggestions of participating older adults:

Growing Wiser was developed in Boise, Idaho, as a companion to a physical wellness project called Growing Younger. Developed by Healthwise, Inc., a nonprofit health promotion organization and cosponsored by the Boise Council on Aging, Growing Younger is a workshop series that focuses on fitness, stress management, good nutrition and self-care. Since 1980, over 2,500 of Boise's "60 and better" population have participated in Growing Younger.

As their physical health improved, Boise's older adults expressed an interest in having a program that enhanced mental health. It became apparent that flexibility of the mind was just as important as flexibility of the body, and that hardening of the arteries is no more damaging than hardening of the attitudes. From this raised consciousness, Growing Wiser was born. (Mettler & Kemper, 1986)

In the programs of Growing Wiser five major topics focus discussions and choice of material: memory, mental alertness, coping with loss and life change, choices for living, and self-Image. The Healthwise handbooks offer a wide variety of suggestions for a more healthful outlook. In particular, the *Growing Wiser* handbook goes beyond the physical to guide the individual towards states of mental wellness. The listing of contents suggests the breadth of its program as it moves through materials covering "becoming a Sage," to dealing with loss and life change, to a final discussion of a senior's world at "home and beyond." (Kemper et al., 1986). And in all the programs there is a nurturing of love and laughter and what Mettler and Kemper name "a call to the Spirit."

This call to the spirit is a feature of many emerging programs across the United States. Speakers who are active in these experimental efforts and who incorporate a spiritual perspective are being invited to share their thoughts at professional programs, notably those of the American Society for Aging (see the Fall 1990 issue of *Generations* for sensitive presentations of the spiritual perspective). At the same time, churches are becoming more active in addressing the needs of senior adults and in providing them opportunity for meaningful participations. Pastor Elbert C. Cole is a leader in this movement. In a featured presentation at a June 1989 American Society for Aging conference in Seattle, Washington, Cole described "Elements of a Model Ministry by, with and for Older Adults in the Congregation" and shared a listing of specific guidelines. These include the following:

1. Our ministry is intentional.
2. We empower older persons for life and ministry.
3. Our meeting places are free from barriers to participation.
4. We affirm the need to stay intergenerational.

In its church program, the congregation supports "A Shepherd's Center" which is part of an integrated network of centers housed in existing churches and temple properties. These centers serve as conduits for existing programs and services. "The goal is for people to be helped by one another and improve accessibility of the resources of a community." Cole summarizes the concept by writing, "A Shepherd's Center is a new social model informed by a healthy view of life after retirement, providing new benchmarks for vital involvement and significant and meaningful living in later years. The concept is believed to be applicable to any ethnic, economic or cultural group of older adults. It takes a commitment of people helping people live a meaningful life" (Cole, 1989).

Another type of group effort that is being developed and promoted in various areas of the United States aims to bridge the gaps between the generations. One such program has been created by Francis P. Larkin, who calls himself a "consultant in intergenerational programs." Operating out of Marmora, New Jersey, the program facilitates intergenerational conferences, an Intergenerational Club, and works with participants, sponsors, the Office on Aging, high schools, and colleges, to help confront misinformation about young and old. Even more importantly, it works to develop cross-generational activities, networking, and friendships.

These are samples of the community and national programs that a therapist can tap in steering the client towards learning, towards "invested caring" in others, towards the stimulation of novelty, and towards the cultivation of new abilities and outlooks. The therapist is encouraged to do what many of us in career development have long been doing—to keep files of information on the abundance of developing resources for persons of all ages and now, particularly, for the older person.

What does this all indicate? That if we let our imaginations run free there are many ways to enter the worlds of our clients to tap their strengths and capabilities and to encourage their innovative potentials. There are many therapies that can be incorporated into these creative explorations: Gestalt, focusing, action therapies of the type I have named above, and spiritual/existential therapy in tune with the orientations of the therapist and the wishes of the client.

GROUP THERAPIES

Here we run into a further abundance—the therapies of marriage, family, and group experience.

Family therapy and the elderly. In the *Family Therapy News* of the American Association for Marriage and Family Therapy, articles are appearing that address the concerns of late-life family members and their roles in the family system. Cleveland G. Shields, writing in the January/February 1990 issue, is representative of those who are contributing in this way. He observes that there are few articles discussing family therapy where the identified patient is an elderly family member, few theories and techniques for this kind of work. To remedy this he suggests an agenda for family therapists to consider:

1. Develop a theory about late life family members and their role in the family system.
2. Develop research on family interactions and the elderly that includes healthy elderly subjects, not just chronically ill.
3. Develop family systems intervention models with the elderly and their families around a variety of presenting problems, caregiving, depression, marital conflict, intergenerational relationship problems, and so on. (p. 5)

I like Shields' suggestions but would caution all of us in the therapeutic field to avoid placing older people in a "them" position, where they somehow stand on the edge of the family system. Many older people are right there in a very active way, serving as listeners, friends to their grandchildren, keepers of the family history. Many older family members are the ones who maintain the traditions, assemble the pictures, and preside over family rituals. They are what Eisdorfer calls "the glue in the tribe"—a very important role indeed!

Because this is so, the family therapist can have a good time with clients in reinforcing constructive connections, confirmations, and communications. In harmony with these ideas, the *Family Therapy Networker* used its July/August 1989 issue to feature family ritual as "The Hidden Resource" in working with the family. And I see this as a very particular resource in bridging the gaps between the generations. Rituals, David Kertzer believes:

- bind memories and images to us long after they are enacted;
- supply a mechanism that allows people to feel bonds of solidarity with others in their society, even others whom they rarely or never see;
- foster continuity in the face of major changes;
- encourage our self image, and the image we have of others through a process of identification between the individual and larger groups, be they ethnic, religious, political or whatever. (adopted from Kertzer, 1989, pp. 24–26)

Kertzer also comments on the place of family elders in the observance and preservation of ritual: "Past is remade into the present with the aid of the sensory stimuli that, through ritual performances, have become rooted deep within our memories," and it is frequently the older members of the family who help carry on the traditions.

Family therapy has the opportunity to draw senior members into the action of family experience in renewing, continuing ways. To foster such renewals, therapists can stimulate the retelling of family stories, the sharing of unique traditions, and the practice of genuine family dialogue. In this kind of shared experience can come new appreciation of what older family members have to offer. This lays the groundwork not only for the enjoyment of ongoing family traditions, but a basic framework for solving family problems when they do arrive. Within a spirit of mutual respect and constructive engagement the family can work through to creative solution.

A *"family meeting" model.* Created by Bonnie Genevay and her staff at Family Services in Seattle, Washington, this model suggests an intensive intervention with a broad representation of the extended family. Genevay describes concerns which shaped this approach:

Bind is defined by Webster as: "to tie or confine, to restrain." Unfortunately, "ties that bind" aren't always blessed! They can lead to premature dependence and loss of self for the older person who is too tightly bound, too soon, by caring family members. This can happen when older adults change rapidly from sufficiency to insufficiency, overwhelming mid-year children with indecision, guilt and feelings of inadequacy, and when professional assessment, support and planning are lacking. (1979, p. 16)

When family members join in acknowledging and facing this shared helplessness, a door is opened for the kinds of planning and treatment that are the focus of the family meeting approach.

With a goal of teaching family skills and opening entry to other kinds of resources, the Aging Consultation Team of Family Services sits down with three or four generations of the family in one room for a three-hour session. The goal is honest communication, definition, delegation, and facilitation. Although this is a one-time consultation, resources are explored for learning and reinforcement: "family counseling, groups for adult children and other family members, groups for older persons themselves, and family 'checkups' (one-time experiences designed to reinforce family strengths and help members learn from other families) and aging family consultations (conferences in which a team of counselors works with the whole family)" (Genevay, 1979, p. 16).

Here the kinds of "dubious protections" (discussed in Chapter 6) are identified and confronted:

- talking *about* aging persons rather than *to* them;
- making plans *for* declining parents without consulting them;

- smothering older family members with more help and advice than is desirable;
- perpetuating old feelings, attitudes, and behaviors;

In addition, negative communication habits are investigated:

- "mind-reading" — when you assume what a person is feeling and wanting without asking;
- avoiding questions of life, death, and meaning;
- unwillingness to share feelings, hurts, questions.

Humor and cross-generational observations (frequently grandchildren pick up things their parents avoid) are encouraged to interrupt errors of overparenting or to soften unwarranted guilts. Although, as Genevay notes, "guilt may have a positive effect in precipitating family change. . . . When the family's energy is needed to address life review, increasing disability, or impending death of the older adult, letting go of guilt is critical" (p. 17).

This model of family intervention is one for all of us to consider in our work with seniors — to encourage the kinds of loving support and family continuities that will enhance and sustain the lives not only of the older persons but of the younger members of the family, as well.

Marital therapy. The kinds of marital therapy we use will depend a great deal on the belief systems and commitments of the couples we see. It is a particular challenge to be in tune with historical period and cultural influences which these men and women bring with them. I have found this true in work with older women clients whose husbands did not want to come in for couple therapy. These particular women were more gender-traditional, reared to be keepers of the home, their children, and their men. They have internalized an ideology that the man is the breadwinner and the head of the household and, as such, needs their protection and focused attention. Trained in this protective stance, these wives hesitate to ask their husbands to come into therapy, and may refuse to share their protests for fear of hurting their partner. Because they are getting older and they want their time to be as satisfying as possible, they are reluctant to shake the marital system they have practiced so long. Nevertheless, helpful work can be done by quietly encouraging the wife to address her own needs and to honor them. This may eventually draw in the partner for beneficial work in communication as well as life planning. What is emphasized is a need to respect the particular value systems which are presented — and the need not to rush in with some contemporary perspective of what a marriage should be.

In an anthropological type of field study, David Fenell (1988) studied 147 couples happily married for over 20 years. With these long-term partners it was found that certain variables had contributed to the success of their marriages. These included: strong, shared moral values, lifelong commitment to the institution of marriage, loyalty to the spouse, a spouse "who is my best friend," sexual fidelity and compatibility, religious faith, a sense of responsibility, and a spouse who is stable and dependable. In spite of these positives there were classes of problems that did occur from time to time: sexual dissatisfaction, disagreements about the discipline of children, unrealistic expectations, not sharing decision-making, a lack of common interests, a loss of trust, financial disagreement, and so on. These listings offer checklists for marital work as clients and therapist identify the problems even as they reinforce positives. I believe marital therapists have a challenge and an opportunity to work with older couples in all these matters. I would also suggest the potential for life-planning which I address more specifically in the next chapter.

Before I close this discussion of "therapies and the therapeutic," I want to name two final therapies which I have discovered in my search for constructive approaches—pet therapy and gardening therapy, which are illustrative of imaginative steps to enhance the lives of those less able.

INTERVENTIONS FOR THOSE LESS ABLE

Animals are becoming known as "four-footed therapists" in work with the elderly. I quote from an article in *Family Circle*:

In the lounge of the Westchester Long-Term Care Affiliate of Beth Israel Nursing Home in White Plains, New York, 20 elderly residents are sitting quietly, waiting. Many are staring into space. Some have dozed off. . . . Suddenly the elevator door opens and out steps a man named Bashkim Dibra, holding two pet-carrying cases. Out of one he lifts a beautiful blue Persian cat named Chickie. Out of the other he picks up Kimberly, a Yorkshire terrier sporting a pink bow, and Goldie, a Chihuahua with huge brown eyes. (Randolph, 1989, p. 186)

It is what happens next that is of importance: "the elderly residents immediately become alert." As they cuddle the animals, kiss them, hold them, talk to them, they show signs of happiness and involvement with the animals. How important it is to touch something soft, warm, and responsive when all too often there is no one to touch. Not only is there this observable, subjective response, there is objective evidence that animals are calming, that they can dramatically lower heart rate and blood pressure, ease loneliness and depression, as well as serve as social catalysts providing a common ground for conversation. Amy Zegas, the director in this particular home, believes the animals do even more:

Because they are brought at regular intervals they provide something for the residents to look forward to.

Gardening is another source of stimulation. The "Disabled Independent Gardeners Association" has its headquarters in North Vancouver, British Columbia. Their stated purpose is "Encouraging gardening, whatever the obstacle." For those individuals who find joy in preparing the soil, planting seeds, pruning trees and shrubs, gathering flowers and vegetables, innovative programs are encouraging gardeners of all ages to surmount any limitation on their capacity for this kind of creative expression. DIGA's concern, as expressed in their brochure, is "not only for people with any sort of physical problem, but also for people who find themselves environmentally disabled, that is, those who find themselves in apartments with little if any patio space or the myriad of other suburban conditions that can and do inhibit gardening activity." Actively promoting these goals, this enlightened organization works with the gardener to create a workable program. Doing this adds not only activity to the life of the person but a sense of control and an interruption of those states of mind and emotion conducive to apathy and hopelessness. Those last assumptions are mine but I would guess that research would bear that out. Certainly anything that adds to a repertoire of personal possibility is of value in dealing with the uncertain, evolving states of the later years of aging.

Most of us are skillful in shutting out the world, and what we do observe we see with a jaded eye. Men or women with the gift of originality manage to keep a freshness of perception, an unspoiled awareness.

—John W. Gardner, 1964, p. 43

The first cool winds of the evening that is at hand begin to blow, even though the summer sun is still burning vividly in the afternoon sky. . . . In short, the adult in his middle years becomes the secret watcher of the implacable clock of the life drama which measures and demythologizes his younger dreams and carries him onward to the dark outlands of a youth-dominated society.

—John A.B. McLeish, 1983, pp. 40–41

CHAPTER 8

Turnings to Take Next

EACH OF US WILL feel the "first cool winds of the evening" in a different fashion. As the meanings of our youth no longer serve us well, as we face ambivalent wonderings about our life options, we will find particular questions gaining ascendence while others fade away. For even as we present a calm face to the world, the mind and emotions move to address the questions stimulated by the unfamiliar in matters of age. Our inner and outer dialogues may be increasingly engaged in integrating what we have been and are with what we are becoming.

In my Preface I shared an inner dialogue stimulated by my arrival at the age of my mother's death. About that same time I found myself engaged in another set of reflections, this time about the associated meanings of aging:

Aging is:

- *being 60 and wondering what comes next;*
- *sensing the body's shifts of energy, momentum and efficiency;*

Aging is a set of wonderings:

- *about tomorrow's unknowns, about possible losses;*
- *about how long we will live;*
- *about whether we will be strong or vulnerable, shattered or intact, when we lose a partner, a job, or a life-style;*
- *about decisions and confrontations;*
- *about discipline—deciding between settling in or continuing to tackle life, doing exercises or giving up;*
- *a set of big questions: where to live, whether to keep on working, whether to have a face-lift, whether to push limits or relax;*
- *a set of daily life choices;*
- *like every other stage of life in many ways;*
- *different from every other stage of life in many ways.*

I further pondered the links between aging and lifelong meaning-making:

Aging is grappling with meaning and meaning-making. Aging is a lot of ordinary living which involves sleeping and eating, working and playing, dozing and awakening. Just like any other period of life—but different! Tasks taking on new colorings within the shifting contexts and social demands of being an older person. Each daily activity screened through shifting filters of perception. Here are the reactions that influence us: we may not feel older but the messages of others tell us we are growing older. And those body messages intrude on our awarenesses.

Not long after creating my own reflections I discovered these words of dancer Mikhail Baryshnikov, which are *his* wonderings about aging:

You know, the physical aspect of aging is so sneaky. It doesn't just hit you—boom—overnight. It starts in your twenties, really. It's the stamina that goes first. And I tell you, it really takes you by surprise. In a way it's like a flower, where first the petals start to droop. And then the leaves start to change, and slowly the flower just wilts away. (E. Levin, 1989)

Probably most of us, then, take time to consider questions of age and aging, particularly as the reminders keep collecting in our consciousness. As a result, many of those who enter "midlife" (however you would define that for yourself) experience restlessness, a vague malaise, a fear that they will never find a meaningful role for their lives, a fear that their bodies are rapidly failing. These kinds of thought are certainly the stuff of the notorious midlife crisis. Whether we agree or not with the label, or the idea that there is one major crisis (and I think that is much too simple), the late thirties and the decade of the forties do seem to bring times of realization that certain tasks and challenges have to be addressed.

Crisis is sometimes viewed in a negative fashion—something to be avoided if possible. But when viewed constructively, crisis can actually be a time for the stimulation of new ideas and explorations—a time of "danger and opportunity," as the Chinese have so graphically portrayed in their calligraphy. A crisis is a turning point, a time to gather personal resources, a time to come to terms with the dreams that will never be realized, the banners of illusion that have to be furled. All too often the person turns away from these questions to settle into the stagnations of a middle age that does not want to face the future. Even worse the turning away may go as far as the couple in their forties who chose suicide because they believed they had gone as far in their success as they could. This is how the news release in *The Seattle Times* described their choice:

The bodies of a wealthy husband and wife, who made a videotape saying they wanted to "end it all" while they were still successful, were found yesterday. Police Sgt. Chet Barry said Anaheim real-estate broker Douglas Ridenour, 48, and his 45-year-old wife, Dana, were found in their million-dollar home after Ridenour's brother made an emergency call. Said Barry: "They decided they reached the age where they have gone as far as they are going to go." (August 2, 1990, A6)

As I reported in Chapter 1, Martin Seligman believes we are seeing a greater proportion of people in their mid-forties who are depressed. According to his theory and findings: "more people have suffered depression—the loss of hope and faith—as a result of an exalted sense of commitment to the self and a concurrent decline in commitment to religion, family, the nation and community." He believes contemporary shifts in values and emphasis make people more vulnerable to feelings of alienation because they are no longer buffered by traditional connections and institutions. Like Seligman, I ponder this, and I wonder further about our culture's strong emphasis on immediate gratification and life-styles oriented to the material, the beautiful, and the physically active, about definitions of "success" that don't leave much room for the reflective, more spiritually oriented processes of aging.

To counterbalance such pessimism it is helpful to take hold of Neugarten's conceptualization of "the executive processes of personality in middle age: self-awareness, selectivity, manipulation and control of the environment, mastery, competence, the wide array of cognitive strategies" (1968, p. 98). What people may need to learn is that middle-aged people have the advantage of experience, of some learned skills for handling success and failure, some capacities for coping with the disappointments of life. Or do they? Although we can't generalize, I do hang on to my belief that there are those creative folks who keep their minds open, use their capacities to question and wonder, do move beyond trouble, do put experiences together in new ways. It seems increasingly important that we tap their wisdom and examples.

It is in a search for examples of the management of turning points — of the "turnings to take next" (and this wonderful phrase is from the title of Freda Goldman's 1965 study of alternative goals in the education of women) — that we find the subjective reportings of the conflicts, of the feelings, of the struggles. These reportings increase our knowledge of the kinds of choices, learnings, and activities that open doors of perception rather than shut down the processes of development. Following are two such studies that have informed my thinking in this matter.

SELF-FULFILLMENT
THROUGH LEARNING

The first study is mine. I have already named some of its findings in Chapter 4 where I discuss the human needs identified by a group of mature, returning college students. But here I focus more directly on the kinds of self-fulfillment that these women experienced in their midlife learnings — learnings that brought transformations in perceptions of self.

The majority of these women reported an emerging sense of identity that came with their new investments in learning — an identity that appeared to be linked to increased participation in life outside home and family. With such participation they began to grow in self-confidence, while, at the same time, they lowered certain boundaries and protections between themselves and others. Many of them commented on a new ability to see themselves — an increased capacity to stand outside their problems with a new objectivity. They were more willing to be "in process," to allow life to unfold without having all the answers in advance of the process.

Their words are revealing:

I am no longer just a recipient of TV ads, of built-in appliance convenience, of my husband's income, of the new media. Now I also partake of and give to these areas. I receive, in return for my work, status, recognition, and monetary pay, for I have earned it.

It has brought poise and confidence and a sense of worth that somehow got buried in trying to guide the lives of others for so many years.

My understanding of people, society as a whole, has increased so tremendously. As a self-fulfillment it was the most powerful groundstone I put down. (Carlsen, 1973)

The reports of these women are pertinent to questions of personal reflection, decision and emerging outlook—and of the turning points of midlife. These women had had to make many choices in their return to school, and it was revealing to sort through these. Some came out of crisis need—a death in the family, lack of money, a divorce, or the personal urgency influenced by a diffused sense of identity. Some came because a degree represented a goal never fulfilled, one that stood as a symbol of personal accomplishment. Others came simply because they needed some educational work to fulfill a job requirement. And yet others invested in midlife educational effort simply because they loved to learn. They didn't want a degree, they were integrating their learning with life and work, with relationships and personal decision making. Above all, they liked the stimulation of ideas and all that goes with that sparking of the mind.

Again, many of these women were working to fulfill needs that are *human needs*: the need to participate, to be respected and acknowledged, to be needed, to find avenues of personal growth and expression, to find a continuity of self, and to find a greater reciprocity of relationship with others. They gave evidence that personal needs demand attention at choice point, whether that point be in young adulthood, the middle years, or the later years of life.

In my work in career development I meet clients whose needs are similar to those named above—the folks who come because some sort of life transition is taking place; or because loss of a work role has removed the structural supports that have previously organized and ordered life activity in a meaningful fashion; or because retirement is on the horizon and has to be addressed. Emotional reactions and more objective evaluations send the signal that new forms of meaning and meaning-making are required.

THE FIFTIES DECADE

A second body of research findings come from David A. Karp who focused specifically on the decade of the fifties in an investigation of the feelings and experiences of a cohort of professionals aged 50 to 60. He asked these interviewees to discuss how they think about themselves, their careers and the processes of aging. Their responses throw some new light on the decade that forms a bridge between midlife and the retirement years.

Karp found it was difficult for these people to express what they named the *paradox of aging*—how difficult it is to convey the contradictions between the way they feel inside and the way they know they appear to others. To portray the paradox these subjects were trying to articulate, Karp introduced the metaphor of "*age as a stranger.*" (I have resonated with this metaphor for it touches the feelings I experienced when I free-associated around the trigger word "aging.") Karp explains his choice:

The stranger notion was drawn from a quite different context in sociology. Among the several brilliant essays written by Simmel (1950) is one entitled "The Stranger." Simmel wrote about the stranger as a distinctive social type. As he conceived it, the stranger to a group or culture (for example the trader in the middle ages or the immigrant to a new culture) holds the distinctive position of being near and distant to a group at the same time. This idea of simultaneous nearness and distance captures well how many people feel about age and aging. (1988, p. 729)

Karp believes that the "stranger" becomes nearer and less distant as a recognition of one's place in this new stage of aging unfolds. Age reminders and age questionings begin to collect and synthesize — indeed, to transform conceptions and images. "Their mutual effect might be likened to that of drugs such as alcohol and tranquilizers which act synergistically, each magnifying the effect of the other when taken simultaneously (Karp, 1988, p. 730). But even as these synergistic, transformational developments occurred these people continued to find the fact of aging "one of life's great surprises, a surprise that is most fully sprung in the fifties. . . . The idea that they are as chronologically old as they are seems foreign. Age, at least in the early fifties, is a stranger. It is psychologically near and distant at the same time" (p. 729).

In synthesizing his data, Karp identified *reminders of aging*: body reminders, generational reminders, chronological reminders, contextual reminders, mortality reminders.

Body reminders: Just as Baryshnikov named his unique reminders of body aging, each of us has our own collection of physical signs. Many of these signs come from the mirror on the wall as our personal image shifts and transforms before our probing eyes. For some people this awareness becomes a serious threat at a relatively early age — in the late twenties, the early thirties, as the person compares and contrasts shifting body image with the impossible ideals presented by our youth culture. Unlike Dorian Gray, whose changing image was locked into his portrait behind closed doors, ours is there for everyone to see, to judge, and to evaluate. With our emphasis on an almost impossible beauty it is all the more difficult, especially for women, whose looks are linked not only to sexuality but to their interest to us as persons. Somehow the older woman fades before our eyes, her total uniqueness muted by negative body perception.

I study the most recent Christmas catalog from a sophisticated local department store. Although a gray-haired man is used as a model, no gray-haired woman appears within the pages. What is the older woman

to feel as she searches for someone to identify with? Or as she reads the
pages of Harper's Bazaar *for July 1990—an issue devoted to the*
"over-40" woman and discovers, once again, gray-haired men but only
one, nearly hidden, picture of a gray-haired woman. (This is in contrast
to earlier issues that seemed to give more honor to the mature face and
figure.)

Body reminders, then—particularly for women—leap from the pages of magazines, newspapers, and colorful advertisements, *not so much*
by their presence as by their absence.

Other reminders include the kinds of illnesses that shake one into
sharp awareness of personal mortality. Karp found it noteworthy that
some diseases are red flags for aging. One man, for example, found a
signal in the onset of prostate trouble—an experience that made him
feel old, for "I see that as an old man's disease."

Karp further notes that the *chronology* of the number 50 is significant; 50, after all, is a midpoint number, a sign that one has lived half a
century. All of us carry clusters of meanings which collect around the
markers of our birthdays. I certainly meet the clients who pay attention
to such things: the "big three-oh", those who see age 40 as a major
turning point, and, as Karp has suggested, the half-century marker of
"50."

I remember my own 50th birthday. It was a wonderful birthday with
friends who shared the same benchmark event. As we drank
champagne we felt an act of celebration launching us into a new and
potentially very fulfilling decade. In sad contrast, I remember another
friend seen on the same journey, a friend who was also celebrating his
50th. His mood was doom and gloom, bitter disappointment, feelings
so malignant and invasive that we could not linger long.

And so it goes. Each of us facing, perceiving, and interpreting the
differing physical and psychological signals of age. These are frequently
reinforced by the *reminders that come from generational difference.*

Karp calls our attention to the host of social-psychological in-be-
tweens, as those in their fifties find themselves midway between children and parents. They are the generation from which grandparents
emerge, the generation that also produces many of the caregivers for
aging relatives and friends. Burdens of responsibility escalate even as
these inhabitants of the fifties continue a degree of responsibility
for their young. They are the "sandwich generation." As they acknowledge signs of the mortality of their loved ones they also become increasingly aware of their own nearness to death. Soon they will be at the
front edge of the generations facing their own needs for help and support.

I am struck by one of Karp's insights, which comes in the form of a wondering: Is traditional conventional wisdom really accurate when it suggests that we keep young by working with young people? "It may certainly be the case that constant contact may keep one in touch with the ideas, feelings, consciousness, and popular culture of younger people. Equally likely, however, is that their presence will call attention to differences in generational status" (p. 731).

I thought of this while living my RV resort experience. Certain age perceptions slipped away as people gathered to swim, play tennis, and dance without the onerous comparisons of body that can occur when doing these things with younger people. But, interestingly, I felt at the same time people were checking each other out, comparing and contrasting to see how they were doing with the business of aging.

As I consider Karp's questioning in the light of my observations, I think of those other experiences that are distinct from body perception, that are intertwined with the wisdoms and learnings of the mind and spirit. If we go into the arenas of the mind, if we keep our thought processes alive and aware, if we continue to act out of curiosity, we may well find ourselves serving as mentors for the young in roles that are enhanced by this connection. We may find our thinking and emotional experience enlivened by exposure to a generation that is still dealing with the unknown and the unexpected, a fortunate interruption to our jaded tendencies to settle into practiced patterns.

Contextual reminders: Becoming the oldest in the group, in the job setting, in the class, certainly reminds us that we are growing older. Indeed, as we move through the decade of the fifties we are occasionally (frequently?) the oldest. Certainly, too, there are the moments of truth: when we join AARP or declare ourselves a "senior citizen" when buying a ticket to the movie. That may well constitute a major "coming out of the closet."

"Fitting in all too well" can bring age awareness. Like moving to the sun belt in the winter season when all the other "snow birds" descend from the north.

It is indeed a strange experience to enter restaurants to find everyone is gray-haired and that the entire format of menu and decor is geared to the elderly. Or to drive down a major roadway in Mesa, Arizona to discover cars shooting by in a spirit of open warfare, to become aware that senior drivers are stereotyped and put down as bad drivers — not as individuals but as a class. I even heard a friend suggest I increase my insurance for my brief stay because I was surrounded by senior drivers. To read the editorial page of the Phoenix/Tempe/Mesa newspapers is to find a battle of the generations, to see the issue of driving skills debated in genuine ageist fashion: the old taking aim at the young; the young firing back in their leveling of accusation.

The older person faces dilemmas in matters of dress. Indeed, the norms for proper attire for older people are falling around us as fashion offers a wide range of choice. Yet, as the body shows its signs of age a certain style sense may be needed to negotiate the narrow boundaries between what is flattering and what is not, what is dowdy and what is not. To see a 60-year old woman in high-heeled boots and mini-skirt may inspire a generational double take — but maybe not. In writing this, I remember a Phil Donahue program during the 1989–1990 season which featured a group of older women dancers. Attractive, with well-proportioned, firmly toned bodies, these women wore leotards and tights and danced a carefully choreographed routine. After they were finished a phone caller responded indignantly, "Ridiculous." The audience rose up in protest in a fascinating discussion of these women's performance which was challenging norms very directly. Standing out in that discussion (and wearing her neatly fitted leather pants!), a woman in her late 60s hotly declared: "That woman is already old!"

And what did she mean? Simply that this woman caller had rejected these women's activity by labeling it "ridiculous." Her thinking was indeed "old" (and ageist) as she abruptly discarded the potential of older women for continuing sensual activity, for the spirited routines of dancing, for the joy of doing the zany and unexpected.

Finally, there are the *mortality reminders*. As one of Karp's respondents cogently noted, "there is a momentum of mortality occurrences in the fifties. People in their fifties find that members of their age cohort begin to die with some regularity. The death of a close friend of the same age, a work colleague, or a former college roommate brings increasing awareness of one's own proximity to death.

In the middle years mortality awareness does come with all the reminders named above. With that mortality awareness does come a sense of the finiteness of time as we come to greater appreciation of the special meaning of choices in the middle years of life. "Once time is recognized as a diminishing resource, people have got to decide what they are going to do with that resource. Inevitable questions arise about the nature of the contributions that can realistically be made at this life point" (Karp, 1988, p. 735). How the diminishing resource is viewed, accepted, and used as raw material has much to do with whether the fifties become a time of a new liberation or of increasing decline.

Transcending the ambiguities and negatives of awareness, many of Karp's subjects *did* talk about the positive features of this emerging state of life:

The notion that people in their fifties feel an "enriched sense of self and a capacity for coping with complexity" (Neugarten & Datan, 1974) was supported by the data. One word that came up frequently as people described themselves was *wisdom*. The attainment of a certain wisdom with age is one of the ways in which the fifties were considered a time of personal liberation. (p. 735)

In tune with this attention to the concept of wisdom came the finding that the fifties are a time of increasing review of the larger themes of life, of the meanings to be explored and put into perspective.

Pertinent to this, I find it interesting to work with the many clients in their forties and fifties who come to wrestle with their purposes and shifting meanings. They are seeking a place in the order of things — for some way to leave a lasting mark on or a meaningful contribution to the world in which they live. The facts of these recurring themes confirm the studies of Karp and of others like Erikson (1963) and Neugarten (1968). At some point in our midlife many of us do become more reflective, introspective, and self-aware. Jung's suggestion that the years beyond midlife are more attuned to questions of the spiritual is also confirmed.

We must remember, however, that age alone does not bring the transition. Development is not automatic. Rather, the shift comes with growing sensitivity to matters deeper than the superficial, money-oriented, impulse-satisfying tendencies of our society. It is to become more in tune with caring for generations and generativities which can counteract the threatened stagnations of age. It is to shift the ways we perceive and process our realities. It is to reorient to the more transcendent as the physical declines. (Study the alternatives in Tables 3.2 and 3.3.)

Even as there is a quickened sense of aging in the fifties, even as the demands and signs of change bring more introspection and redefinition, there is still potential for the new and the renewing, the rewarding, enriching, and unfolding, in the experiences and states of age. In fact, it would seem that the many new examples of creative, middle-aged people are pointing us towards experimental adventures never dreamed of before. Colonel Sanders started his Kentucky Fried Chicken business when he was in his 60s; an advertising man, healthy and vitally alive in his purposes, enters a seminary upon his retirement from business in order to use his accumulated resources to help others; an 83-year-old man starts painting and pottery-making after years in a service role. These examples, coupled with the falling of retirement regulations in the 1980s and 1990s, are transforming our conceptions of retirement. With the shifts in definition and arrangement, the so-called "retirement" period seems to be emerging as a relatively new and relatively uncharted developmental stage.

RETIREMENT:
A NEW CAREER STAGE?

Retire? That's like hanging up your soul on a nail and closing the door. I don't know enough about life to start worrying about death, and I'll stay in it until they come for me. This is a crazy way for a grown man to make a living, breaking myself up with my own stories, but as long as I make so much money they ain't gonna lock me up. (Red Skelton as quoted in Hawthorne, 1977)

Obviously, many of us won't earn the money Red Skelton makes or have the option of keeping our work roles going until the day we die. But his ideas are important—that if we quit being challenged, if we hang up our souls on a nail, we are indeed closing the door on life.

Retirement decision-makings grow out of midlife decision-makings. Even more, they grow out of the reflective, self-discovery processes that are possible at any age. The earlier the better, for it is in developed self-awareness and self-understanding that fruitful directions for purposes and talents can be chosen. These kinds of decision-makings are the stuff of the kinds of therapeutic work I do in career development and life transition—therapeutic work that takes on a particular salience as one becomes aware of time limitations and wrestles with the feelings of becoming older.

With the transformations that come with the closure of a job role there is genuine possibility for a new "career." For *career* is not the same as job (at least not within the transformational approach I use in career development; see Carlsen, 1988). Using the original metaphor of *career* as "street, path, the chariot on which one rides" puts the concept of career into a perspective beyond the mechanical, survival elements of money and regular hours of 8:00 am to 5:00 pm. It has to do with personal meaning, with personal direction, with organizing principles for the ordering of life.

John Crystal and Richard Bolles (1974) write of the "three boxes of life," which have locked us into simplistic images of appropriate successive progressions: the student stage, the work stage, the leisure stage. With traditional enactments of these stages we are frequently thrust into successive orgies of a very particular type of experience with little time and energy remaining to incorporate others. There is little opportunity within these traditional passages for a more imaginative mix and match of study, work, and play. And, although lifelong learning experiences are leavening people's lives, the work role still dominates much of the American scene making us relatively unprepared for abrupt leaps into the leisure frequently forced upon us by the retirement edict.

But *there is a leavening* even as the patterns continue. People are becoming more aware of the need for the "mix-and-match" (and I frequently help people design "mix-and-match" careers), especially with new attention to exercise routines and stress reduction programs. (Sometimes these very programs become their own form of "work" rather than leisure.) Elderhostel programs are stimulating the learning juices of many older Americans even as they spread out across the world. (Studying the catalog of classes is fascinating.) People are allowing themselves the occasional leave of absence or time off to go to school.

We are challenging the meanings of retirement. In fact, I challenge the word itself. *Retirement* is a perplexing word! The thesaurus in my computer lists a rather strange (and somewhat awful) set of synonyms: abdication, departure, resignation, exile, isolation, leisure, quarantine, relaxation, rest, retreat, seclusion, solitude, withdrawal. Certainly leisure, relaxation, rest, retreat, solitude, are not so negative. But to fill one's time with only those? To devote the rest of one's life to an excess of these experiences? Doesn't that destroy any sense of vital investment in the business of living? It certainly does from my perspective — and, apparently, very much from that of Red Skelton.

The word "retirement" was first applied as an economic term by Germany's Bismarck in the 19th century. The concept and its application was adopted in America during the Depression, at a time when 25% of the population was unemployed. It was an aid to stimulating the work activity of younger people even as older people were eased from their occupational roles. Perhaps a structure of retirement was useful at that time, but what seems remarkable is that we have continued to make the age of 65 our line of demarcation both for being "old" and for being "retired."

Jules Z. Willing (1981) puts it this way:

If a person thinks of retirement as entering old age, he draws all sorts of erroneous conclusions about what is happening to him. He attributes some of the temporary adjustments of retirement to the permanent onset of old age and creates a self-fulfilling prophecy in which he confirms his identity as an old person. (p. 170)

We know that we grow older; we don't know when we become old. I think it may be said that we become old when we declare ourselves to be old — and that is why I think it is so important to stop speaking prematurely of ourselves as old. (p. 173)

Fortunately, retirement is being redefined. In the 1980s and now in the 1990s, the requirements for retirement ages are falling. Already new regulations are in operation in many places, and it won't be long until mandatory retirement is an experience of the past. No doubt these shifts will bring new problems and challenges in the marketplace, but perhaps those dilemmas and possibilities will be worked through from a less generalized perspective on what constitutes "old." With shifting guidelines and regulations, people will be increasingly challenged to define and redefine what they want for their lives. With rising life expectancy there will be a period of 20 to 30 years for career reinvestment. And there will be divisions within subdivisions as people define more fully the shifting tasks and demands of old age.

CONFRONTING THE CHOICE
POINTS OF AGING

Recently I reread the report of the TIAA-CREF's (Teachers Insurance and Annuity Association, and College Retirement Equities Fund) study on retirement (Milletti, 1984). What Mario Milletti summarized there adds fuel to my emphasis on creative, preparatory work for aging. Although this study found 90% of the academic respondents satisfied with their post-retirement lives (and, yes, this is a select population, but with many of the same concerns as the rest of us), there were those who shared concerns about the abrupt leap from full-time work into retirement:

The abrupt "break" between working and retirement can be disconcerting. There is some initial feeling of being cast adrift and "out of the swim" writes a 68-year-old man. "This feeling soon passes." Not so for others. "Even after seven-and-a-half years of retirement" says a 72-year-old woman, "I am still not reconciled to a life of leisure and find few attractions in my life."

These respondents send two messages, among others: (1) that many are satisfied with life after retirement, but (2) many are also concerned that the break be less abrupt, more planned, more gradual. In their commentary, these former academics alert us to some of the problems which can result if the individual does not implement a planned transition: (1) the retiree may discover serious drawbacks in a lack of daily structure and firm deadlines; (2) without personal involvements in new contacts one's circle of intimates may decrease; (3) there may be a lack of stimulation from the young. Once again, these respondents emphasize "retirement should be a gradual process, not an abrupt shift."

Whether the decision-makings of the later years are linked to a work role or not, this is a time of many choices: places to live, money needed, health arrangements, continuing structurings of each day, renewing experiences with family and friends to keep the mind and body as alive and alert as possible even as they begin their decline. This is the time, then, of sorting the kinds of life-style options available, of making the kinds of decisions that will set a revised style more fully in motion.

Downs and Roll's (1981) thoughtful book is filled with important suggestions for both the individual and the therapist who are examining the questions of aging. Though these writers don't fit the category of "gerontologist," each brings a rich background of experience: Hugh Downs with his own retirement from regular broadcasting in 1971, his role as a spokesman for retired people and their issues, and as moderator of his Emmy Award-winning talk show *Over Easy.* Richard Roll, on the other hand, brings an M.B.A. from Harvard Business School and his work as president of Best Years Resources, Inc., a New York publishing firm specializing in pre-retirement.

The last section of *The Best Years Book* (and some might argue with their title), speaks directly to choices and life-styles. Pertinent to our exploration of creative cognitive development and life planning are the chapters "Learning and Growing Don't Stop with Retirement" and "Your Second Career: Work as a Leisure Activity." In these chapters Downs and Roll offer both caution and suggestion:

... planning a rich, full lifestyle for the future is a critical part of avoiding upheaval. If you know where you're headed before you get there, you can make the transition from job to retirement far more smoothly. You won't be facing a threatening void; instead, you'll be gaining the opportunity to devote more time to familiar activities, along with the new interests that come your way. If you are able to do many different things, you'll have the necessary resources to adapt to changes when they occur. (1981, p. 259)

Downs and Roll encourage the older person to incorporate "ten keys" for choosing activities. Here I enlarge on these themes:

1. *Build continuity into your life.* This will provide a shape, a structure, a helpful level of routine, a balance between being completely spontaneous and having a sense of a connecting thread.
2. *Build to peak moments, to small and large completions.* This can be the gardener planning a garden, the silversmith creating a pendant, the musician practicing for the next concert. For the writer, of course, there is the movement in the shaping of a story. For a family member, it can be planning for the next reunion with loved ones. However simple, what is needed is some sort of rising cadence that takes one towards a climax—a climax that creates positive tensions and motivations in a stimulation of the possible.
3. *Maintain growth.* This can mean skill development or the cultivation of new outlooks and learnings. It incorporates the experience of becoming better at something.
4. *Exploration that helps to keep curiosity alive.* The RV adventurers are out keeping curiosity alive as they face daily the

unexpected event, scene, and human contact. These enactments of new exploration would seem to be important practice in facing small dangers and decision-makings (like being
in an RV when it is five degrees below zero on Christmas eve,
or driving down a bumpy road not knowing if your "rig" can
make it!).

5., 6., and 7. *Build balance into life by juxtapositions of the social
and the private, the indoor and the outdoor, the structured and
the flexible.* This requires self-knowledge and creative exploration, for each of these terms will have to be individually defined. What is private for one person may be very public for
another. What is structured for one will be flexible for another. By sorting these contrasts the individual gains more understanding of self.

8. *Build "worthwhile activities" into the schedule of events.* This
means fulfilling the human "need to be needed"—a need that
becomes a central concern for many older people, a concern I
will address more directly in Chapter 11 in my discussion of
creative models for aging.

9. *Find a harmony between the passive and the active.* There is a
slowing down in aging which requires adjustment, and it may
be all too easy to settle into a passive position. All the above
activities can be used to foster the adjustments of these balances.

10. *Find an economically rewarding activity to "turn a profit."*
Again in my RV wanderings I was struck by the imaginations
of these older adventurers that produce new entrepreneurial
activities, many highly sophisticated: the artist who collects
sands from around the world, using his search for unexpected
textures and colors to provide times of adventure and exploration for him and his wife. The resulting sand paintings,
created in a variety of beautifully crafted bottles, are exceptional in their beauty and design (yes, he had been a highly
respected artist before he retired from more formal work). I
also saw the man who makes wooden signs for recreational
vehicles, setting up his workshop in leisure parks, in flea mar-
kets, in gatherings of every kind. These people are models of
the entrepreneurial adventure; they demonstrate ways to earn
money while having a little fun and enjoying a time of new-
found independence and leisure.

Auren Uris's *Over 50: The Definitive Guide to Retirement* (1979) also
offers helpful stimulus to creative exploration. In it he summarizes a set
of life-styles to consider:

Bearing the torch: This includes helping others, being an activist, serving as a volunteer, working with family members. There are no "shoulds" here. It is a matter of exploring before committing too deeply as one identifies what one really wants to do.

Blissfully at leisure: This means tapping the full meaning of the word "leisure," which comes from the Latin root, "to be permitted." In order to be happily at leisure requires a plan, an appreciation of the pitfalls, and understanding of what is novel and interesting for one's self. Auris cautions that an abrupt switch from a heavy work load to unstructured leisure can be a big jolt. Here all the suggestions from Downs and Roll and the TIAA-CREF respondents become particularly helpful. A focused career development search that creates a profile of interests, skills, values, and needs, is also an important adjunct to effective planning (see Chapter 11, Carlsen, 1988).

Traveling: Uris suggests the individual "experiment and explore," gather information, examine the budget carefully, keep flexible in terms of time, attitude, and approaches.

Continuing education: Uris calls this a "different kind of journey." He sees this as a development of new skills, possible improvements of those already learned, an improvement of memory, and an opportunity to keep the mind in trim. (I write of learning programs in Chapter 11.)

Passions new and old: This means building a vital, involving life around a passionate interest: music, children, teaching, study, history, being a courtroom observer, writing letters to the editor, finding a new and engaging hobby (best started earlier than the retirement era, however).

This topic of retirement planning is a rich and engaging one—a challenge for both client and therapist to carefully consider, a reminder that "retirement" may well be a new stage of vocational development. Those of us who specialize in career development can treat retirement counseling in the same manner we do any other career counseling. My model, which is fully explained in *Meaning-Making*, has many approaches to consider (see Table 8.1). Here is self-search as the client discovers, sorts, and names profiles of skills, interests, values, and needs. Once these are identified the creative part begins: the clustering and shaping of these "personal ingredients," as I call them, into some sort of meaningful form, into purposes and directions and choices—whatever it is that will work for the individual person. Development can and does continue if the person wishes to explore new potential in later life. In such creative search vocation as "calling," and career as "path," can take on many new meanings.

TABLE 8.1 Career Development Plan*

I. *Identity Clarification*

Defining skills, interests, values, and needs is the first task. The following tools are used to facilitate the process:

Interview:	Gathering history in a search for patterns of vocation, interests, skills, needs, and values. At this time attention is given to any self-defeating attitudes that may be present.
Testing:	Strong-Campbell Interest Inventory Myers-Briggs Type Indicator Career Assessment Inventory Rokeach Values Test
Autobiographical Exercises:	Review of significant experiences "Who am I?" Fantasy exercises

II. *Developing a Plan:*

Research:	Through library research, interviewing for information, reading, collecting want ads, attending professional workshops, perspectives are broadened and unique job possibilities are brainstormed and defined.
Resume:	As job descriptions take shape, resume writing is begun, meshing the personal profile with focused job goals.
Time Plan:	A time plan is developed showing the "shape" of exploration. At this point there may be several types of plan according to varying job goals. Pros and cons are discussed using techniques of decision making.

III. *Active Search:*

Much of this stage is in the hands of the client. Role playing of interview techniques, supportive feedback, decision making, and continuing brainstorming provide increased clarification of the search.

---

*This sequence is adapted to the needs of each individual. Although a "typical" series consists of four sessions, this can vary considerably. If depression or anxiety is present, or if relationship concerns are complicating the decision process, these will be looked at as a part of the career therapy process.

In closing, I turn to a man who I consider to be a remarkable example of the creative. His words reinforce all that has been written above:

I still believe that creativity is the whole essence of one's being. I am eighty-two, almost eighty-three, but I have been, and am, creative. And that means that I am young—young in mind and young in heart. Creativity is the most important element in the human being. I do not care what a person creates, be it beautiful handiwork, beautiful carpentry, beautiful metal pieces, beautiful poetry, beautiful music, I do not care. The important thing is that he [and she] has created something and is able to say, "This is mine." (Chapple, in Wilson, 1985, pp. 8–9)

Stanley Chapple, noted music educator, orchestra conductor, and consummate musician, is now dead, but his words linger on.

God made man because he loves stories.

—Elie Wiesel, 1966

... the meaning of what exists is constantly placed in sus-
pense by a totality that does not yet completely exist. But the
totality that does not yet exist relies on the individual things
that do exist...

—Stuart Charme, 1984, pp. 47–48

To live over people's lives is nothing unless we live over their
perceptions, live over the growth, the change, the varying intensity of the same — since it was *by* these things they themselves lived.

—Henry James (in Strouse, 1986, p. 183)

CHAPTER 9

Narrative as Meaning-Making

SEVERAL YEARS AGO I found new understanding of personal identity when I attended a workshop with social historian Theodore Roszak,
in the quiet, idyllic setting of Princeton University. All of us listened
attentively as he talked of "reflective autobiography," in which we locate
a point in personal history where we touched feelings of uniqueness for
the first time. He described such a moment as a "universal experience"
of childhood when identity is experienced and affirmed, whether by a
sense of personal aloneness, by a strong emotional response, or by the
sudden awareness of one's name.

To start us on this inner journey, Roszak reported one of his own
experiences as a little boy who lay in a wheat field, all alone, looking up
at the stars. In this dusty, secluded place he found a sense of uniqueness as well as a private vision. Planted within his memories were
images which would stay with him into later life, guiding him, inspiring
him, identifying him.

I was moved by Roszak's description to reach into my own memories. I recalled one special time as a little girl at the top of a California redwood tree. Here was the tomboy, five years old, high in her perch, looking through a green window onto the world far below. Nearby, in the closeness of the small branches was my friend Bob. Bob and I had found this natural sanctuary together and had christened it "our place." And we had gloated quietly, as children will, when a friend's efforts to climb the tree ended in ignominious failure, reassured that our place at the top of the redwood was indeed ours, secure from unwanted intrusion.

Sitting there in my workshop group some 45 years later pondering this child of so long ago, I began to understand what Roszak was talking about when he described those early experiences as roots of how we make sense of ourselves. I also agreed with him that each of us, either consciously or unconsciously, is reaching across the years to connect with childhood experience, to name and rediscover the genuineness of those moments, and thus to bring early learnings and conditionings into the fabric of understanding of current life.

Thus I come to an exploration of narrative process and life review. Here is the comparing and contrasting, the sifting and sorting as we work to make sense of life. Here are the meaning-makings which strive for personal order and significance. Here are the present-day processings of goals, purposes, intentions, potentials which offer springboards to the future, even as we integrate the stories from the past.

Whether life histories are gathered through the dialogues between therapist and client, by the researcher studying the lives of particular individuals, or by the individual engaged in private autobiographical work, they offer a significant means for *learning what a person is about*:

What a person is about—what do I mean by that? I mean something which I think you all understand immediately, the strange fact that for each person certain things seem to *matter*; matter more than other things. Matter, meaning what? Meaning that there are certain things which they seem to pursue more than other things; that either with persistence or else off and on, they behave in a certain manner which indicates they are after something or they are up to something, as the saying goes, or hung up on something. (Buhler, 1977, p. 20)

These "things that matter" have certainly guided me in focusing on identity questions and creative expressions. They certainly guide the scientist in her laboratory or the artist in his studio. They certainly guide therapeutic questionings that search for a passion, a guiding purpose, a pathway of personal significance.

To shape one's story requires an attention to what matters—a selection process that picks and chooses from among the different possible story lines, the different players who can star in the drama, and the various interpretations of what the story is about. In this manner, telling one's story is a coming to terms with what it all means, an opportunity to express feelings linked to the unfolding experiences as well as to confront the various ways one can interpret the story. Here is a renewing, ongoing opportunity to work through to new understandings of oneself even as one engages in creative self-expression.

Charlotte Buhler, noted for her study of biographical histories, linked personal storytelling to the processes of meaning-making; she strongly believed in the "phenomenon of people wanting 'to live for something,' which becomes for them life's meaning" (Buhler & Massarik, 1968, p. 21). And she further believed that people gain something in the process of naming and integrating their experiences. By doing this they more directly confront their ultimate beliefs and goals as well as their times of crisis and disenchantment. For indeed, "most people want desperately to believe in something, regardless of whether their lives have been ever so *disorganized* or *conflicted* or that they have found *integration* and *peace*" (Buhler, 1977, p. 27).

Operating out of these assumptions, she devoted a great deal of her research and writing to explorations of human goals and needs as they are integrated within an "intentionality" that unites personal life themes and gives them a sense of coherence. From these studies she concluded that those "who worked themselves through to any kind of creative doings, felt better about themselves and about life, even if some of their problems or conflicts remained unresolved" (1977, p. 23). Why did she believe this? Because "any kind of creative activity is experienced by the person as a self-expression in which *feelings* are released in such a manner that the result is a *product*"—a product that carries within it the ingredients of one's life story.

LIFE IS A STORY

To create a personal narrative is to act on the metaphor "life is a story," which linguist George Lakoff and philosopher Mark Johnson believe is rooted deep not only in our culture but in the cultures of the world. In their words: "It is assumed that everyone's life is structured like a story, and the entire biographical and autobiographical tradition is based on this story. What do you do? You construct a coherent narrative that starts early in your life and continues up to the present" (Lakoff & Johnson, 1980, p. 172).

To tell one's story of life is to search for the common elements of the actor/participants, the parts they play, the stages of their development, the linear sequences of history and chronological time, the causes and effects, and the naming, shaping, and living of purposes and potentials. Here are the mixtures of alternatives, options, possibilities, ingredients, substances, capacities, and power. Here, too, are the failures, the losses of meaning and personal drive, the disenchantments, the crises, the awakenings born of destructions. As these are formed into narrative, the author of experience, the person in process, is remembering some things, forgetting others, highlighting, downplaying, all according to the cognitive and affective forces working together to create the story.

Narrative has to do with what we take to be true:

Reality is what we take to be true. What we take to be true is what we believe. What we believe is based upon our perceptions. What we perceive depends upon what we look for. What we look for depends upon what we think. What we think depends upon what we perceive. What we perceive determines what we believe. What we believe determines what we take to be true. What we take to be true is our reality. (Zukav, 1979, p. 328)

Perception is what makes one historian tell the story of history in her way and another in his way. Jean Strouse (Zinsser, 1986, p. 172) describes what this history-making, this biography-building, is like as she quotes from Lytton Strachey in his preface to *Eminent Victorians* (1918):

It is not by the direct method of a scrupulous narration that the explorer of the past can hope to depict that singular epoch. If he is wise, he will adopt a subtler strategy. He will attack his subject in unexpected places; he will fall upon the flank, or the rear; he will shoot a sudden, revealing searchlight into obscure recesses, hitherto undivined.

What creates the excitement in well-shaped biography is an unexpected portrayal of the events, a perception, an emotional response, a new synthesis breaking forth into the light of the biographer's day. In the words of Strachey we can "row out over that great ocean of material, and lower down into it, here and there, a little bucket, which will bring up to the light of day some characteristic specimen, from those far depths, to be examined with a careful curiosity." The very act of lowering the bucket brings us closer to ourselves, to the sense of our life as an integrated whole. It is a learning and a practice, an adventure and a discipline that helps us to come to know ourselves better and to bring into our agings and dyings the understandings and continuities which will help us live our lives more effectively.

Numerous ways suggest themselves for dipping the bucket. We can enter our life review by examining the places where we have lived, the railroad stations from which we have departed (as suggested by a railroading class sponsored by the Center for Creative Retirement), the people who have fed us our cookies, the situations that have shaken our images of self. Our dipping in the bucket can be a naming of persons, places, events, wishes, fears, dreams, beliefs, insights, the citing of first awarenesses (like the stories collected within "early recollections"), examples of conflict, "touchstones of reality" (Maurice Friedman's wonderful terminology, 1972), evaluations, questionings. We can wander our narrative ladders from concrete experiences, which can be observed from the outside, to those that represent our dialogues with self and with the universe. In those latter explorations is the stuff of mystery.

Sam Keen adds other exploratory themes to incorporate into our repertoire of questionings:

1. What invisible cultural myths guide and inform you?
2. What is your personal myth?
3. Where did you come from?
4. What have you forgotten?
5. Against what must I struggle? Who is my enemy? [And Keen answers: "My hell includes writers of IRS forms, advertising agencies that lie for pay and producers of TV sitcoms that aren't funny and demean the human spirit."]
6. What is the nature of the good? Who are the heroes and heroines? What ought I do? (Keen, 1988, pp. 43–49)

Then there are the kinds of questions I might use for people in life transition or in active career development search:

- Who am I as a person? Titles, descriptors, negatives, positives.
- First awarenesses: homes, illnesses, family, relationships (my own experience at the top of the redwood tree, for example).
- Chapters of life: Make it an exercise to divide personal history into developmental stages and assign titles to the stages and/or chapters.
- Crisis times that brought you to this transition.
- Shifting beliefs — or the beliefs that have remained strong.
- Questions to be answered.

Recognizing that our themes of questioning can change with shifting contexts and shifting chronology, we can use Havighurst's "demands" or Peck's life questions as stimuli for autobiographical work. Or we can play with Neugarten's suggestion of "salient issues" in later adulthood:

1. The use of experience.
2. The structuring of the social environment.
3. Dealing with perspectives of time.
4. Examining ways to shape the major themes of love, time and death.
5. Coming to terms with changes in self-concept, and changes in identity as one faces success, contingencies of marriage and relationship, parenting, career development and decline, retirement, widowhood, illness and personal death. (Neugarten, 1968, p. 139)

These issues, demands, and challenges suggest the value of wrestling actively with life questions in the building of the continuities of self. In this manner the self is explored within an ongoing dynamic of life, and is seen as an evolving series of salient challenges to be addressed, clarified, and acted upon. With these kinds of explorations the person may become less threatened or overwhelmed by the difficulties that do come, somehow gaining a more overarching conception of what life is about.

NARRATIVE AND
THERAPEUTIC PROCESS

Indeed, to tell the story of one's life *is* to create a product, a self-expression, an emotional release. Because this is so, I continually use narrative process as an integrative tool in psychotherapy. In fact, the very acts of interviewing, asking questions, playing back and forth between the past and the present, engaging the dialogue, and sharing feelings are very much a storytelling experience. Whether I collect early recollections, help my client design a genogram, or encourage forms of writing that use the theme of "Who am I?", I am stimulating expressive dialogues with self and life. By choosing these methods I also hope to teach my clients to incorporate storytelling into personal meaning-makings well beyond the therapeutic experiences in my office.

The narrative style of thinking is a developmental, meaning-making, kind of thinking. It attends more to process than to product, more to facilitation than to treatment, more to aging as a lifelong evolution than a stage or state of life. This cognitive approach agrees with my husband's thoughtful insight, "Aging as stage divides us; aging as process unites us." And it underscores the excitement and adventures to be found in a process which first brings into awareness the elements of one's life, and then fits the pieces together into a cohesive whole. It is self-discovery in partnership with self-creation.

Incorporating what Jerome Bruner (1986) calls the narrative mode, this biographical approach accesses the side of the mind devoted to the "irrepressibly human acts of imagination that allow us to make experience meaningful. This is the side of the mind that leads to good stories, gripping drama, primitive myths and rituals, and plausible historical accounts" (from the dust cover of his book). To acknowledge and honor these acts of imagination is to break loose from our more linear, analytical, logical forms of psychotherapy to stimulate the whimsical and the intuitive — and thus, the unexpected.

Narratives can be assembled through the techniques of writing or through the verbal processes of storytelling. Indeed, Sam Keen, who has done a great deal of professional work sorting our personal myths, calls psychotherapy a species of storytelling "closer to theater, the novel and the dramatic arts than to science or medicine" (1988, p. 45). As he puts it, "in psychotherapy a troubled person hires a private theater and

an audience of one (or lately, a group) to recollect and re-enact a lifetime of forbidden and untold stories. One day, after many quite ordinary 50-minute hours, magic may happen"—a magic when the spell is
broken, when a cognitive leap takes place, when one way of seeing the
past is transformed as one "feels and sees something new" (Keen, 1988,
p. 45). I have named such a transformation in my opening paragraphs
in *Meaning-Making* when I describe the "chilling, poignant moment"
when the client "no longer *is* the problem, but *has* the problem, thus is
able to hold it, objectify it, and deal with it with a new construction of
that problem" (Carlsen, 1988, pp. 3–4).

These cognitive/emotional transformations do carry the essence of
magic—but they arise out of the hard work of the data gathering,
patterning, and closure which confront and stimulate the cathartic
awakenings of personal memory, the validatings of perception, the de-
fusings of volatile emotions, and the reframings of blocks to creativity
and development. By telling the story, verbally or in writing, the individual begins to make sense of the whole even as he or she exposes the
vulnerabilities of the particular.

Supplementing verbal process, writing offers its own particular rewards, often bringing the rich results of values articulated,
needs expressed, and intuitions accessed. Why is this so? Writing seems
to gather and translate what Arieti has called the "endoceptual" experience—that inner world of unnamed memory and impression that has
never been put into concept, in other words, "that which we know but
which we don't know that we know." "This may be particularly true for
sensitive, intuitive observers. For these people, who may have a hard
time explaining their intuitions or their emotional reactions, writing
becomes an effective means for translating preconscious, nonverbal
experience (what Arieti calls 'endocept') into objective material available for analysis and thought" (Carlsen, 1988, pp. 118–119).

Our writing can break us loose from simplistic categories, offer
stimulus for new connections of thought and idea, and open new windows into how we make sense of things. Indeed, "to write is to categorize, to compare and contrast, to select one word or idea over another.
To write is to evaluate, to stand back, to become the more objective
observer. To write is to join one body of memories with another, one
place in personal history with the experience of the moment" (Carlsen,
1988, p. 119). In these varieties of ways writing can stimulate "mindfulness" (Langer, 1989), stimulate dialectical thinking (Basseches, 1984),
and suggest new creative synthesis.

My clients are frequently relieved, less fearful, as they come to know
themselves in more interesting and intimate ways through the narrative
experiences of therapy. By arriving at a new sense of personal coherence they more fully engage the present (the static in perception seems

cleared), more directly shape new possibilities for their futures, more willingly allow the unfolding of processes which do not often name themselves in advance. In making sense of their past they may well counteract what Alfred North Whitehead calls our "human style," which is "to mourn the past and worry about the future, while all the time the Sacred Present is passing us by, half-used, half-enjoyed" (cited in McLeish, 1983, p. 37). What this all seems to constitute is the fulfillment of what Stuart Charme (1984) calls the "biographical instinct" which reflects the "universal human need to be meaningful, and reveals the cathartic effect of meaning" (p. 72).

In summary, then, therapeutic explorations using narrative as both process and technique create a dialogue between the self and history. It is a dialogue that can help to identify those life experiences and life patterns that have shaped personal identity and have contributed to a sense of consistency and continuity of the self. It is the realization that many of those internalized learnings are still operating to guide the person towards choices and directions. By naming these influential forces the therapist may help the client to discover and cultivate a new ability to contrast those learnings that are disruptive and interfering with those that are helpful and enriching. And in the experience of telling the story, the person may yet challenge the patterns rather than leave them operating as the saboteurs of experience.

A SEARCH FOR
THE "AUTHENTIC STORY"

In the shared experiences of developing such themes, therapist and client are looking for the "authentic story," uncluttered by the stories of others. This means unblocking the family taboos, the restrictions of culture, the "thou shalt nots," the "shoulds" and "oughts" that interrupt the spontaneities of personal construction. But even as I write "authentic story," I realize that perhaps there is no such thing— perhaps the story is always in process, always under construction; perhaps it is an illusion that we will ever name that which is "authentic." But at least we can heed Erving Polster's warning that in the telling of the story:

Some are fooled into mistaking the tales for the events themselves, repeating them over and over as though that will restore the old event itself. Some tell stories when they should have conversational exchanges. Some distort the events that actually happened. Some tell stories that are marvelous elaborations on what was only a simple experience; for others the most complex event is worth only a grunt, the punctuation mark for a story to be imagined. Some people are wary about telling those things which they are afraid will make them look bad. (Polster, 1987, pp. 22–23)

Yes, all those possibilities can interrupt the meaning-makings of storytelling. Simple repetition is not enough. Simplistic perceptions are not enough. What is needed is an invested sorting and naming that can transform the story, that can compare and contrast, incorporate both the negative and positive, face both joy and pain. How well the individual handles this may well highlight contrasts between those who are open to experience and those who are not.

In a social-cognitive analysis, David J. Sperbeck and Susan Krauss Whitbourne (1985) have found marked differences between open and closed individuals in how reminiscence is processed. Those persons who carry strong biases as to how they interpret past and present will edit their memories in ways that will shut out some of the raw experience for reminiscence. "It may be predicted that for persons extremely closed to experience, the predominant goal of processing and interpreting personal information into remote memory would be preservation of a stable knowledge base about the self" (p. 108).

What can bias the person? Sperbeck and Whitbourne suggest the following: (1) recalling personal history in terms only of how one relates to events (an egocentric perspective, in other words); (2) viewing oneself somewhat simplistically in seeing that one has done well in those events of history; and (3) carrying built-in resistances to shifts in self-concept and self-perception (here would be the cognitive blocks described in Chapter 5). These researchers further name a correlation between being closed to new experience and being behaviorally rigid, maintaining a restricted fantasy and emotional life, and being ideologically dogmatic.

In contrast to the person who has restrictive filters for processsing personal experience, the experientially open individual enjoys novel situations, has a playful approach to ideas and problem solving, and appreciates experience for its own sake. Here is the person who is able to process personal experience in relatively unbiased ways, who is open to life experience, who can enter into new adventures and new mysteries. According to Sperbeck and Whitbourne, the older person who is creative in his approaches to personal living is better able "to incorporate relevant personal information of both a positive and negative nature (in terms of its implications for identity) into a unified view of past life. . . . it will be those with a more flexible approach to their life experiences who will ultimately adapt most fully to the existential issues in old age" (1985, pp. 107–108).

Narrative process opens the mind as it sorts and integrates experience. It serves a valuable purpose, therefore, in cultivating a more flexible approach to life experience and, even more, in shaping a readiness for the coming of death. Robert Butler is one of those who has taken narrative process and framed it as life review. This next section explores some of its values and therapeutic applications.

LIFE REVIEW

The life review as a looking-back process that has been set in motion by looking forward to death, potentially proceeds toward personality reorganization. Thus, the life review is not synonymous with, but includes reminiscence; it is not alone either the unbidden return of memories, or the purposive seeking of them although both may occur. (Butler, in Neugarten, 1968, p. 488)

Robert Butler has been a strong advocate for the use of life review as an integrative experience in facing one's death. According to his definition, life review is a "looking-back process that one sets in motion by anticipating death . . . a major step in personality development. Memory serves our sense of identity: it provides continuity, wisdom and serenity" (1971, p. 51). Further affirming the value of this particular form of narrative process, Butler quotes Goethe who noted that "he is the happiest man who can see the connection between the end and the beginning of his life;" and asserts that "the act of recall can renew our awareness of the present and restore our sense of wonder" (1971, p. 51).

Butler's assertions have stimulated many to explore the value of life review in work with older people. Among those who have sorted and refined his ideas are Victor Molinari and Robert Reichlen, whose review of the literature examined some of Butler's more sweeping statements (1985). Among the points they make is that life review is a particular form of reminiscence in which the past is actively evaluated, and in which conflict is necessary for resolution to occur. They also believe that life review is not unique to old age nor is it necessarily linked to matters of death and dying. And although much of the literature on life review suggests beneficial treatment effects, research still needs to be done to help us more fully understand the kinds of benefits that may accrue.

Whatever the continuing questions, life review does seem to be valuable because it is an active personal expression, an ego activity, and a way to order one's memories and impressions in the face of the changing circumstances of one's life. In times of grief, life review may be the meaning-making enterprise that integrates and makes sense of the scattered searchings and wonderings within the mourning process. Like mourning, "reminiscence can involve obsessive recounting and reiteration; like mourning, reminiscence can appear to be reflective of self-absorption and introversion; and, as in the case of mourning, reminiscence can result in an ability to relinquish what has been lost" (Molinari & Reichlin, 1985, p. 89). By respecting the repetitive rememberings in reminiscence as possible grieving, caretakers, therapists, and family members have an opportunity to engage the individual in finding answers, settling questions, and more clearly understanding the disruptions of personal experience.

I find the 1971 report of Irving Janis particularly helpful here. He and his associates discovered that survivors of disasters have had a self-shattering experience. Although they had felt invulnerable before the disaster occurred, they found a new, very uncomfortable, and threatening sense of vulnerability which they had not felt before. Shaken by this interruption of their personal systems of meaning and interaction, they needed to make sense of the experience, to create a new image of its place in the events of their lives. As a result, their minds moved into high gear, into an obsessive, repetitive problem-solving to try to make sense of all that had occurred.

If Janis' research findings apply to younger victims of traumatic experience, don't they also apply to those vulnerable older people whose lives may have shifted dramatically as a result of some serious loss? Is it so unusual that the older person in a nursing home, for example, who has been wrenched from home and family, frequently not listened to, frequently humiliated in depersonalizing routines, is repeating and repeating memories and questionings? Is it so unusual that someone who has experienced a cerebral accident, for example, or the loss of a home, is trying quite desperately at times to make sense of it all? I think we have a long way to go before we fully appreciate the cognitive and emotional insults that assault the aging person and that require new resolutions of personal identity and meaning.

The "connection between the end and the beginning"—isn't that what we are after? Like my experience in Roszak's workshop when I named an important image which reformed some perceptions of myself? Like Buhler's subjects who identified what really mattered? I think so. And life review can certainly constitute a coming to terms with one's past—the grievings, savorings, reportings, puzzlings—all to work and rework the integrity of one's life story. And if the person is willing and able, he or she can address more directly the consequences of growing older and of facing death. Once again, how the person deals with all of this appears to be tied to how the person processes life, how flexible and open he is to life experience, how much she continues to live in the present of life (Sperbeck & Whitbourne, 1985), (and, I would say, how much he or she is acknowledged in what is being said). This means, too, that effective, healthy life review does not mean settling into a dwelling on the past.

In defining the value and meaning of life review in both individual work and group process, a set of goals can be named: to assemble the pieces of personal history into a coherent story; to find some sort of bridge between the interpersonal and the intrapersonal, between that which is good and that which is not so good; to continue unto death the processes of meaning-making which are at the heart of the human endeavor; to enter into the mystery of life even as one allows for it, plays with it, and incorporates it. As Carl Jung puts it:

A human being would certainly not grow to be 70 or 80 years old if this longevity had no meaning for the species. The afternoon of human life must also have a significance of its own and cannot be merely a pitiful appendage to life's morning. (Jung, 1960)

GROUP PROCESS AND LIFE REVIEW

Because storytelling is facilitated in the listening as well as in the telling, group experience is one of the more helpful ways to stimulate the creative syntheses and self-expressions of life review. And not just "life review" but the active, ongoing, autobiographical, memoir-building exercises that many people have practiced through large parts of their lives. But these, once again, can take on new flavor and enjoyment in sharing with others — in classes, small self-exploration groups, in the history-building of special projects.

In March 1981, an innovative project was set in motion at the Pierce Country Library in Tacoma, Washington. Funded by a grant from the National Endowment for the Humanities, this "living history project" was called "All My Somedays." The purpose was to draw together a group of older people to write stories of their lives. These individual biographies were assembled into small books which included pictures, poetry, whatever the individual wanted to include. Frequently these stories described the significance of these individuals within the more encompassing histories of their surrounding communities. Ronald J. Manheimer, director of this project, offered these explanatory comments to the *Tacoma News Tribune*:

People undervalue their own knowledge, oftentimes because they don't have a frame for it. They can't connect it to other experiences or larger meanings. But ordinary people are the characters of American history, not the famous. These are people that others can relate to.

I'm hoping that when people begin to reflect on their histories, they will find their place in public history and a sense of continuity in a meaningful way. My first interest is in sharing life stories and propagating the feeling that life has meaning. (Sunday, February 15, 1981)

Not only did these participants find some of that more global contextual meaning, they also discovered new relationships and new connections with those who shared this writing effort. Manheimer acknowledged these experiences of new connections as he further commented that this living history project enhanced the lives and feelings of the older people who participated. What these people gained from their group experience was a "warmth, a closeness, an intimacy that most of us have never experienced, even with our dearest friends" (p. 4).

Robert Butler has found similar results in his applied therapeutic work with life review. Using a variety of techniques, an extensive autobiography is taken from the older person and family members. The use of the tape recorder is helpful in preserving the story, and the creative process can be enhanced by using family albums, scrapbooks, memorabilia—anything, in other words, that will stimulate and connect crucial memories, responses, and understandings in the aging patient.

Using biographical tools like those above, Butler and his colleague Myrna Lewis have also conducted age-integrated psychotherapy groups with participants of all ages. The focus within these group experiences was the resolution of personal crisis: "from near normal to pathologic reactions to adolescence, education, marriage or single life, divorce, parenthood, work and retirement, widowhood, illness and impending death" (1982, p. 19). Dealing with life crisis issues from a life cycle perspective, the individuals were able to ameliorate personal pain as well as stimulate new experiences of intimacy and self-fulfillment. Additionally, the older participants were able to contribute "models for growing older, solutions for loss and grief, the creative use of reminiscence, historic empathy, and a sense of the entire life cycle" (p. 19). Butler and Lewis found the intergenerational approach particularly helpful in providing an opportunity to "recapitulate the family, something woefully missing for many older people."

These stories and reports affirm the value of the biographical approach in helping older people to remember and reshape their personal stories—and, thus, their personal understandings of identity and significance in the order of things.

As I close this discussion of narrative process, I offer a counterbalance to possible assumptions that life review occurs primarily with the facilitations and ministrations of a therapist. Many older people are joining together spontaneously and independently to tell their stories to one another. In settings provided by community colleges, adult evening programs, and organizations such as the Older Women's League, they are opening themselves to the autobiographical experience. With the availablity of leisure time and with appreciation of what it means to tell their stories, many are doing what they may have practiced earlier in their lives, while others are experimenting with this creative expression for the first time. Whatever the circumstance or motivation, people are bridging the gaps of personal history and personal intimacy as they make sense of themselves in imaginative new ways.

[The approach to death is] the most supremely interesting
moment in life. . . . It is as simple in one's own person as any
fact of nature, the fall of a leaf or the blooming of a rose, and
I have a delicious consciousness, ever present, of wide spaces
close at hand and whisperings of release in the air.

—Alice James, in a letter to William James
(in Strouse, 1986, p. 182)

Back in the late 1950's and 1960's, the experts were saying that
old age was a time for a man or woman to "disengage"—to
mute their intensities, diminish the life-roles they had played,
in short, to prepare for death. . . . Who were these savants of
aging to tell me when to disengage at the very moment when
I felt the fire of battle, like Nelson at Trafalgar? Who were
they to tell me to prepare for death, when death was exactly
the adversary I had to confront and somehow outwit?

—Max Lerner, 1990, p. 158

CHAPTER 10

Meaning-Makings Unto Death

IT IS ALL TOO EASY to practice the cognitive habits of our culture—
what Ernst Becker (1973) has labeled our *denial of death*. Unless we
acknowledge and allow for the unknowable in death as well as its unpleasant, distasteful physical manifestations, we may continue the all
too common practice of relegating the dying person to a corner to die
in loneliness and fear. Unless we look deep within to examine our own
anxieties we may also avoid sensitivity to the possible losses the dying
person is facing: "the loss of experiencing, the loss of people, the loss of
control and competence, the loss of the capacity to complete projects
and plans, the loss of body, and the loss of the dream" (Kalish, 1985, pp.
49–50). Even further, unless we come to terms with *how we are* in
relationship to the meanings of death, we may inadvertently negate our
potentials for life.

Indeed, if we are to avoid the hypocrisy and the superficiality that
may keep us distant from the dying person, it seems important to
decide how far we choose to move along the helping continuum from

detached observer to involved participant. Informed choice on our part requires a growing understanding of the physical conditions of death, varying meanings of death, and an increasing understanding of our own emotional reactions to touching, smelling, and holding the dying patient. In such appraisal we may gain the sophistication of insight to determine how reluctant, naive, anxious, denying, or just plain ignorant we are. At the same time we may also find ourselves captured by the mystery and wonder of this most ultimate and intimate of human transitions to the degree that we are increasingly drawn into the needs and concerns of the dying person.

It is a matter of following the Delphic injunction, "know thyself," in the manner Samuel Klagsbrun suggests for his hospice staff:

I think that hospice staff should periodically examine themselves on a spiritual or philosophical level. They must address crucial questions like, Why am I doing this kind of work?, What's in it for me?, and Where am I going with my life in the hospice system? A number of staff people I have met have found themselves in emotional difficulties by virtue of not having examined these questions in their lives. (1982, p. 1264)

Entering this chapter with that challenge I look around to identify questionings, wonderings, ways of reacting. I also look around to consider denials and avoidances, and thus, our ageisms in this most dramatic of exits. Whether the swinging door slams shut with finality or whether it is a doorway into another series of meaning-makings is not at issue here. Rather, I report on a few contrasting experiences, a few contrasting perspectives, to stimulate reflection, to face and sort ever so briefly our own reactions in the matters of death.

TO LEARN ABOUT DEATH

Ambivalence is a common response to the concerns of death—a mixture of response that calls on us to peer through differing windows of perception, to expose ourselves to various ways that people interpret and assign significance or insignificance to death, and to honor "the desirability of suspending our personal convictions long enough to learn what other people truly think and feel about death" (Kastenbaum, 1986, p. 35). And that isn't easy! In a culture where death is frequently a taboo subject, where personal feelings and trainings all too easily pull us back, it requires a certain effort to ask the questions appropriate to the answers we seek—or to even name the answers we seek. The cool, objective stance of the researcher may not work—nor may a romantic stance that fails to acknowledge death's dehumanizing physiological processes.

William Liss-Levinson writes bluntly about our tendencies to go to extremes in these approaches to death.

Death, although always a part of our lives, was seen for many years as a taboo subject. Now we have swung the pendulum the other way. Death is being discussed in every magazine and publication, on every television and radio show. This in and of itself is not dangerous. The ways in which the topic is presented, however, reflect a romanticization that far exceeds reality. I think I will scream if I see one more butterfly symbolizing death as a transition, ultimately characterized by the soaring skyward of this fragile insect. Death is not by its very nature beautiful or dignified. (1982, p. 1267)

Acknowledging these extremes we can gain expanding insight and knowledge from many sources: personal observations; a study of clinical cases; collections of controlled observations; interviews and questionnaires; psychological autopsies; observations of culturally established rituals; the study of myths; and in the gathering of the images, symbols, and creative expressions from the worlds of literature, music, and art (Kalish, 1985, pp. 15–22). But even more vital—we can learn a great deal about death by talking to, listening to, and relating to the person who is dying. In this manner we are exposed to intimate, subjective experience.

In these days we *are* learning and we *are* paying greater attention, for we have come a long way in the development of death-awareness since the few early writings of the 1920s and 1930s. Although much of that early exploratory material was ignored, essentially having little impact on the delivery of supportive services to the dying and bereaved, it was a sign that explorations were under way (Kalish, 1985, p. 12).[1] Gradually, neglect has been replaced with increasing attention to the concerns of the terminally ill. Herman Feifel's *The Meaning of Death* (1959) has been influential in turning professional attention towards death-awareness. In addition, a number of health and behavioral scientists, as well as practitioners, have been working hard to identify the problems, to start explorations into these concerns, and to spread their findings not only to other professionals but to the general public. Organizations have been developed (e.g., Association for Death Education and Counseling in Hartford, Connecticut) and international conferences promoted and sponsored by such groups as King's College in London, Ontario, and by the Prince and Princess of Wales Hospice in Glasgow, Scotland. These offer important education and resources for the interested professional.

---

[1]Notable among those leaders were Richard Kalish and Robert Kastenbaum whose early newsletter covering developments in the emerging field of thanatology resulted in the journal *Omega*.

The 1960s saw strong growth in the death-awareness movement. This was the time when Elizabeth Kubler-Ross appeared as an advocate for more intimate, supportive involvements with the dying person. In the late '60s a popular article showing her work with dying patients captured the attention of the American public. Her 1969 book, *On Death and Dying*, added much impetus to death-awareness. Whether we agree or disagree with her linear model of the stages of death, she did much to bring the taboo subject of death out of its closet. She has also contributed greatly to our sensitivity to the anxieties and concerns of the dying person—and to the potential for meaning-making and growth unto death.

At the present time there is a growing stream of books, reports, and journal articles which directly address the topics and systems of death. As a culture we seem more willing to talk about death, especially when we face the difficult ethical questions raised by contemporary medical technology. As treatment paradigms face off against the feelings and wishes of the dying person, there are increasing demands for compassionate palliative care that can facilitate death with dignity. Because these issues directly concern each of us, because they touch a range of responses from the emotionally involved to the objectively detached, we do well to assume a dialectical perspective that allows for the different sides to each question and to recognize that questions have a way of piling upon each other in a manner that makes simple edicts and statements inappropriate.

Creatively opening ourselves to the mysteries of death may bring us to that which is called "spiritual." Whether or not we think in this manner, whether or not we use the language of the spiritual, we are in an era when more and more gerontologists and caregivers are recognizing the need to pay attention to spiritual concerns. In fact (as I have mentioned previously), the Fall 1990 *Generations* (the journal of the American Society on Aging) devoted its entire issue to the exploration of "Aging and the Human Spirit." Guest editors Thomas R. Cole and James W. Ellor shared a "conviction that the 'larger questions' about human life—questions about meaning, significance, and value—must be addressed by the discipline of gerontology and by individuals who work with elders" (p. 4). Building on this conviction, Cole described his encouragement of caregivers to enter the less tangible world of the spiritual—"to stretch toward the human side of what they are doing."

If they only pay attention to the instrumental work of care, they're going to miss something for themselves and the people they are caring for. Without overwhelming them, you want to remind them that they are not just dealing with a solvable problem, but with the mysteries of life and death. And approaching mysteries requires a different way of being—a certain awe. (1990, p. 5)

To find that *certain awe* takes us beyond technical expertise into private exploration. Here our answers don't fall into neatly framed categories. Here we may have to face doubts, ambivalence, shifting motivations, and our own willingness/unwillingness continuum to join the mysterious and unexplainable. As we do this, however, we have the opportunity to explore our own potential to meet the following goals:

- To help people think more about death so that they can better prepare for their own deaths.
- To help people know more about the dying process so that their own may be less distressing.
- To help [people] understand their feelings about the deaths of others so that they can be more effective in relating to others who are dying and more capable of doing their own grieving later.
- To help [those of us] who wish to work in a professional or paraprofessional capacity with the dying and the bereaved.
- To help [those of us] who work in the innumerable fields that touch on death, dying, or grief to know a little more and think a little more about [our] roles.
- To help people [and that means us] grapple with one of the major philosophical problems — the meaning of death. (Kalish, 1985, p. 22)

But are we reluctant to approach death? It would seem so. In his book, *Death, Grief, and Caring Relationships* (1985), Kalish quotes LaRochefoucauld, a philosopher who wrote some 300 years ago that "the human mind is as little capable to contemplate death for any length of time as the eye is able to look at the sun." But Kalish argues with this, even as he suggests that after reading one hundred pages or more his readers may find themselves better able to face and absorb the intensity of the radiations from the death experience. Even with this assurance, however, he gives his readers plenty of psychological, emotional space for determining and naming their own reactions and resulting choices:

For a few people, the sun will still be painfully blinding, and I would encourage them to find some way to avoid the sun. Even those of us who have been studying, writing about, talking about, and working with death and the dying for many years find there are times when it shines too brightly, and we retreat for a while. You too may find such times. Or you may find that you need to retreat completely. If so, please do. [To read and study about death] is not an endurance test or a mark of personal worth. (Kalish, 1985, p. 6)

What seems evident to me is that our traditional trainings have not prepared us for work with death and dying. We have been asked to keep our emotions clean and clear, our values neatly categorized, our abilities to be detached nicely maintained. But those guidelines do not prepare us to work in the arenas of death. Not only are we asked to approach and engage the emotional power of the dying person, not only are we asked to join with the grieving survivor, we are asked to come to terms with pieces of personal history and emotional memory that bob to the surface of our consciousness and that influence how we react. If ever there were a challenge for our dual roles as aging/dying persons, aging/grieving persons, aging/helping persons, it is in naming ourselves, in choosing a level of participation, and in finding our particular delicate balance in our relationships to the dying person and the dying process.

WINDOWS INTO DEATH

Leo Tolstoy's remarkable story, *The Death of Ivan Ilych* (1960), gives us a point of departure for considering how far we choose to move along the continuum from detached observer to involved participant in the drama of death. His is a tale of participations and observations, of detachments and intimacies, of those who turn their backs or stigmatize Ivan in his desperate search for answers, and those who join him in the most intimate joustings with approaching death.

Central to this story is Ivan's growing awareness that he is indeed dying, an awareness that intensifies into a dialogue not only with his pain and his desire to know, but a deepening dialogue with death — with It. This dialogue, though Ivan's alone, is interactively responsive to the dynamics of those around him — his colleagues and friends, his doctors, his wife and family, who never fully enter his world; and his manservant, Gerasim, and Vasya, his son, who actively join him as he confronts his severe physical deterioration and his agonies about death.

Part of Ivan's death-making experience is an increasingly desperate reaching for answers and validating connections — consultations with doctors, his reading of books, the checking out of those around him, his growing pain, intense introspections, growing terror, active reminiscing. This is meaning-making in high gear as he tries to make sense not only of his systems and his relationships, but also of his past life in the light of his dreadful present. And what "tormented Ivan Ilych more than anything" was his increasing awareness that he was very much alone, often misunderstood, often alienated:

There was no deceiving himself: something terrible, new, and more important than anything before in his life, was taking place within him of which he alone was aware. Those about him did not understand or would not understand it, but thought everything in the world was going on as usual. That tormented Ivan Ilych more than anything. (p. 125)

In this manner "he had to live . . . all alone on the brink of an abyss, with no one who understood or pitied him" (p. 127). He also had to live with silences and distortions, the living of lies:

This deception tortured him—their not wishing to admit what they all knew and what he knew, but wanting to lie to him concerning his terrible condition, and wishing and forcing him to participate in that lie. Those lies—lies enacted over him on the eve of his death and destined to degrade this awful, solemn act to the level of their visitings, their curtains, their sturgeon for dinner—were a terrible agony for Ivan Ilych. And strangely enough, many times when they were going through their antics over him he had been within a hairbreadth of calling out to them: "Stop lying! You know and I know that I am dying. Then at least stop lying about it!" But he had never had the spirit to do it. (p. 137)

Only two individuals emotionally and physically joined Ivan: Gerasim, the butler's young assistant, who offered him comfort out of a simple, compassionate spirit that gave help "easily, willingly, simply, and with a good nature that touched Ivan Ilych. Health, strength, and vitality in other people were offensive to him, but Gerasim's strength and vitality did not mortify but soothed him" (p. 137). Gerasim willingly performed the necessary, often disgusting menial tasks, and quietly, patiently, held Ivan's legs on his shoulders for long periods of time in order to relieve Ivan's physical pain. Ivan's son, Vasya, also entered this intimate environment. Although he was frightened and filled with pity, his emotions were genuine and his concern eased his father's psychic suffering just a little bit more.

Ivan's death comes after a dramatic period of questioning of life meaning and relationship—"What if my whole life has really been wrong?" (p. 152)—and of three days of horrible screaming. At the end Tolstoy brings redemption to Ivan, who loses his terror of death, awakens to a new sense of compassion towards those around him, and finally arrives at the moments of dying when "in place of death there was light" (156). In death Tolstoy has given Ivan a victory.

For me the genius in this story is Tolstoy's ability to attend to the universal even as he attends to the unique—to probe the deepest of feelings at the same time he is able to step back to examine human vulnerability and complexity. For these reasons and many more I find *The Death of Ivan Ilych* a poignant statement of the collisions between life and death, between health and illness, between those who care and those who reject, between a sense of personal significance and a sense that what one has lived has no meaning.

Another window into death comes from a student nurse who found it important to share her feelings with her professional colleagues: "By my sharing my feelings with you, you may someday be better able to help those who share my experience":

The dying patient is not yet seen as a person and thus cannot be communicated with as such. He is a symbol of what every human fears and what we each know, at least, academically, that we too must someday face. . . .

But for me, fear is today and dying is now. You slip in and out of my room, give me medications and check my blood pressure. Is it because I am a student nurse myself, or just a human being, that I sense your fright? And your fears enhance mine. Why are you afraid? I am the one who is dying!

I know you feel insecure, don't know what to say, don't know what to do. But please believe me, if you care, you can't go wrong. Don't run away—wait—all I want to know is that there will be someone to hold my hand when I need it. I am afraid. Death may get to be a routine to you, but it is new to me. You may not see me as unique, but I've never died before. (in Moustakas, 1977, p. 118)

"You may not see me as unique, but I've never died before." What powerful words! They capture the agony of separateness that may be a part of a person's dying. And they call us who are helpers to care and to understand as we increase our capabilities to humanize and connect with those who are terminally ill. As we do this we are more than detached observers; we are drawn into the roles of *participant/observers*.

PARTICIPANT/OBSERVERS

Death places us in various interactive positions vis-à-vis its mysteries. As we watch TV with its huge array of killings—everything from the corpses on "Murder, She Wrote" to the daily reports of mayhem on our streets and casualties in the confrontations of war, it is little wonder that we frequently detach ourselves from the graphic realities of death. Reluctant to face emotional/psychic pain we all too easily step away from the colors, smells, excretions, and absurdities of death.

We gain sensitivity, I believe, by telling our personal stories of experiences related to death. These experiences may be limited or they may be extensive, superficial or profound, detached or intensely involved. Included in these processings may be pieces of family history, religious symbols, or artistic portrayals that touch on death in particular ways. Here, too, may be more searing remembrance that has left its mark on our consciousness.

In sorting my movements along the helping continuum, I have found it valuable to tell my own stories in tracking personal movements from detachment to involvement.

After I earned my Ph.D., I worked for a short time as a "Manpower girl" (weird juxtaposition of titles!) for a mortuary/cemetery management company. I was the temporary "girl Friday" who typed the bills listing caskets, burial plots, monuments; the one who transcribed letters for the president and sent reminders of past due accounts. Absolutely naive in matters of death, I observed the workings of the staff with a kind of bemused wondering. When I watched one of the managers adopt a "stained glass voice" when sitting in consultation with a bereaved person, I found myself fighting cynicism. When I heard the staff playfully debate the merits of vertical burials as a possible way to save space, I found myself collapsing in helpless laughter. When I listened to their black humor as it emerged side-by-side with a genuine wish to be of service, with a wish to make a profit, with a wish to protect themselves a bit through their humor, I found myself confused, perplexed with the whole issue of profits from death.

Then there were the many years I served as an organist for funerals and memorial services, sitting on my bench hidden amid the flowers, sometimes coughing and sneezing in allergic reaction. Though I felt sorry for those who sat in mourning, it was all very unreal, a part of my job, definitely detached from any intimate interface with bereavement and death.

Although awarenesses have grown, sensitivities developed, much of this is knowledge by description rather than knowledge by experience. I have heard about the deaths of grandparents, I have heard the reports of the lonely circumstance of my mother's sudden death from a heart attack, I have heard about my father-in-law and mother-in-law who each died in hospital settings.

But I began to move closer to the intensities of dying when my brother-in-law died of an aneurism. The night he died, we, his family and friends, sat in an impersonal waiting room while the medical team worked several floors above. After waiting for several hours we learned our brother was dead and that the surgeon had gone home for the night! Although we were appalled at the insensitivity of that man, we were greatly helped when one of his colleagues (who was also appalled) took it upon himself to return to the hospital late at night to field the questions and angers built up during our long hours of waiting.

The edge of my involvement and sensitivity in matters of death was further sharpened at my father's bedside a few weeks before his actual death. Though I was not present when he died, in this preparatory time there were little dyings and little returnings that stimulated unusual questions and awakened awareness of the mysterious and the unexplainable. For example, there was the experience of seeing my father fight the phlegm in his lungs even as his eyes lighted into a rapture I had never seen before, of hearing him exclaim "Mary, you can not know what I know now. But someday you will understand." And the experience of seeing the light in his eyes fade as he took on the tired, dismayed look of someone who realized he was still caught in the painful, terribly frustrating, seemingly never-ending processes of dying.

During my father's time of dying I also learned about the ageisms that cluster around death: the pulling away from the dying person, the repugnance, the stereotyping of the capabilities of that person, the *active rejections, the abandonments. He was put in a hospital room at the end of the corridor where nurses seldom appeared, where personal care was all too frequently left to inexperienced, embarrassed family members who were not trained or prepared for such intimacy. I remember the IV that slipped from his veins to spray him with fluid and how long it took for help to arrive. I remember his gaunt emaciated body shivering because he was wet and had no blanket. In all fairness, I also remember the sensitive doctor who stood quietly in the wings, available as needed, and responsive to our request that no heroic measures be employed. Indeed, it was a curious time, a curious mix of that which was negative and sometimes disgusting and of that which was amazing and quite wonderful.*

Let us take time, than, to sift and sort our death-related stories even as we look about for other stories, other examples, to open our eyes to the different ways that people die, and to the different ways that we can relate to the dying person.

One such story comes from Nancy Burson (1990), an artist whose bedside watch with her dying mother made her vividly aware of the colors, the smells, the sounds of death. Before Burson decided to maintain her vigil, a substitute nurse took her by the hand and said, "I don't want you to watch your Mom die — it's an image you'll live with the rest of your life." Burson agrees that this nurse was right, "but not in the way she thought."

Because she was so visually oriented Burson paid particular attention to the colors of death and learned much from caring, informed nurses. For example, as Burson's mother neared death one of her nurses observed that "There's a kind of marbling of the skin that happens on the back or legs a few hours before." Later, as her mother's foot turned blackish-purple another nurse commented that "People usually die in parts unless it is a very sudden death. It's usually the extremities that go first — feet, then hands." This was a moment of emotional trauma for Burson: "I felt betrayed. . . . How could it be that I was 35 years old and didn't know dead people turn colors? I was sure she was trying to frighten me."

As the dying process proceeded Burson also smelled the smells, observed the shifts in breathing process, the accelerations of heart rate, the fever, the moaning, that were part of her mother's dying. It was not an easy time. But then, at the climactic moments of dying, she observed her mother in a different way:

Suddenly a new expression came over her face, and Lisa [her nurse] leaned over her to see it. "Look at that smile," she said. "That's unbelievable." It was the biggest, most complete smile I had ever seen. . . . She looked incredibly happy. She squinted slightly, then relaxed her eyes and mouth. "She's gone, Nance,"

Lisa said. "No, she's not," I said. "She's still here." The air in the room was dense—filled, I knew, with her presence, her spirit. (1990, p. 71)

Burson continues: "I felt her spirit lift very slowly from the bed and pass in layers through the ceiling. . . . There was no last gasp. . . . She wasn't the horrid color I had imagined. She was gray." And, finally, "At the same time that I felt my mother's spirit lifting, I felt my own body become heavier and heavier. By the time a doctor came in to pronounce her officially dead, I ached all over. Part of this, I knew was stress, but I also couldn't help feeling that she had left me something, some part of her spiritual self or perhaps new life." In these amazing moments Burson felt that her Mom had "found a way to make my wait worthwhile" (1990, p. 71).

"Making the wait worthwhile" would seem to be an important goal for us as helpers. In the times of passing from life to death can come particular opportunity for survivors to find their way back into life. That is what Burson seems to have told us.

BRIDGES BETWEEN
DEATH AND LIFE

The "hospice movement" has been providing unique support in bridging the gaps between life and death, and between death and life. Here can be found caring attention to the needs both of the dying person and the family and friends who often feel helpless in their efforts to help. More than a place, hospice is a philosophy of care that is based on the premise that when the quantity of life is limited, the quality of that life must be optimal. Thus, when we define a particular type of terminal care as "hospice care," we refer to the concepts and activities that combine to help the dying person to "live until he or she dies." Founder Cicely Saunders stated it this way: "You matter because you are you. You matter to the last moment of your life, and we will do all we can not only to help you to die in peace, but also live until you die" (Butterfield-Picard & Magno, 1982, p. 1258).

When put into operational terms, this means that hospices differ from the traditional models of care for the terminally ill in several major ways:

1. This philosophy of care emphasizes support and assistance as it provides an environment that helps the patient/family unit to retain as much decision control as possible.
2. The patient is able to discontinue many aspects of conventional care. Thus, acute interventions and cure-directed therapies are replaced by palliative care.
3. In its provision of palliative care, hospice emphasizes "the con-

trol of pain in its psychological, social, and spiritual as well as physical dimensions, and attention is given to the alleviation of other distressing disease symptoms."

4. An integrated team includes physicians, nurses, psychologists, social workers, and volunteers.
5. Every effort is made to emphasize the "normal" surroundings of a home, even if the patient is in an inpatient facility.
6. As long as is possible the patient is cared for in his or her home with a hospice team promoting and supervising that care.
7. Both before and after a patient's death, specialized bereavement care and counseling is offered to the family members. (Paraphrase of Butterfield-Picard & Magno, 1982, p. 1255)

Elin Brockman and Dianne Hales (1990) quote Florence Wald of the Connecticut Hospice in New Haven who describes the atmosphere that has been the goal in their residential setting:

"Environment," Florence says, "is vital. We wanted the setting to be as homelike as possible." Patients are encouraged to bring their own clothes and other possessions, and live in spacious rooms; in the communal living areas there are fireplaces and kitchenettes.

Just about anything goes here. . . . patients' children are always made to feel welcome, along with other relatives. Even family pets may visit. . . . No one is ever turned away for lack of money. (Brockman & Hales, 1990, pp. 15–17)

How well the goals of hospice have been accomplished in the New Haven center is answered with words like these of a widower whose wife had just died: "To me, hospice is people. Every time I needed help – someone to talk with, someone to answer questions – they were there. They taught me the meaning of love, which is giving of yourself" (1990, p. 17). Further illustration is in the story of an Irish woman who died in another hospice. Knowing death was imminent, she sent out for a bottle of champagne to be shared with staff workers, family, and friends. "There is no way that I am going to be left out of my own wake," she laughingly exclaimed. Not only did she bring an act of celebration into her final moments, she gave a gift of joy to those who joined her. She also seeded a memory for my colleague of a death shaped by enlightened medical care and compassionate sharing (Sandra Elder, personal communication).[2]

Recognizing that not all hospices have the money, staff, or energy to fulfill the ideals named here, it is good to see those that do (see thoughtful analyses of related questions in Klagsbrun, 1982, and in Liss-Levinson, 1982). The Hospice of Victoria, British Columbia, is a model of a

[2]See Herman Feifel (1977) for another remarkable story of death – this time complete with autobiographical writing and pictures.

highly successful program. In its residential setting, which is at one end of a hospital wing, there are attractive outlooks on gardens that provide an aesthetic view at the same time they provide quiet. Here individuals can be alone or share with family and friends. Supporting the patients and families are carefully chosen, well-trained staff members and volunteers. Integrated teams care for their residential patients as well as for those who choose to remain at home in the care of their families.

Educational material is given to family members to educate them in matters of death. "When Death Occurs at Home" is the title of one leaflet that describes in concrete, practical language "what to expect, what to do" when death occurs at home (and they warn us that every individual dies differently and simplistic generalizations should not be made). According to this handout the person who is approaching death may:

1. Sleep longer periods and sometimes have difficulty waking.
2. Have a decrease in appetite.
3. Become confused and unable to recognize familiar people or surroundings.
4. Become restless, pull at bed linen and clothing or may "see" things.
5. Have difficulty swallowing or "forget" to swallow.
6. Have irregular or shallow breathing.
7. Have irregular pulse or heartbeat.
8. Develop "wet" sounding breathing.
9. Be unresponsive to voices or touch and may appear to be sleeping with eyes open.
10. Lose control of bladder or bowels.
11. Have cool legs and arms with the skin acquiring a mottled blue/purple appearance.

Signs that the person has died:

• There will be no response.
• There will be no breathing.
• There will be no pulse.
• Eyes will be fixed in one direction; they may be open or closed.
• There may be loss of control of bladder or bowels.

Finally, suggestions are made for the various practical steps that have to be taken at the time of death. (And isn't it a fact that most of us have never witnessed a death, don't know what to expect, and have never learned physical techniques for taking care of the dead person — techniques that most people knew in the eras before our specialized medical settings?) I like the leaflet's emphasis in these matters: "There is no hurry to do this. Spend as much time with your loved one as you wish. If you feel you want help with the things that need to be done, don't be afraid to ask." And so the survivor is given a first boost back into life.

As a result of her study of the meaning of death in Amish society,

Kathleen Bryer concluded that "separation of the family from the dying patient can promote feelings of frustration and despair; health care and mental health professionals must be sensitive to the meaning of death for the dying, their families, and themselves" (1979, p. 261). Her study has shown how much attention Amish families give to a philosophy of life and death, and how lovingly and carefully they prepare for death throughout their lives — everything from washing and ironing the death linens in advance of one's death to following supportive guidelines in helping and supporting the bereaved. Bryer believes that the "meaning of death in Amish society serves as an important principle in determining the quality of life among them" (p. 261). (And certainly for us a most important model!)

What is noteworthy is the similarity between the philosophies and goals of the Amish people and those of the hospice movement. These seem to offer central guidelines for all of us in working with the overlapping systems of death and living, of the terminally ill person and those who survive. Bryer summarizes these "most helpful aspects of coping with death" as suggested by the Amish families: "(a) the continued presence of the family, both during the course of the illness and at the moment of death; (b) open communication about the process of dying and its impact on the family; (c) the maintenance of a normal life-style by the family during the course of the illness; (d) commitment to as much independence of the dying person as possible; (e) the opportunity to plan and organize one's own death; (f) continued support for the bereaved for at least a year following the funeral, with long-term support given to those who do not remarry" (1979, p. 260).

There is much to be learned here if we are to avoid simplistic treatments of grief such as the giving of tranquilizers, the offering of pat advice or reassurance, and the too easy imposition of formulas for grieving. The tasks are complex because the survivor has to redefine and reintegrate the meanings of death and loss into the processes and meanings of life. And, although bereavement brings a difficult and painful transitional time for most survivors, it offers the impetus for new interpretation and integration of life. In the words of Kathleen Bryer: "Familiarity with the face of death brings with it a reordering of the priorities of life, thus granting to death the ultimate importance it deserves" (1979, p. 255).

In his studies of the grief of widowhood, Parkes (1972) found major changes in self-perception and role expectations paralleling developmental transitions from adolescent to adult. What occurs is the destruction of old assumptions about life and meaning, a reassessment of one's personal power and significance, and major shifts in self-esteem. In this manner the "old identity is dissolved and replaced by a new one" (Parkes, 1972). This is certainly the stance of my constructivist position, although I see the new identity in more transformational terms — what was there before is taken and put together in creative new ways that constitute a *reconciliation* of the new and the old rather than a *replacement* of the old.

GRIEVING: A MEANING-MAKING PROCESS

A few definitions are needed here: "Bereavement is the event in personal history that triggers the emotion of grief. Mourning is the process by which the powerful emotion is slowly and painfully brought under control" (Grollman, 1974, p. 3). But "when doctors speak of grief they are focusing on the raw feelings that are at the center of a whole process that engages the person in adjusting to changed circumstances." Here is the bereaved person facing deep fears, considering the prospects of personal loneliness, and sorting the hurdles to be faced in building a new life. Here is the survivor trying to reassemble the puzzle when a central piece has been lost, when a system of life and meaning has been shattered and scattered. "Grief is a whole cluster of adjustments, apprehensions, and uncertainties that strike life in its forward progress and make it difficult to reorganize and redirect the energies of life" (Grollman, 1974, pp. 2–3).

Persons in grief have a whole jungle of emotions in their guts which need to be expressed in some way. Sometimes openly, sometimes by talking, sometimes by crying, sometimes poetically, sometimes through ritual: there are many ways, but people must have the opportunity to express real feelings because unresolved grief is a destructive horror. (Nichols & Nichols, 1975, p. 93)

What is to be remembered is that recovery and redirection are not immediate and timetables vary enormously. Many variables influence this — the character of anticipatory grieving that has already been accomplished, how the survivor deals with the chronologies of life expectation, whether the death was sudden or prolonged, how well the dying experience has been supported and worked through, what kinds of practical supports are available, what kinds of life experience and philosophical, spiritual orientations exist for the grieving person. In grief, generalizations cannot be made.

Unfortunately, writes Glen Davidson, M.D. (1984), misguided expectations can interrupt or distort the person's recovery — pieces of misinformation like the following:

1. *"Mourning lasts from 48 hours to two weeks."* This is not accurate, says Davidson: "Research into bereavement has made it clear that the mourning process is complex and the period of mourning lasts far longer than most people expect" (p. 16).
2. *"Keep busy! Don't think!"* Although keeping busy can be help-

ful, too much activity can increase both vulnerability and disorientation and decrease the ability to solve problems. "Medi-
cally speaking, the need to become very busy after the loss of a
significant other occurs when the endocrine complex is high in
the bloodstream, during the period of *searching*" (p. 17).

3. *"This is a private matter."* "The irony of this way of thinking is
   that persons who have to remain 'private'—cut off from the
   very people they need—do become disoriented and crazy." In
   times of grief, people need basic cues of orientation to keep
   them in touch with healthy living and connection (p. 17).

4. *"Mourning is for women only."* "The misperception that men
   are not as greatly affected seems to be based on societal expectations that men need to show their grief minimally in order to
   demonstrate their manliness" (p. 18).

5. *"Forget it!"* This is highly inappropriate advice to give those
   who are grieving—indeed, one of their common fears is that
   they *will forget.* All too often this "advice to forget is given not
   for the sake of the advised, but for the comfort of the advisor.
   Such advice only disorients mourners further" (18–19). In my
   own work this last point was borne out as a widow and I strug-
   gled with the synthesizing of her memories of her husband
   with the evolution of her new identity as a woman who was
   more than "widow." During this time she found it puzzling
   that close friends often resisted or negatively evaluated her
   evolution out of "widowhood." What they seemed to say was
   "forget," even as they covertly admonished "don't forget." One
   wonders if they were still involved in their own unresolved
   grieving.

After studying 1,200 mourners over a two-year period, Davidson
identified *shock and numbness as a common first reaction.* This can
include: (a) feeling stunned, (b) resistance to stimuli, (c) conflicting and
competing emotions, (d) impeded functioning, (e) difficulty in making
judgments. In an effort to make sense of the loss the bereaved person
may struggle with the telling of the personal story as questions vie with
each other for attention: whether to tell, how to tell, whom to tell. Here
can be high-intensity gathering of the facts of the story—checking with
doctors, attendants, witnesses. "Being able to know the facts, to visualize the setting, and to confirm your loss are all needed at a time when
your own perceptions of reality are most distorted" (Davidson, 1984, pp.
55–56).

Behaviors of searching and yearning tend to dominate in the first
four months. During this time the grieving person may become acutely
aware of sensory stimuli, direct anger at other people, and maintain

guilt towards self. This is an ambiguous time, a testing of what is real, a time when disorganization and depression intertwine with restless, impatient searching and yearning (p. 59).

The bereaved person may adopt negative roles — that of the derelict, that of the invalid, and that of the despairing survivor. I think here of Huston Smith's five stages of meaning. Meaning may indeed become organized around the trouble that dominates the survivor's life — a negation of the hope, endeavor, and trust that are required to take the person towards new roles. (Remember the widow I described above? Her task was to find a role that transcended grief and widowhood.)

This is the time for nurturing, supportive social networks, and careful attention to physical care — a well balanced diet, enough fluids, regular daily exercise, and time each day for rest. This is the time for the survivor to face the reality of loss, to continue the active experiencing of grief, to find new adjustments to an environment in which the deceased is missing, and to gradually withdraw emotional energy and attention from the deceased to reinvestments in the everyday business of life. If the grieving person has persistent thoughts of self-destruction, if he or she fails to take care of personal health, abuses alcohol or drugs, and is dominated by long-term depression, more intensive efforts like psychotherapy or even hospitalization may be required.

Davidson found that those who were most successful in resolving grief — those who were able to translate their mourning into "outreach, compassion, new relationship" — had learned some very specific skills:

- being able to call emotions by name
- coming to terms with personal faith
- understanding basic survival needs
- finding a sense of personal esteem
- developing an ability to relate to others
- fostering a desire to improve coping skills and deepened understanding of life
- improved understanding of how human beings function, feel, and take meaning from life
- the arrival of the ability to enter into someone else's suffering. . . . "in the compassion of reciprocating concern for each other, people not only become reorienters for others but their own wounds are healed." (p. 98)

In terms of the developmental transition from love to the capacity to care, that last seems particularly important.

But even as I report Davidson's sequence I caution against seeing any stage framework as fixed or inevitable. A process perspective is more workable for it allows for the alternating currents of emotion, thought, and behavior. The unique expressions of these dynamics have been named by Sandra Elder and Karen Martin (personal communication, 1991) who emphasize the individuality and fluid unpredictability of grieving. Rather than a staircase of stages of grief they envision the Möbius strip that is never ending, ever-recyling. Using this model, they see personal meaning-making as the catalytic bridge from despair, protest, or detachment, to the awakenings of new growth within hope, investment, and exploration.

Of necessity, this look at states of grief and processes of grieving has omitted much important material. Caregiving, of course, is one large topic for examination (see Hooyman, 1986, for example). And I call particular attention to Eisdorfer and Cohen's significant contribution to the literature on Alzheimer's disease. Their book, *The Loss of Self* (1986), is rated "outstanding" by *The American Journal of Alzheimer's Care* for its knowledge and sensitivity. And its chapter, "Death and Dying," has contributed to my own understanding of the exquisite forms of grieving that have to be faced within the Alzheimer experience.

The ongoing psychological death of the patient causes profound grief, and the grieving is very much like the reaction to terminal illness, but with one major difference. The patient appears healthy, looks very much like he used to look, and is likely to be alive for many months or years in this peculiar state of physical health and psychological decline. It is not easy to deal with the invisible changes that alter behavior and mood and destroy the husband, wife, patient, or friend whom one has known for years. (1986, p. 260)

In a spirit of respect for those who grieve and for the complexities of the dilemmas that have to be resolved I bring this chapter to a close.

SECTION IV

Learning From Our Elders

The soul that has no fixed goal loses itself; for as they say, to be everywhere is to be nowhere: He who dwells everywhere, Maximus, nowhere dwells.

—Martial (in Montaigne, 1986, p. 21)

How do we keep from "growing old inside"? Surely only in *community*. The only way to make friends with time is to stay friends with people. If I try to deal with time by myself, I lose. Absolutely. Of that I am certain.

—Robert McAfee Brown, 1980, p. 18

In the course of objectifying, quantifying, and categorizing a human experience, subtleties are necessarily lost; the vague, the ineffable, and the indescribable must be omitted, and what is concluded may be accurate without being true, may represent the experience yet omit the essence of it, which is the humanity of the person whose experience it was.

—Jules Willing, 1981, p. 38

CHAPTER 11

Pioneers in a New Prime of Life

T O COUNTER TENDENICES to dehumanize the old through our statistics and our clinical descriptions of emotional states ("low self-esteem," "role loss," "stimulus deprivation," for example), it seems essential to enter the real world experiences of older people — activities, adventures, reflective wonderings, emotional expressions, innovative experiments.

In this chapter I work to do just that as I assemble a sampling of creative role models — a sampling to awaken us to the wide array of possibilities available to older people. And there are many. This abundance is a significant part of our "quiet revolution": older adults taking charge of their lives in imaginative new ways — to learn, to teach, to give, to share, to adventure, to produce, and to cultivate and maintain human relationships.

Within these models there are no simplistic equations that old equals useless, that old equals noncreative, that old equals disengagement. *These people are engaging life.* Here are the real-world examples of our "new pioneers": the gentle and not-so-gentle leaders who are daring us to focus on new images of aging; the individuals who are modeling creativity in everything from product to process to life experience—in ways that neatly graphed creativity curves (those of Lehman, 1953, for example) do not even begin to discern. Within these models can be found the glimmerings of new attitudes towards old age, attitudes that point us (however slightly) toward an "unashamed acceptance of being old and recognition of old age as offering a new stage of life fulfillment" (Monroe & Rubin, 1983, p. 20).

I have looked for the kinds of creativities that may certainly be linked to an artistic product, but are more often illustrations of the adroit capabilities of the human being to engage the present. These seniors are modeling courageous and innovative problem solving, sensitive human networking, imaginative interactions with personal crisis, passionate joustings with the problems of aging, and the maintenance of curiosity and intellectual growth. In studying these models I have uncovered examples which affirm John McLeish's statement that "creativity is the key to good aging"—that creativity is a process representing a dynamic interaction between the unique individual and the "materials, events, people, or circumstances of his life" (1976, p. 34).

Through all this I maintain an attitude congruent with these words:

In no sense can we regard our inquiry as scientific, if by scientific, one means an impeccable methodology that meets all or most of the requirements of experimental procedure. Our inquiry has no such pretensions; its principal aim has been a serious interest in a preliminary understanding of creativity *as experience*, which we regard as largely subjective, though nonetheless capable of communication and understanding. (Rosner & Abt, 1972, p. viii)

Creativity as experience. That is our theme here.

CREATIVITY WITHIN LEISURE

With extensions of health and life span people are being handed the gift of *time*. And time can be a perplexing challenge because former generations have not generally had that gift to play with. *How, what, where,* and *why,* then, are shaping questions for the older person to consider. How am I going to spend this time? What sorts of things can I do with my time? Where do I want to live out that time? And what motivations, what purposes, what focused activities will give me a "why" for my time? The issues of *time,* then, become a creative problem to be resolved if leisure is to be a meaningful experience.

Writing for seniors in its *Guide to Leisure, 50-Plus* magazine puts it this way:

The most precious gift in the world is time. Time to do anything you want to do, whenever you want to do it. . . . Time gives you the golden opportunity to meet new friends, get involved in new activities, travel to new places. It's your chance to create, innovate, help others, be valuable in the community. It's your time to grow as a human being. (1981, p. 2)

All well and good. But the leisure-time dream can sour, the hoped-for recreation deaden in its abundance — at least for some. This is the rub: unless a person actively engages the questions of meaning, abundant time can become meaningless. These are the same meaning questions that can surface at other major life turning points when the ordering structures for time and connection are interrupted. The graduating university student, the middle-aged person entering a new career, the retiree phasing out of an active work role — all these individuals need to ask *"Who am I?"* and *"What do I want to do with my life?"*

Narrowing those larger, more overarching dilemmas, here are some guiding questions suggested by the *50-Plus* booklet:

1. Does this activity do more for me than just kill time?
2. Does this experience stimulate me and enhance my skills?
3. Does this activity raise my status in the eyes of others?
4. Does this activity raise my feelings of contribution and self-worth?
5. Does this activity demand a good deal of my energy (mental and/or physical)? How much do I want to give?
6. Does this activity constantly offer me fresh challenges?
7. Does this activity make me feel "alive" and/or "good inside"? (Adapted from *50-Plus*, 1981)

"Cashing in on Late-Life Leisure" is the title of the February, 1985, issue of "Your Money and Your Life," a newsletter from the Savings Bank of Puget Sound assembled by Joan Gaines, creative director, and her staff. This publication puts it this way: "We can invest our leisure, save it, spend it or waste it. The opportunities are endless, limited only by our attitude, our imagination and perhaps by that other asset — money" (and, I would add, health, energy, and circumstance). I quote from among the possible choices for the older person to consider in a listing from "a" to "z":

Arts. No need to be a stay-at-home! There are senior discounts for movies, concerts, plays and other performances; ask at the box office.

Computers. You too can join the computer generation. Just sign up for a class at a community college, senior center. . . .

Investment Clubs. Pool your research efforts and investment dollars by starting a club with like-minded investors.

Just stay at home. Enjoy the simple pleasures of cooking, sewing, puttering in the garage, watching the ball game or gardening. No need to feel guilty!

Politics. Join with others to work for legislative reform or start your own campaign. If you want to improve conditions for seniors, contact the State Senior Lobby, OWL/Older Women's League, Grey Panthers, or the AARP/American Association of Retired Persons. (Savings Bank of Puget Sound, 1985)

All excellent selections. But once again, each person has to come to terms with personal choices and levels of need for investment and abstraction, privacy and connection. What many discover, however, is that invested activity can open new doors, lead to "flow" experiences when the mind is fully engaged, stimulate personal novelty (an important goal for creative aging), and promote the kinds of life interactions that provide new purpose and a more active living in a fully invested present. Building a repertoire of involvements and related skills also provides backup choices when one body system falters or fails.

My husband and I saw this adaptability enacted in the experience of a neighbor. This man invested his leisure in golf, a game he thoroughly enjoyed and which enabled him to spend many entertaining hours with his friends. All that changed the day he had a heart attack on the golf course. Fortunately, immediate medical care saved his life. What happened next is pertinent to our story. As his strength gradually returned he invested his emerging energies in learning silversmithing. He found he liked his new activity and it kept his mind from dwelling on physical concerns. Building on innate talents, he was soon producing beautifully designed and finely crafted chains, pendants, and rings. He had found an important alternative to the vigorous activity he had enjoyed before.

Thus, even with a basic optimism, the aging person still has to come to terms with interruptions of plans, the unpredictabilities of health, the uncertainties brought by shifting contexts and relationships.

In knocking down myths about aging and in trying to undo the wrong our culture has laid on its elders, there is the danger of appearing to say "Aging is a figment of our imaginations: if we think positively and live right, we can go on indefinitely as though we are thirty-five." To infer such nonsense from anything in this book would be to have misread it. No one lives forever. (Downs & Roll, 1981, p. 381)

As I have stated before, when I cite models for creative aging I do so against the backdrop of such reality—but I get the strong feeling that those who age creatively have that well in mind when they tackle the challenges of age.

INVESTED CARING — THE ESSENCE
OF VOLUNTEERING

Here I adopt Erikson's language of care and caring.

From the point of view of development, I would say: In youth you find out what you *care to do* and who you *care to be* — even in changing roles. In young adulthood you learn whom you *care to be with* — at work and in private life, not only exchanging intimacies, but sharing intimacy. In adulthood, however, you learn to know what and whom you can *take care of*. (1974, p. 124)

I see evidence in my studies that such caring is indeed an integral part of the only happiness that is lasting: "To increase by whatever is yours to give, the good will and the higher order in your sector of the world. That, to me, can be the only adult meaning of that strange word *happiness* as a political principle" (p. 124).

In the spirit of this generative capacity, psychiatrist Robert Coles writes about "Our Time for Giving." He quotes Anna Freud at 84 years of age:

I wish I had given more reflection and study to elderly people. . . . Toward the end of life I think certain psychological truths become especially clear — because we have less energy to hide ourselves! Many men and women who are called "old" and "retired" are living up to the best in themselves, and it's a pity we don't ask for their help. They have much to offer the world. (1988, p. 88)

In his commentary on Freud's ideas, Coles adds his own:

We have had our great dreams, and we have seen some of them, inevitably, come to naught. As we add years to our lives, we begin to appreciate the preciousness of life and its vulnerability. We no longer can wrap ourselves in that expansive egoism of youth. . . . Instead, we are likely to settle for the pastoral rather than the prophetic outlook — to seek our satisfactions in daily deeds rather than grand designs: the small gestures toward one another, the concreteness of an hour's involvement in the life of another person, as opposed to the big (and lengthy and abstract) discussions about what should or should not be done in general. (p. 88)

Coles believes it is natural "to extend ourselves to others — touching them and helping them in the here-and-now of their lives and ours. . . . No cosmetics or health regimen or program of exercise, no expenditure of money and influence, can really nourish and sustain that humanity — only a kind of moral exercise, so to speak, will do the job: the flexing, the strengthening, of our generous impulses through their regular use" (p. 88). I call this *invested caring* — not passive, not detached and observing, but actively involved in the contexts of people and community. This theme of invested caring organizes the material I present here.

To study the history of volunteering in our country is to look at the earliest traditions and philosophies introduced into our country from the time of the Mayflower Pact. Here is the pledge of our early founders "to work—not for money, but for 'a just and equal life.'" Adopting these words, educator Ethel Percy Andrus vowed "to work not for profit, but for good" as she organized the American Association of Retired Persons. Following her lead and living out its motto "To serve, not to be served," AARP provides vigorous leadership in organizing and administering a wide variety of programs. Through its initiative, tens of thousands of older citizens have taken hold of their lives in new ways, serving society at the same time they have found a measure of satisfaction for themselves.

Through AARP's computerized Volunteer Talent Bank people are helped to match interests and skills to a particular role or task. An active research and publishing program informs this work. Volunteers and volunteer coordinators can learn a great deal from such booklets as "Educational & Community Service Programs" (AARP, 1989), and "Older Volunteers: A Valuable Resource" (Warrick, 1986). The latter publication provides a practical examination of both obstacles and facilitations of the volunteer role—an examination that considers carefully the needs of those who volunteer. In the words of one man: "When I volunteer, I am committed to the organization I work for. But I need that organization to feel committed to me, too." And, another, "We volunteers need tangible goals. We need to know when we succeed and when we fail."

In addressing such questions AARP encourages feedback and sensitive interaction between volunteers and professional staff. In this manner volunteers can learn new roles and understanding of what those roles involve. Both staff and volunteers can then more fully appreciate the unique capabilities the older volunteer brings to the task—skills born of life experience, strong motivations, conscientiousness, dependability (impressive attendance records, low turnover rates, and steady performance), and availability. What do the volunteers ask for in return? Full integration into the program, staff support, growth opportunities, recognition rather than being patronized, payment of out-of-pocket expenses, attention to physical work needs, and appropriate liability insurance coverage.

Following these guidelines, many seniors are being trained for new and relatively sophisticated volunteer roles—peer counselors, for example, to encourage older folks to use community mental health centers.

At AARP, volunteers are retired accountants who counsel older taxpayers in filling out their returns. They are homemakers and retired educators teaching health maintenance and good driving skills, retired legislators and lawyers representing older consumers' interest on national boards, and men and women of all backgrounds helping shape laws to fit the needs of older citizens. They are the people who help other older men and women better their lives. (Warrick, 1986, p. 1)

I have described the AARP program rather extensively because it is a model of seniors working for seniors. But there are other programs that go beyond that emphasis; the Center for Creative Retirement in Asheville, North Carolina, is significant among these. Funded, sponsored, and housed at the University of North Carolina, this center organizes and offers well developed programs to take post-retirement persons into the individual and collective lives of the community. Under the imaginative leadership of Ronald J. Manheimer, a team of affiliates trains leaders for community programs, teacher/helpers for the public schools, and mentors for college undergraduate students who can gain from dialogues with senior specialists in their fields of interest. In addition, the UNCA Center offers a variety of sophisticated learning programs both at the university and in the community even as it spearheads leadership training for similar centers across the United States.

In similar fashion, other volunteer activities are being generated across the nation in a wide variety of locations. Here are some samples:

1. Seniors who go into schools to fill educational gaps and to reduce the pressures put upon teachers.
2. Volunteers who deliver library books to the homebound and use the occasion to begin a life review with the person they're visiting (AARP's Reminiscence Program in Rochester Hills, Michigan, for example).
3. Volunteers in programs that stimulate dialogue and interaction across the generations. (In one example, the University of Pittsburgh sponsors a Generations Together program. Here, students in the third and fourth grades are paired with adults old enough to be their grandparents. The purpose is to foster intergenerational friendship.)
4. Programs that use the nurturing capabilities of older people to fill in the gaps of day care, of physical touching for babies, of listening ears for latchkey children who reach out for someone to answer their questions and ease their fears. (Children's Orthopedic Hospital in Seattle, Washington, sponsors an Auntie-Uncle program which uses a variety of volunteers, including seniors, to provide focused "tender loving care" for premature babies whose parents have had to return to homes in other areas of the country. These "aunties and uncles" come in every day for a minimum of one hour to play with the babies, cuddle them, bathe and feed them.)
5. Those who work to teach adults who cannot read and write.

(The Laubach Literacy program is noteworthy. Its techniques and philosophy "Each One Teach One" have created considerable constructive impact. This is another cross-generational program which has depended heavily on its older volunteers.)

On many local levels there are volunteer bureaus, community social service organizations, church groups, schools, cultural insititutions, hospitals, and political action programs (which I will explore more fully below). Then there are the popular national programs run under the sponsorship of ACTION, the federal agency that coordinates major volunteer efforts. These ACTION programs include the following: Peace Corps, VISTA (Volunteers in Service to America), RSVP (Retired Senior Volunteer Program), Foster Grandparent Program, and the Senior Companion Program.

Other programs include SCORE (Service Corps of Retired Executives) and ACE (Active Corps of Executives), which are both sponsored by the Small Business Administration. Nonprofit organizations include The International Executive Service Corps, which sends volunteers with business expertise into developing countries across the world. Further opportunity for personal sharing can be found in the programs of the American National Red Cross, the Federation of Protestant Welfare Agencies, the National School Volunteer Program, CARE, National Conference of Catholic Charities, and the United Way of America.

Political activists invest their energies and talents in a variety of ways — some widening their scopes to national and international concerns; others speaking out in causes close to home. In either case, these people are often passionately involved in issues which can range from those of the environment to those of national security to those of the legislative concerns of older people. Claude Pepper was such a leader. Working within the legislative framework he endeavored ceaselessly to better the living conditions of the seniors and the poor in our country. Despite losing his wife and despite having heart problems that necessitated his using a pacemaker the last seven years of his life, Pepper maintained an intensive work schedule until he died at 88 from cancer. A remarkable model of informed, ethical, sensitive activism, Pepper holds the record for serving longer than any other member of the United States Congress.

Maggie Kuhn is another model for political activism. Founder of the Gray Panthers, her story was effectively summarized in *The Nation*:

It was in 1970 that Maggie Kuhn, then editor of a Presbyterian social justice journal, and several friends faced a dual challenge: how to participate actively with young people in the struggle against the Vietnam War and how to resist forced retirement at 65. From that confluence of political commitment and aging emerged an imaginative, passionate movement, which placed the artificial division between young and old—ageism—alongside racism, sexism and militarism as one of the great oppressive forces of the era. At first burdened with the high-church title, the Consultation of Older and Younger Adults for Social Change, they were dubbed the Gray Panthers by a New York talk show host. The name stuck, along with a motto that said it all: "Age and Youth in Action." (1990, May 28, p. 727)

This editorial highlights the *cross-generational* emphasis of the Gray Panthers that incorporates a passionate refusal to pit the interests of the old against those of the young. In work for decentralized health service, for intergenerational home sharing, for the abolition of retirement cutoffs, for an alert awareness which monitors attitudes towards the old, Maggie Kuhn continues her leadership even as she moves through her eighties (she became 85 in the summer of 1990). Still barnstorming around the country, brimming with rage and ideas, she seems the ultimate example of the inspired, creative activist.

On a smaller scale I tell the story of the Giraffe Project, an organization created by John Graham and Ann Medlock of Langley on Whidbey Island in Washington. A November 1988 article in *50-Plus* gave this history:

In five years, some 252 Giraffes [people who stick their necks out for the common good] have been tapped, each having been nominated by one of the project's 2000 members who pay $25 a year to support the project's work. The criteria for commendation include typical Giraffe qualities—compassion, humor, courage, action beyond the call of duty and service for the common good. (p. 15)

The winners of the Giraffe award are models of enlightened activism, chosen because they have taken social, financial, or physical risks in actions that are not "violent, unconstitutional or solely self-serving." The winners are publicized on more than 500 radio stations and most recently, in a PBS documentary. Among those selected: a woman, age 90, who has fought environmental battles in the Northwest; a couple in New York who selectively have provided seed money of $100 each to nearly 8,000 small businesses in 100 countries around the world; a gem expert who has spent her own money to help the San Carlos Apaches set up a development plan to make their gemstone mine financially independent. What is especially remarkable about this Giraffe program is that the dedicated contribution of a single husband-and-wife team has spread so far, a demonstration of their avowed purpose to provide inspiration to others.

Then there are the participants in the Habitat for Humanity International, which has as its subtitle, "Building houses in partnership with God's people in need." This is a cross-generational program, founded by Millard and Linda Fuller in Americus, Georgia in 1976, that addresses the need for decent housing in the world. Habitat works with low-income families to build comfortable, simple dwellings that would be otherwise unaffordable. Habitat's reliance upon volunteer labor and donated materials significantly lowers costs for new homeowners. In addition, Habitat makes no profit on the homes and charges no interest on homeowners' 15-year to 20-year mortgages.

What I find particularly appealing about this program is its no-nonsense "theology of the hammer," which requires a 500-hour "sweat equity" from its new homeowners who work side by side with Habitat volunteers. What this highly successful program offers for seniors who wish to volunteer (and these include Jimmy and Rosalynn Carter) is further opportunity to contribute, to keep active and fit, and to find remarkable returns on new investments in caring. Here is the opportunity to be a part of a program whose 1990 goal is to build or rehabilitate 4,300 houses worldwide.

I close this discussion of volunteers with an expression of appreciation for the work of the Older Women's League. Founded by Tish Summers and Laurie Shields in 1980, built on its battle cry, "Organize, don't agonize!", this organization provides a mutuality of support for its members as it also works vigorously for the rights of all older women. Its newsletter, *The Owl Observer*, reminds us of what it is to be old and a woman in America—not always a coveted position in the order of things. This organization also stimulates a wide variety of volunteer activities to aid and enhance the life experiences of women in need.

These varied contributions serve to remind us of what a vast resource there is in our elders. They also remind us that many of these folks are not waiting to be asked—they are simply going ahead quietly to invest in others, many times following a pattern started early in life, at other times exploring this personal investment for the first time. Whatever their choice, these senior adventurers have much to teach us about the processes of living creatively.

MIX-AND-MATCH

But creative aging is not all hard work and heavy-duty, invested caring. It is a mix-and-match of many things. In fact, for many people, the more mix there is the more fulfilled the person may be. In this regard I remember the the handsome older couple whose recipe for a "good life" consists of work, play, and children. Every year this man and woman settle into an Arizona retirement community for three months, work in a national park as guides for another three months, and then spend the remainder of their time in a home base where they can enjoy their family and friends. This formula works well for these people—but there are no set prescriptions for the good life. Some will choose to mix travel, learning, and time with families — or work and activism — or recreation and learning — or artistic creation with spiritual exploration.

And we mustn't forget PLAY—*genuine play*, that is, which unites the mind, body, and spirit in spontaneous, joyous, personal expression. One example of such a union is the folk dancing adventure. It is really quite amazing to see the spirited congregations of people learning their calls, dancing their steps, planning their wardrobes, and following the impulse to continue to learn, to travel, and to share with others. What better way to keep the entire person alive than to engage in an activity that requires a dedication of time, perseverence, intense learning, and focused concentration — and that stimulates joyous connections with others.

The conclusion here is that whatever the choice, there are many combinations for the person to consider.

LIFELONG LEARNING

I like Merlyn's words of wisdom in T.H. White's *The Once and Future King*:

The best thing for being sad is to learn something. That is the only thing that never fails. You may grow old and trembling in your anatomies, you may lie awake at night listening to the disorder of your veins, you may miss your lonely love, you may see the world around you devastated by evil lunatics, or know your honor trampled in the sewers of baser minds. There is only one thing for it then — to learn. Learn why the world wags and what wags it. That is the only thing which the mind can never exhaust, never alienate, never be tortured by, never fear or distrust, and never dream of regretting. Learning is the thing for you. (1987, p. 183)

Parker J. Palmer uses this passage in his writing as he calls learning a "magic of sorts, a healing, an empowerment, a conduit of grace, a wellspring of health and wholeness, of life itself." Even more, he considers learning both the result of working through life's difficulties and a way to "move in and through those travails to the life on the other side" (1989, p. 6). Whatever our reasons for experiencing learning — whether we like to take part in philosophical, spiritual discussions like these or prefer to gather a body of concrete skills — many of us are discovering the stimulus to the mind and the energy renewal which comes from new learning at any life stage.

Strong evidence of these combinations are to be found in the Elderhostel program. Taking inspiration and practical models from the youth hostels of Europe and the folk schools of Scandinavia, Marty Knowlton, a well-known social activist and educator, launched the program in 1975. He saw the important links between simple residential settings and the adult education programs offered by the folk high schools. Since its beginnings in 1975, Elderhostel has grown to over 190,000 hostelers in 1989, enrolled in all 50 states, all 10 Canadian provinces, and over 40 countries overseas. Currently, more than 1,000 different colleges, universities, and other educational institutions proudly offer their best programs to eager and challenging students.

The student population for Elderhostel is drawn from individuals 60 years or older, together with their spouses, but a companion, 50 years old or older, may accompany a participant who is at least 60 years of age (here is one time when age is a definite requirement and an advantage!). These students personify the Elderhostel philosophy, which states: "We're for elder citizens on the move, not just in terms of travel, but in terms of intellectual activity as well. Our commitment is to the the belief that retirement does not represent an end to significant activity for older adults but a new beginning filled with opportunities and challenges." Evidence for that statement is certainly seen in the excitement of those who attend, and in the large numbers who are engaging the joy of learning "from Cicero to computers . . . politics to poetry . . . from Maine to Manitoba . . . Wollongong to Wales" (Elderhostel Catalog, 1990).

I have already reported on the multi-faceted program of the Center for Creative Retirement in Asheville, North Carolina. Another such program geared to lifelong learning is the Duke Institute for Learning in Retirement in Durham, North Carolina. In their brochure they write about the possibilities which retirement can provide: "Time not only for travel and leisure, but also for the active pursuit of knowledge and understanding. Time to renew former interests, to discover untapped creative and intellectual abilities, to stretch the boundaries—in short, to learn." These learning adventures are not just something done to and for seniors, but adventures that include a mutuality of experience, of sharing, and of teaching. The Duke Institute writes that half of its classes are taught by members of the Institute (adults over 50 who wish to pursue academic interests); the other half of the classes are taught by a mix of university faculty, retired faculty, graduate students, independent scholars, and community experts.

In Canada similar programs are beings developed. For example, at Saint Mary's University in Halifax, Nova Scotia, a group of adult educators and seniors have established a community resource bank, Experience Unlimited, which enables retired individuals to share their knowledge and skills in a variety of voluntary meetings and activities. Their flyer lists these objectives:

- To encourage participation in lifelong learning
- To further the concept of the "University of the Third Age"

- To become more aware of the heritage and traditions of our peoples, our province and our country
- To promote greater friendship, cooperation and communication among lifelong learners.

Across the continent in the city of Bellevue, Washington, the Telos program has continued active learning programs for more than fourteen years. According to its literature, "In 1971 Bellevue Community College became interested in the problems of the 'Aging' and started classes on the BCC campus on 'The New Image of Aging.'" With the motivated actions of a cross-generational group of leaders, and with Helen Ansley as "the catalyst who saw the vision of what such a program could be and do" (and Helen is still a catalyst as she moves into her 90s), the Telos program was fully launched in 1976. Emblazoned across the cover of each quarter's program is the following: "TELOS means in Greek, Fulfillment. The TELOS of an acorn is an Oak tree." The senior students who continue personal development within its programs are considered the fruits of this tree. In the manner of St. Mary's, Telos suggests a set of goals:

- To offer the older citizen opportunities for individual self-appraisal and for planning a way of life designed to attain the maximum degree of self-realization and enrichment in the years ahead.
- To create a stimulating and rewarding environment for the older citizens in which they can keep alive their interest in life, broaden their horizons, and develop and maintain an image as one of continued growth and development.
- To assist the elderly in coping with problems associated with old age by making available appropriate classes, consultations, or counseling.

Comparable programs can be found not only in other parts of the Puget Sound area but in small towns and big cities across America. This seems to be a genuine renaissance in our time as older people seize the opportunity to learn, and as they demonstrate the sophisticated capacity of the older learner for a wide range of learning experiences. These people are indeed "pioneers in a new prime of life."

Independently, many seniors are developing programs of their own. Some of these are being organized under the umbrella sponsorship of the Good Sam Club. This club has a large membership of RV owners and is a model of cooperative enterprise. Offering insurance programs, park ratings, and helpful tips for effective travel and living, Good Sam's official publication, *Highways*, which published its 24th volume in 1990, provides interesting commentary on a population many know little about.

Pertinent to our topic, the Good Sam Club has a chapter that is devoted to computer learning. Several times a year the "Computer

Sams" assemble for a camp-out, choosing a facility that has lots of indoor space for tables and chairs, and sufficient electrical capacity to power 20 or 30 computers and printers. What reporter Beverly Edwards discovered was that only a few of the participants had been introduced to computers in the business place, "the rest had learned about computers on their own, in classes and through the Computer Sams. And they are still learning" (Edwards, 1990). The members apply their knowledge in the same kinds of ways the rest of us do: for keeping files, writing letters, maintaining business accounts, making banners for a party—and in some special ways, as a means for personal therapy and connection with others. One participant indicated that the computer was an important therapy tool for her husband, who has muscular dystrophy. "The games he plays on the computer keep him going" (p. 49).

In a more formally constructed program called SeniorNet, a non-profit computer network has been designed for adults over 55. According to Marvin G. Katz (1990), SeniorNet is the "first nationwide program to help older persons join the telecommunications revolution." Its avowed purpose is to build an electronic community for older people. Founded in 1986 at the University of San Francisco, by the end of the 1980s this program had reached over 26 sites in 13 states and in Canada. Volunteer coordinators have trained more than 3,000 people (55 and over) to use personal computers. Grants from a wide variety of corporations have provided helpful financial support for this unusual, innovative learning enterprise. What is particularly gratifying about this program is that it enables house-bound elders to chat with friends across the continent. It also makes these people feel more a part of the technological world in which they live.

As I close this section on learning I call your attention to a unique group of lifelong learners that Ronald Gross calls "independent scholars." His descriptor has personal overtones for me because it has given some meaning to my drive to study, research, and write, without the support of a formal professional community. In *The Independent Scholar's Handbook—How to Turn Your Interest in Any Subject into Expertise* (1982), Gross gives a model of the independent scholar, a collection of shared stories from his own experience and that of his students, and a wealth of practical suggestion for anyone who, like myself, finds themselves captured by an idea to be explored. On a personal level, Gross provides an empathic acknowledgment of the isolation, potential loneliness, and lack of support that is frequently the lot of the person who works on her/his own. I found both affirmation and hardhitting advice in his words.

I close this section on lifelong learning with these words of advice that Max Schuster gave to Gross when he first started his work at Simon and Schuster:

Begin *at once*—not today, or tomorrow, or at some remote indefinite date, but right now, at this precise moment—to choose some subject, some concept, some great name or idea or event in history on which you can eventually make yourself the world's supreme expert. Start a crash program immediately to qualify yourself for this self-assignment through reading, research, and reflection. . . . I don't mean the sort of expert who avoids all the small errors as he sweeps on to the grand fallacy. I mean one who has the most knowledge, the deepest insight, and the most audacious willingness to break new ground. (In Gross, 1982, pp. xii–xiii)

That is definitely a path to creative aging!

WORK THAT BRINGS REMUNERATION

In the realms of vocation, words become a little ambiguous. The Random House Dictionary (1969) defines *vocation* as "a particular occupation, business, or profession; calling . . . a strong impulse or inclination to follow a particular activity or career." Within the concept of this definition is the idea of a commitment of a major portion of time, energy, and interest. This may or may not be tied to monetary return, and thus includes not only paid employment, but homemaking activities, volunteer work, and all the leisure-time activities named above which involve an investment of real interest, time, and commitment. Those last are the key variables in naming *vocation*.

Work, on the other hand, does not carry quite the same concept of being a "major focus of a person's activities and usually of his thoughts" (Roe, 1956, p. 3). Rather, the Random House Dictionary defines it as "effort directed to produce or accomplish something; labor; toil." It thus refers to more specific activity, but does not necessarily include a sense of valued meaning. Work may or may not be tied to monetary reward (Carlsen, 1973).

The "why" of work is much more complex. Many theorists have pondered these "why's", searching for the meaning of work in the lives of men and women. Anne Roe, for example, wrote:

The old concept of economic man has proved totally inadequate to explain why men work as they do, or what it is they are working for. That men work just to make a living is obviously not true. It is sufficient to point out that, if this were true, as soon as food and shelter had been assured, work would stop. . . . Studies of morale in industry and of job satisfaction have shown that much more is involved in and expected of a job than a pay check. (1956, p. 23)

Ginzberg (1968) has commented that an individual must be more than a consumer—that work adds a dimension of meaning to his or her relationships, and that meaning adds depth to the living of life. Thus people come to the questions of work with widely varying needs.

I call *career* one of these needs: to have an organizing principle for one's life, a source of meaning, a "path or street, the chariot on which one rides on the street" in the original metaphorical meanings of the word. Like vocation, career engages the whole person in providing a sense of significance and meaning for life. And like vocation, career can provide a vehicle for invested effort as long as one lives.

Whatever the ambiguities in these words, older people frequently want a part in the world of work. Their motivations may be various: a structure for everyday life, a sense of contact with others, a feeling of being needed and respected, and/or an opportunity to keep on earning money. Money, we must remember, is closely entwined with feelings of worth in our society. Many older people do not have a need for money and status, but many do.

The motivations and opportunities for work are being actively explored by researchers within the business community. *Generations*, the Journal of the American Society on Aging, devoted its Summer 1989 issue to an exploration of these matters. In that issue, guest editors Robert Levin and James Weil agreed that business has many opportunities to contribute constructively to the well-being of older adults. Both also agreed that employers will become increasingly involved in aging issues. Optimistic that business can be helpful in solving dilemmas of health care, housing, and financing, Levin and Weil also defined opportunities for business to employ adults in innovative, creative ways.

Even as the business world explores new products and services for older people, they are also discovering that older employees can actually help them bring about a profit. At least that was the experience of The Travelers Companies. These affiliates implemented a model retiree reemployment program which won the approval of aging advocates. "What has prompted the interest of other firms, however, is the finding that using retirees as temporary office help has saved the company an average of $1 million annually since the program's inception" (R. Levin, 1989, p. 67). This company, in its response to human need, found a synergistic reward which helped its own bottom line.

The imaginative efforts of modern business may help resolve some of the problems faced not only by seniors eager to keep on working, but by an economy overloaded by shifts in demographic proportions. Population shifts are reshaping the balances of the working population, national budgets are threatened by the aging baby boom group, all at the same time retirement laws are removing the pressure to quit work. Although many people will not choose to work, many others will find a sense of continuing value and financial advantage in maintaining a job. It is to be hoped that the business world will be imaginative enough and sensitive enough to generate a variety of options for today's seniors.

If we look around for examples of older people who have reinvested in the work role there is an abundance to choose from. And there are a number of research findings to back up the specific examples:

- Productivity does not decline with age; older employees are as productive as most employees in most jobs.
- Workers 45 and older have attendance records equal to or better than those of most other age groups. The American Council of Life Insurance, for example, found that these employees took an average of only 3.1 sick days per year.
- People 55 and older account for only 9.7 percent of all workplace injuries, despite the fact that they make up 13.6 percent of the labor force. (1984 AARP study of workers 45 and older, cited by Rosenblum, January 1989, pp. 27–34)

Further findings from the AARP survey revealed that one third of the over-60 people they interviewed would like to continue working. Financial benefit is part of it, but many choose continuing employment not only for the intrinsic elements of their job, but as a way to feel active and useful as well (Rosenblum, 1989).

Another survey, this time by Public Agenda, a nonpartisan public affairs research organization, found that most men and women prefer to work well past the age of 65. But many do not want to continue in the same jobs they have held for a lifetime; they want some spontaneity and novelty in their work life and a chance to express themselves more creatively. Studying these findings and using the criteria of people's needs for work renewal, the magazine *New Choices* listed 10 job opportunities for the 1990s (January 1989, pp. 32–33): (1) financial planner, (2) travel or leisure professional, (3) corporate-classroom teacher, (4) receptionist, (5) medical record technician, (6) food-service worker, (7) actuary, (8) child-care worker, (9) real estate salesperson, (10) contract or temporary worker. Some older people are more imaginative than that. For example: Merrilyn Belgum left social work at the age of 64 to go into comedy. She had the talent and gumption to make the turnaround, plus the creative humor which could make her a success. "Since her decision to retire in 1985 to pursue comedy full-time, Belgum's given more than 500 performances in 16 states, from Louisiana to Minnesota, and in Victoria, British Columbia" (Rosenblum, 1989, p. 31).

Then there is Willie Kocurek, who entered law school at the age of 67. He had three personal goals: "I had to graduate. I had to pass the bar exam. And I had to be alive on both occasions." (With humor like that who can lose!) After owning an appliance business for 46 years he opted for "renewment" rather than retirement. The shift into studying and writing term papers and taking tests was not easy, but he maintained a personal discipline which enabled him to keep going. He also found his nearly 50 years *outside* school invaluable preparation not only for his study but for his new role: travel, dealings with finances, book-keeping, employees, customers, advertising—all had helped him to keep his mind alert through his entrepreneurial years. Now 78 years of age (in 1989), he suggests: "Keep your body and your mind razor sharp. And always have something in the wings" (Rosenblum, 1989, p. 34).

In addition to volunteering, investing in learning, experimenting with new careers, today's older adults are frequently active in sports and exercise programs, testing new cuisine, producing art work, learning new hobbies, exploring the spiritual realms, writing books, traveling the nation and the world. And then there are the creative RV explorers. After nine months as a visiting member of this nomadic population I have considerable respect for these adventuresome people, much appreciation of what an important contribution this way of life is making to their vital investments in life.

THE RV EXPERIENCE

The life of a traveler is a very fulfilling life-style for many older people—in fact, so fulfilling that a 1986 joint research study by AARP and the U.S. Travel Data Center showed that the 50-plus traveler accounts not only for 30% of all travel, but for 72% of recreational vehicle trips. This way of life fulfills a variety of purposes: learning, adventure, novelty, independence, personal stimulation, connection, physical activity, low cost living. Many participants are also acting directly on needs for independent choice, their "own place," a chance to go rather than to sit back and wait to receive whatever time their families and friends have available to share. Their travel decisions and experiences are a way to seize the moment and to feel more in control of their lives. Some feel they are giving their children a gift by creating their own independent lives (for some of the people we talked to this statement carried a certain tone of poignancy).

Beyond such active expression of personal needs, these people travel because they love to travel. They like the excitement of coming upon a new campground, meeting a new friend, seeing the sunsets, mountain tops, ocean beaches, that they have only dreamed about earlier in their lives. Many of these people have been small business owners, farmers, school teachers, service providers—the occupants of America's middle class in the the very best sense of the word. I don't know the demographics of this population but my observations would suggest a group predominantly white, predominantly married, and generally traditional in their outlooks on life. But there are many exceptions, as single people and minority travelers join this adventure and as wealthy executives and professionals appear on the highways in their very impressive homes on wheels.

Some of those who choose the mobile home life also choose to be "full-timers," selling their homes to wander the land. For many this works well, but for others the decision is premature and they soon head home, realizing that that is not their particular adventure. Wise counsel suggests that a rental RV makes a good beginning, giving a chance to sample different parts of the country, different types of resorts and options.

And it really is very interesting to meet the variety of people who are out there. On our journey my husband and I met two vigorous and delightful retired school teachers in northern California. In a middle-sized "rig" they had been traveling for over two years and "loved it." Initially they had maintained a home, using renters and house sitters for its security — but after many unpleasant hassles they decided that it was ridiculous to try to keep up two residences. While wandering the back roads of the nation these women share the chores, do most of their own repair work, and seem to be thriving on their nomadic life-style. What is to be noted is that these two highly educated, capable women took time to live out their alternative choices before fully severing their roots.

One of the results of being a "full-timer" is an independence from the ties of real estate and local legal systems. But that is not always so good. Letters to *Highways* in August 1990 shared these insights:

It recently occurred to me that the approximately 1 million full-timers have not been included in the 1990 Census. I have been unable to locate any full-timers in my travels who have been contacted by census takers or who have received a census form in the mail.

* * *

When are we, the genuine 100 percent full-time RV society, going to become legitimate, recognized and accepted in this world of truly diverse factions? 1999? 2022? Never? Now? . . . Being as we really don't have roots or ties in any of the existing United States, and being as we seem to travel into all 50 states, thereby enhancing their coffers, and being as we need to license our vehicles, want our right to vote, want to carry health insurance policies without hassle, and don't want to be told we must have a phone number or else, I'd like to suggest that there be a 51st (fictitious) state especially for full-time RVers.

Shades of the 20th/21st century! Problems never dreamed about just a few years ago — problems that may become a new focus for the activism of older people.

Though some critics wonder if "frail" older folks should be out driving, most are doing well. A feature article in *Highways* (June 1990) describes "Good Sam's Centenarians." Writer Ellen Brandt asks us to realize that "since centenarians probably represent the most resilient genetic strain within each generation, they actually tend to be healthier, both mentally and physically, than many people decades younger. They tend to stay active and maintain an optimistic outlook and a love of life" (p. 31). So, who knows, that man or woman out there driving that rig may be older than you think!

No doubt the majority of RV travelers mix their traveling with other life-styles, maintaining a home base and, frequently, a job in another area. Some bring lifelong learning into their experience as they attend special Elderhostel programs or as they participate in learning programs in RV parks and at rallies sponsored by the various mobile-home clubs.

What are these people modeling for us? Creativity, certainly; courage and a spirit of adventure; a willingness to try out something new; and, I would suggest, the demonstration of the generative capacity to care. I found all these qualities demonstrated in the Mesa RV resort where my husband and I lived for three months as a part of our research and writing leave. I had time to observe and participate in a community where the majority of the residents were actively involved (remember, I didn't have access to the stories behind closed doors). Some of them were studying lapidary and silversmithing, others were practicing music, singing in choirs, playing tennis, hiking around the park night and morning. In the middle of it all there was a spirit of friendship and a genuine concern for supporting each other. (If you consider that the backdrop of this age is the coming of death, that support is not so surprising.) In spite of the emphasis on leisure time and vigorous play, many of these folks took time to give of themselves in a variety of ways.

KEEPERS OF THE NEIGHBORHOOD

And so I close this story. Certainly, many older people do not leave their home communities, preferring to use their original home base for leisure-time and work-time explorations. They maintain a continuity with work histories, neighborhoods, families, and friends. And they may assume intangible roles by being what *Seattle Times* writer Susan Gilmore calls "keepers of the neighborhoods"—people who contribute to the continuity, spirit, and well-being of those around them. I read this as an honoring of the significant part older people can play in keeping us in touch with history, in bridging the gaps between the generations, in passing along wisdom, both abstract and concrete, and in keeping all of us alert to the tasks and challenges of aging. Obviously, some seniors will be bitter, self-absorbed, blocked in their developmental process. These people are not constructive models for aging. But, close by are those other older individuals who are still learning, growing, and creating. We have much to learn from these people whom Eisdorfer labels "the glue in the tribe" and whom I continue to call our pioneers in a new prime of life.

I want to close on an upbeat note as I quote this whimsical poem from the Fall 1988 schedule of classes for North Seattle Community College's Senior Adult Education Program:

The Versatile Age

The old rocking chair is empty today,
For Grandmother no longer is in it.
She's off in her car to her office or shop,
And busses around every minute.
No one shoves Grandma back on the shelf,
She's versatile, forceful, dynamic,
That isn't a pie in the oven, my dear,
Her baking today is ceramic.
You won't see her trudging early to bed,
From her place in the warm chimney nook.
Her typewriter clickity-clacks thru the night,
For Grandma is writing a book.
Grandmother never takes one backward look
To slow down her steady advancing.
She won't tend the babies for you anymore,
For Grandma has taken up dancing.
She isn't content with crumbs of old thought,
With meager and second-hand knowledge.
Don't bring your mending for Grandma to do;
Grandma has gone back to college.

—Anonymous

We who are old know that age is more than a disability. It is an intense and varied experience, almost beyond our capacity at times, but something to be carried high. If it is a long defeat it is also a victory, meaningful for the initiates of time, if not for those who have come less far.

—Florida Scott-Maxwell, 1968

I like spring, but it is too young. I like summer, but it is too proud. So I like best of all autumn, because its leaves are a little yellow, its tone mellower, its colors richer, and it is tinged a little with sorrow and premonition of death. Its golden richness speaks not of the innocence of spring, nor of the power of summer, but of the mellowness and kindly wisdom of approaching age. It knows the limitations of life and its content. From a knowledge of those limitations and its richness of experience emerges a symphony of colors, richer than all, its green speaking of life and strength, its orange speaking of golden content and its purple of resignation and death.

—Lin Yutang, 1935, pp. 347–348

CHAPTER 12

Our Elders at the Conference Table

REPEATEDLY I AM STRUCK by the power of ideas like those above— ideas that shake perceptions and awaken me to the bittersweet complexities of old age. These are not passive older people staring off into some mythical sunset. These are passionate people—a man and a woman, representative of those who live long and dare much, whose creative expressions are outlets for complex sortings of mind and spirit. Their words shake any simplistic summary of what aging is about even as they suggest what is possible.

THE BITTERSWEET QUALITIES OF OLD AGE

Florida Scott-Maxwell's *The Measure of My Days* (1968) is her private notebook, a notebook that records the experiences of an 82-year-old woman as she encounters her own aging. It is a passionate, revealing book, which shares shifting thoughts, emotions, and continually unfolding understandings. It is not a book about the past; it is a book that engages the "now" experiences of her life as she measures the sum of her days. Her insights challenge, they illuminate, for she confronts the serious dilemmas and conflicts of her times. Even more important-ly, she shares an astonishment at how intensely she was engaging the experiences of her 80s. Those intensities stimulated the writing of her notebook:

When I was sewing, or playing a soothing-boring game of patience, I found queries going round and round in my head and I began to jot them down in this note book which I used to use for sketching. The queries were insistent, and I began a game of asking questions and giving answers. Answers out of what I had read and forgotten, and thought my own, or out of my recoils and hopes. If the modern world is this, then will it become so and so? My answers must be my own, years of reading now lost in the abyss I call my mind. *What matters is what I have now, what in fact I live and feel* [italics added]. (p. 7)

Her story of "what in fact I live and feel" fluctuates from humor to sadness, from energy to exhaustion, shaking hope even as she offers hope. She shares the closings of old age even as she points to its open-ings. Back and forth she moves, catching us off guard as one moment she lifts and the next she sets down—a choreographed dance of integri-ty vis-à-vis its despair.

I am getting fine and supple from the mistakes I've made, but I wish a note book could laugh. Old and alone one lives at such a high moral level. One is surrounded by eternal verities, noble austerities to scale on every side, and frightening depths of insight. It is inhuman. I long to laugh. I want to be enjoyed, but an hour's talk and I am exhausted. (p. 8)

So she leads us on and I, for one, come away shaken yet infused with a new spirit of hopefulness which I had not expected—a hopeful-ness that encourages me towards a modicum of the courageousness required for a meaningful old age. This is a quiet courageousness which Lin Yutang has captured in his commentaries on the human condition. His gentle, beautiful words at the beginning of this book and, now, at the beginning of this chapter, catch the paradoxical juxtapositions of age. The result? With his earthy humor and insight he shakes me even as he warms me:

> In my young days,
>   I had tasted only gladness,
> But loved to mount the top floor,
> But loved to mount the top floor,
>   To write a song pretending sadness.
>
> And now I've tasted
>   Sorrow's flavors, bitter and sour,
> And can't find a word,

> And can't find a word,
> > but merely say, "What a golden autumn hour!"

> (1935, p. 348)

These words bring me to May Sarton who declared, after recovering from her stroke at the age of 73, "I had not realized until now what courage it takes to grow old." This persevering spirit was evident as she started a new journal in April, 1986, just three months after she became ill: "It may prove impossible because my head feels so queer and the smallest effort, mental or physical, exhausts, but I feel so deprived of my *self* being unable to write, cut off since early January from all that I mean about my life, that I think I must try to write a few lines every day" (1988, p. 15).

"All that I mean about my life" — those are the roots of the wisdoms shared here, of the enactments of courage that demonstrate very strongly that these wise people are not closing off life. Indeed, in the words of Sarton, "There is much I still hope to do. And I rejoice in the life I have recaptured and in all that lies ahead" (p. 280).

THE COURAGE TO GROW OLD

Sarton's theme, "the courage to grow old," is the same theme Phillip Berman explored with a group of writers born between 1897 and 1923. Although some of those he first contacted objected to the idea that it takes courage to handle the varying, natural phenomena of aging, others responded with interest and creative expression to the the questions raised by that theme. Heartened by their response, Berman, who initially doubted his own enterprise, eventually "fell back upon my original conviction that it takes courage to live fully and vitally at any age, and that each stage in life presents us with different sets of challenges" (1989, xi).

To read the essays in Berman's book is to understand some of the challenges that older people face — but even more, to realize how varied the responses can be to the processes of aging and the coming of death. There is Mary Francis Shura Craig who confides that "age has always seemed relatively immaterial to me" (Berman, 1989, p. 5); Dame Hyacinthe Hill who writes about humor and a "rebellion against the ordinary, through a bravely joyous embracing of the comic spirit" (p. 42); and Robert E. Lee who says that what gives him the courage to grow old is "The Grand Perhaps" — the enjoyment of "the doubt, the uncertainty, the magnificent issue of the game" (p. 71).

These are statements from the younger contributors to Berman's collection. What about the older respondents? What do they have to say? Margaret Cousins, born in 1905, shares the results of some important realizations at the time of her retirement — realizations that reshaped the way she lived her life: "To maintain my independence I felt that I must seek a simpler existence. For the first time, I experienced the necessity of courage as the fountainhead for old age. Courage persuaded me to examine the possibilities, make choices, devise new plans, and render accomplishment of them possible. Courage fueled optimism" (Berman, 1989, p. 209). She took her courage and optimism as the impetus to change everything in her life — her city, her housing arrangements, her former use of a car. As a result, she entered into "one of the most exciting periods in my whole life and I am profoundly grateful for the experience" (p. 210).

Dramatic restructuring of one's life takes a certain kind of attitude, an optimism that orients one to the future, and a "faith in living" — a faith that life's compensations "will multiply with time." This, writes Leland Stowe (b. 1899), is what aging requires. He sees this as more than a courage to grow old. It is a life equation which brings its own reward — an equation that one's attitudes and personal habits result in the kinds of motivations one carries; that one's motivations plus goals plus dreams are what shapes one's character — and that all of these are "cindered into solid bricks for the passageway into growing old" (Berman, 1989, p. 303).

For British journalist, social critic, and theologian Malcolm Muggeridge the attitude is an acceptance of the mystery of death within a belief that "our existence here is related in some mysterious way to a more comprehensive and lasting existence elsewhere" (Berman, 1989, p. 258). But even as he states his hope he describes his waiting for death as being like "a prisoner waiting for release, like a schoolboy when the end of term is near" — and so, he longs to be gone. (As I finish this book in November 1990, I read that at the age of 87 Muggeridge is now indeed gone.)

Psychologist G. Stanley Hall made it his project to probe the meanings of age, sharing his observations and insights in his book *Senescence* (1922). Eighty years old at the time he assembled his insights, he considered this late-life work a complement to his *Adolescence* published in 1904, a work which "could not have been written in the midst of the seething phenomena it describes, as this must be. We cannot outgrow and look back upon old age, for the course of time cannot be reversed" (1922, p. vii). For him "to learn that one is old is a long, complex and painful experience. Each decade the circle of the Great Fatigue narrows around us, restricting the intensity and endurance of our activities."

Hall named some of the painful processes which he discovered and acted upon: "My first and hardest duty of all is to realize that I am really and truly old." "Emerson says that a task is a life-preserver, and now that mine is gone I must swim or go under." It "slowly came to me that I must, first of all, take careful stock of myself and now seek to attain more of the self-knowledge that Socrates taught the world was the highest, hardest, and last of all forms of knowledge." For Hall this meant taking a physical inventory, checking out the various ways he could grow old, but he came to the conclusion that "physicians know very little of old age"—that it was his alone to "pursue the rest of my way in life by a more or less individual research as to how to keep well and at the top of my condition." He called it his "body-keeping" to be maintained if he were to stay fit or even alive (1922, pp. xii–xvii).

Hall modeled ways to tackle the dilemmas of aging as he sorted through his physical goods, discarding some things, saving others. Very difficult was the sorting of his library as he faced the "frustration of activities once thought possible but which now seemed to be no longer so. . . . This riddance of the residue of superfluous printed matter is not unlike anti-fat regimens, which are disagreeable but strengthening" (p. xviii). Even as he did these sometimes onerous chores, he observed that such breaks with the past "have a certain insurance value not only against ultra-conservatism but against the inveterate tendency of the old to hark back to past stages of life." Part of his sorting, synthesizing, and confronting, was the writing of his autobiography—an enterprise he encouraged because it helped him to advance "my understanding of the one I know best of all," an enterprise that constitutes a pleasant and useful service older people "can render to themselves and perhaps their posterity and friends, if not to the world at large."

In this manner Hall named old age "a stage of development in which the passions of youth and the efforts of a life career" reach fruition and consolidation; a period of life that brings "a certain maturity of judgment about men, things, causes and life generally, that nothing in the world but years can bring, a real wisdom that only age can teach" (1922, p. 366).

A real wisdom that only age can teach: Those words suggest what B. F. Skinner calls "knowledge by experience," and which he contrasts with "knowledge by description:"

Philosophers distinguish between knowledge by acquaintance and knowledge by description. Readers of this book will find a little of each. I have been acquainted with old age for a good many years, and Dr. Vaughan knows very well how it has been described. Much of what follows, in part from my paper on intellectual self-management, describes my own solutions to the problem of growing old. The rest, primarily the contribution of Dr. Vaughan, is a selection from the literature on aging. (1983, p. 15)

Skinner's words and ideas take us from the abstract wisdoms that can be gleaned from our elders to those which deal very directly with the practical.

PRACTICAL WISDOMS FOR AGING

Burrhus Frederic Skinner, better known as B.F. Skinner, died August 18, 1990 after a distinguished career in psychology. Just a week before he died, he was awarded a "Citation for Outstanding Lifetime Contribution to Psychology," which was unprecedented in the 99-year history of the American Psychological Association. I cite these facts because they affirm one man's active, continuing contribution to his profession. Though some will disagree with his assertions, most will honor him for what he accomplished and contributed to the field of psychology.

Here I honor Skinner for his active joustings with the unique challenges of his own aging; for being very candid in sharing personal techniques that helped him offset some of his emerging physiological limitations, techniques that helped him to continue his intellectual work. He summarized many of these suggestions in a paper, "Intellectual Self-Management in Old Age," presented to the American Psychological Association in August 1982 (Skinner, March, 1983). Because of his strong theoretical orientation he chose to look at his own aging through the processes of the behavioral and the environmental rather than the abstract and the introspective. In doing this he was able to give some very helpful suggestions for the practical and the mundane in our negotiations with age.

Skinner emphasized our need for a *"prosthetic environment* in which, in spite of reduced biological capacities, behavior will be relatively free of aversive consequences and abundantly reinforced" (March, 1983, p. 239). Each of us will enhance aging, therefore, by attending to all that goes on around us in making our surroundings as supportive as possible. (And those around us are encouraged to support *us*.) Then he speaks of all the little steps we can take in adjusting to possible memory loss, to increasing fatigue, to possible tendencies to pad our verbiage (remember that Skinner was defining his own problems). In making suggestions, Skinner is delightfully candid in a manner quite revealing of his own wrestling with limitation: If preparing a paper, "read relevant material and reread what you have written." Keep reference books within easy reach. Be content with fewer good working hours a day. "You will do much better if you speak only simple sentences." Be alert for "fatigued verbal behavior" that is "full of cliches, inexact descriptions, poorly composed sentences, borrowed sentences, memorized quotations, and Shakespeare's 'wise saws'" (p. 241). (And aren't these good suggestions for any age?)

In his presentation Skinner encouraged the reading of good literature that reinforces the reader in sustaining invested interest for longer and longer periods of time without requiring the quick reinforcement that cheap literature may provice. He also encouraged the senior scholar: "If your achievements as a thinker have been spaced on a favorable schedule, you will have no difficulty in remaining active even though current achievements are spaced far apart. Like the hooked gambler, you will enjoy your life as a thinker in spite of the negative utility" (p. 243).

B.F. Skinner and gerontologist M.E. Vaughan expanded this paper into the book, *Enjoy Old Age: A Program of Self-Management* (1983). I call this book wise as it mixes the behavioral and the poetic, that which is both operationally defined and that which can be called philosophical. Even though Skinner objected to the cognitive and the nonbehavioral, he did acknowledge differing types of knowledge and language:

In every field of science there are two languages. The astronomer speaks one when he tells his children that after the sun has gone down, the stars will come out; he speaks another to his colleagues. . . . Students of behavior also speak two languages and are much more often misunderstood when they do. Everyday English is suffused with terms that have come down to us from ancient ways of explaining human action. They cannot be used in any kind of rigorous science, but they are often effective in casual discourse. (p. 15)

(Remember Erikson's choice of less precise, less easily operationalized language because he believed that the "everyday words of living languages, ripened in the usage of generations, will serve best as means of discourse" (1961, p. 151).

Before leaving Skinner and Vaughn's treatise on aging, I share a few more of their suggestions: What to do when memory fails? Hang the umbrella on the front door knob and accept the challenge to actively work with the memory problem. What to do about failing eyesight? Explore books of larger type, use brighter light bulbs. What to do to reduce common annoyances? Use a small cart for carrying things, make certain rooms are warmer and clothing heavier, install a door opener. In other words, "Attack old age as a problem to be solved":

- In particular, we are not exhorting you to enjoy old age by an act of will. You must be *inclined* to act in enjoyable ways. (p. 36)
- Learning to pace yourself as an old thinker may, in fact, give you an advantage over impetuous youth. A measured pace is advisable at any age. (p. 66)
- Old age is rather like fatigue, except that you cannot correct it by relaxing or taking a vacation. (p. 69)
- We recover from fatigue when we are at leisure, but the extent of the recovery depends upon what we do. (p. 71)

In the last chapter of this interesting little book, Skinner and Vaughn give us a brief treatise on the "grandeur and exquisiteness of old age." (This is indeed poetic, philosophical language from a behaviorist psychologist!) The authors write that the "wisdom valued most in old people concerns old age itself. If you are really enjoying your life in spite of imperfections, you may find yourself an authority. People will come to you to learn your secret, and you would be churlish not to divulge it" (pp. 145–146). Isn't that what we want—our elders at the conference table? I find that thought encouraging.

But some would object to Skinner's naming of techniques for old age. Max Lerner certainly did not agree with Skinner when he wrote a "responding credo" to Skinner's APA lecture with the title, "Sorry Skinner— It's All in Your Mind" (1982). Or when he wrote this statement in 1990:

Too many life-course thinkers—Jung was a notable exception—got caught on the spike of aging and let some of the most fruitful years pass by with hardly a nod. One could understand this in Skinner, a stern behaviorist who disbelieved in anything that smacked of subjectivism. But I felt it important, while asserting the aging revolution, to recognize the stirring changes taking place in the consciousness of Western societies, and redraw the lines of division in order to celebrate the last half of the journey. (Lerner, 1990, p. 153)

What Lerner has written is an important point/counterpoint reminder that no statement about aging can speak to all of us; that no summary of approaches or conditions can summarize what is an extremely individual process for each one of us. In reading these contrasting statements, my choice is to learn some helpful behavioral lessons from Skinner even as I listen to the more encompassing conceptual message from Lerner. As I do this I will continue to follow my subjectivist path that honors the creative power of the human mind and spirit.

FURTHER WISDOMS

These explorations of the practical and the possible are joined by another set of wisdoms, this time from *Senatus*, published by the South African Council for the Aged, June 1974. This little essay is a communication from one group of elders to others around the world.

We should not belittle ourselves. Every elderly person has years of achievement at his back—success, yes and failure too, joy and sorrow, learning and doing, and crowning all, a store of wisdom that only the living of a life can bestow.

. . . we form a unique section of present society. The only part that has knowledge of the great span of life, and therefore an obligation to contribute in greater measure to a fuller understanding to those around us of what it is all about. (*Senatus*, 1974)

Let us then be alert to the fact that the responsibility for the acceptance of the older person has become squarely placed on his own shoulders and he must now become the architect of a new understanding of his role in today's society.

Then these seniors offer a listing that is very much concerned with an attention to and a caring for others:

1. Speak to people.
2. Smile at people.
3. Call people by name.
4. Be friendly and helpful.
5. Be cordial.
6. Be genuinely interested in people.
7. Be generous with praise — cautious with criticism.
8. Be considerate with the feelings of others.
9. Be alert to give service. What counts most in life is what we do for others.
10. Add to this a good sense of humor, a big dose of patience, and a dash of humility and you will be rewarded.

For some, that recipe for age may seem simplistic — and for others, certainly not. What it represents for me is a summation of the small gestures of everyday life that can make people's lives just a little bit easier, just a little bit more satisfying — a summation that comes from a group of wise elders from another culture, from another part of our world.

These suggestions make me think of a wise older man whom I met in the Still Life Cafe in the Fremont District of Seattle. He sat there quietly in the middle of the coffee house, amid the mix of people and conversation and then leaned across to ask me if these people represented the style of many younger people in Seattle. I looked around at the jeans, the long skirts, the boots, the long hair, the curious juxtaposition with those in business suits, obviously on their lunch hour from surrounding neighborhoods. Then I thought of the "punk" style of the University District just a few blocks away. He was making me think and look in a new way — not surprising when I discovered that he had been in the theatrical world most of his life and had acquired a learned attention to behavior and style.

The words that came next struck me even more. He spoke of a continuing investment in life, of his interests in many areas, of his living in the now of everyday stimulation and activity. But then he sadly acknowledged that many of his friends were dying, leaving him more alone as he grew older. A solution? "Diversify, diversify," was his pointed suggestion. I carry his words and his image with me as further reminder that in the widening of our minds, of our interests, of our investments in new activities, in the fostering of new cross-generational friendships and contacts, we can be alive to the moment in the manner he modeled so effectively.

Final Thoughts

I return now to some final thoughts about the creative and the spiritual—of the dynamic interactions of the tangible and the intangible, the applied and the abstract, of that which we can know directly and of that which we can never know. These translations confront our "somethings under the sun," our grapplings with freedoms born of limits. These processes also take us back into the mysterious, into the unknowable, into the paradox that even as we gain solution we will never find solution.

To bring these dialectics into some sort of closing order, I turn to two creative artists whose combining of the creative and the spiritual keep them in the "sacred present." Even though they are in their 80s they don't speak or write of age in their interviews and creative expressions. Rather, they address organic, living processes which they have integrated into their own expressions not only of the artistic but of life.

In an interview for *The Seattle Times/Seattle Post-Intelligencer's* "Guide to Senior Activities" supplement, Northwest sculptor James Washington Jr. spoke from his 80th year. At that time, he saw his work progressing as it incorporated universal symbols into stone "to get people to think." If they think, he believed, they just might stumble across their own spirituality. Not worried about his own physical problems, Washington saw the human being incorporating three natures: physical, mental, and spiritual. "Without the spirit the other two simply are not enough." "Whatever you do mentally or physically—whether writing or sculpting—you must be able to breathe spirit into it so that it becomes yourself objectified." *Yourself objectified!* Is that what this aging is about? Possibly so.

Consider the wisdom of architect and artist, George Nakashima, born in Spokane, Washington, in 1905. Named 1990 *Alumnus Summa Laude Dignatus* by the University of Washington, this man set forth his philosophy in his 1981 book, *The Soul of a Tree*—a philosophy of organic unfolding, of quiet rhythms of life and matter, of a deep respect for the integrity of the creative material, of an allowing of a process that incorporates "natural edges, knots, and other deformities into the finished product."

After internment during World War II as "Americans of Japanese descent," Nakashima and his family settled into a secluded 35-acre compound in New Hope, Pennsylvania. There, living a life of his own design, he has continued his architectural work and his crafting of unique pieces of furniture which incorporate rare and often ancient logs and roots from around the world. With a deep respect for the integrity of his materials, Mr. Nakashima allows the shape, color, and grain of these beautiful woods to guide him to the finished forms.

Through decades of effort he has designed buildings and crafted pieces of furniture "which grace private homes and public buildings, both sacred and secular around the world" (University of Washington 1990 commencement program).

In his book Nakashima writes:

There was no other way for me but to go alone, secure with my family, placing stone upon stone, seeking kinship with each piece of wood, eventually creating an inward mood of space, then bit by bit finding peace and joy in shaping timber into objects of utility and perhaps, when nature smiles, beauty. (Nakashima, 1981, p. 194)

Those simple, carefully chosen words suggest metaphors for creative aging—metaphors not linked to any age stage but to the ongoing processes of naming and creating ourselves. If we can just allow the "stone upon stone"—if we can just embrace the unfolding emergence of who and what we are.

Which affirms for me once again how much we can gain by selecting those wisdoms that are appropriate to us and by honoring those who have shared them with us. Perhaps we can return our elders to the conference table, perhaps we can give them a contemporary reframing as our "wise ones." Whatever position we take, by studying *wisdom* we gather *wisdoms* and internalize *wisdoms*—a journey from that which we can only observe from the outside to that which is uniquely ours.

REFERENCES

Achenbaum, W. Andrew, & Levin, Jeffrey S. (1989). What does gerontology mean? *The Gerontologist, 29,* 3, 393–400.

Adams, James (1979). *Conceptual blockbusting: A guide to better ideas.* New York: Norton.

Adams, James (1986). *The care and feeding of ideas: A guide to encouraging creativity.* Menlo Park, CA: Addison-Wesley.

Adelman, R.C. (1988). Editorial. *Journal of Gerontology, 43,* 81–82.

Adler, Alfred (1958). *What life should mean to you.* New York: Capricorn Books.

Adler, Alfred (1969). *The science of living.* Garden City, NY: Doubleday/Anchor Books.

Adorno, T., Frenkel-Brunswik, E., Levinson, D., & Sanford, R.N. (1950). *The authoritarian personality.* New York: Harper.

Alexander, C., Langer, E., Newman, R., Chandler, H., & Davies, J. (1989). Transcendental meditation, mindfulness and longevity: An experimental study with the elderly. *Journal of Personality and Social Psychology, 57*(6), 950–964.

Allport, Gordon (1935). Attitudes. In C.C. Murchison (Ed.), *A handbook of social psychology.* Worcester, MA: Clark University Press.

Allport, Gordon (1955a). The general and the unique in psychological science. *Journal of Personality, 30,* 405–422.

Allport, Gordon W. (1955b). *Becoming: Basic considerations for a psychology of personality.* New Haven, CT: Yale University Press.

Allport, Gordon W. (1962). Psychological models for guidance. *Harvard Educational Review, 32*(4), 373–381.

Allport, Gordon W. (1968). *The person in psychology: Selected essays.* Boston: Beacon Press.

Allport, Gordon W. (1979). *The nature of prejudice* (special ed.). Menlo Park, CA: Addison Wesley.

Alvarez, Julia, & Oldham, Pamolu (1979). *Old age ain't for sissies*. Cameron, NC: Crane's Creek Press.

Amabile, Teresa M. (1989). *Growing up creative: Nurturing a lifetime of creativity*. New York: Crown.

American Association for Retired Persons (1986). *Truth about aging: Guidelines for accurate communications*. Washington, DC: AARP, Special Projects Section Program Department.

American Association for Retired Persons (1988). *A profile of older Americans*. Researched and compiled by Donald G. Fowles. Washington, DC: AARP.

American Association for Retired Persons (1989). AARP educational and community service programs. Washington, DC: AARP.

Ansley, Helen (1990). *Life's finishing school: What now? What next?* Sausalito, CA: Institute of Noetic Sciences.

Antonovsky, Aaron (1979). *Health, stress and coping*. San Francisco: Jossey-Bass.

Antonovsky, Aaron (1988). *Unraveling the mystery of health*. San Francisco: Jossey-Bass.

Antonovsky, Aaron, & Sagy, Shifra (1990). Confronting developmental tasks in the retirement transition. *The Gerontologist, 30*(3), 362–368.

Arieti, Silvano (1976). *Creativity: The magic synthesis*. New York: Basic Books.

Arluke, Arnold, & Levin, Jack (1984, August). Another stereotype: Old age as a second childhood. *Aging*, Article 12, U.S. Dept. of Health, Education and Welfare, 73–77.

Ashmore, Richard D., & Del Boca, Frances K. (1981). Conceptual approaches to stereotypes and stereotyping. In D.L. Hamilton (Ed.), *Cognitive processes in stereotyping and intergroup behavior* (pp. 1–35). Hillsdale, NJ: Lawrence Erlbaum Associates.

Astin, Alexander W. (1977). *Four critical years*. San Francisco: Jossey-Bass.

Atchley, Robert C. (1971). Retirement and leisure participation: Continuity or crisis. *Gerontologist, 11*, 13–17.

Atchley, Robert C. (1972). *The social forces in later life: An introduction to social gerontology*. Belmont, CA: Wadsworth.

Atchley, Robert C. (1983). *Aging: Continuity and change*. Belmont, CA: Wadsworth Publishing.

Atchley, Robert C. (1989). A continuity theory of normal aging. *The Gerontologist, 29*, 183–190.

Axford, Roger W. (1983). *Successful recareering: How to shift gears before you're over the hill*. Lincoln, NE: Media Productions & Marketing.

Baltes, Paul B., & Brim, Orville G. Jr. (Eds.). (1982). *Life-span development and behavior*. New York: Academic Press.

Baltimore Longitudinal Study of Aging (1989). *Older and wiser*. Washington, DC: NIH Publication No. 89-2797.

Barrett, James H. (1972). *Gerontological psychology*. Springfield, IL: Charles C. Thomas.

Barron, Frank (1963). *Creativity and psychological health: Origins of personal vitality and creative freedom*. Princeton, NJ: D. Van Nostrand Co.

Barron, Frank (1979). *The shaping of personality: Conflict, choice, and growth*. New York: Harper & Row.

Barron, Frank (1988). Putting creativity to work. In R.J. Sternberg (Ed.), *The nature of creativity: Contemporary psychological perspectives*, pp. 76–98.

Barron, F., & Harrington, D. (1981). Creativity, intelligence, and personality. In M.R. Rosenzweig & L.W. Rorter (Eds.), *Annual review of psychology* (Vol. 32, pp. 439–476). Palo Alto, CA: Annual Reviews.

Basseches, Michael (1984). *Dialectical thinking and adult development*. Norwood, NJ: Ablex Publishing.

Beck, Aaron T. (1967/1978). *Depression: Causes and treatment*. Philadelphia: University of Pennsylvania Press.

Becker, Ernest (1973). *The denial of death*. New York: Free Press.

Bedrosian, R.C., & Beck, A.T. (1980). Principles of cognitive therapy. In Michael Mahoney (Ed.), *Psychotherapy process.* New York: Plenum Press.

Beisser, Arnold (1989). *Flying without wings: Personal reflections on being disabled.* New York: Doubleday.

Beisser, Arnold (1990). *A graceful passage: Notes on the freedom to live or die.* New York: Doubleday.

Bellah, R.N., Madsen, R., Sullivan, W.M., Swidler, A., & Tipton, S.M. (1985). *Habits of the heart: Individualism and commitment in American life.* Berkeley: The University of California Press.

Bengston, Vern L., & Schaie, K. Warner (Eds.). (1989). *The course of later life: Research and reflections.* New York: Springer.

Benson, Herbert (1987). *Your maximum mind.* New York: Avon Books.

Berman, Phillip L. (Ed.). (1986). *The courage of conviction.* New York: Ballantine.

Berman, Phillip L. (Ed.). (1989). *The courage to grow old.* New York: Ballantine.

Bianchi, Eugene C. (1982). *Aging as a spiritual journey.* New York: The Crossroad Publishing Co.

Birren, James E. (1983). Aging in America: Roles for psychology. *American Psychologist,* 38(3), 298–299.

Birren, James E. (1985). Age, competence, creativity, and wisdom. In R.N. Butler & H.P. Gleason (Eds.), *Productive aging: Enhancing vitality in later life.* New York: Springer.

Birren, James E. (1988). Aging as a counterpart of development. In J.E. Birren & V.L. Bengston (Eds.), *Emergent theories in aging.* New York: Springer.

Birren, James, & Cunningham, Walter (1985). Research on the psychology of aging: Principles, concepts, and theory. In James Birren & K. Warner Schaie (Eds.), *Handbook of the psychology of aging* (2nd ed., pp. 3–34). New York: Van Nostrand Reinhold.

Birren, James E., & Schaie, K. Warner (Eds.). (1985). *Handbook of the psychology of aging* (2nd ed.). New York: Van Nostrand Reinhold.

Bischof, Ledford J. (1976). *Adult psychology.* New York: Harper & Row.

Blank, Thomas O. (1982). *A social psychology of developing adults.* New York: Wiley.

Blau, Zena Smith (1973). *Old age in a changing society.* New York: New Viewpoints.

Bogdonoff, Morton D., M.C. (1969, December 4). People need "date with tomorrow," says doctor. *The Seattle Times.*

Bortz, E.L. (1954). New goals for maturity. *Journal of Gerontology, 9,* 67–73.

Bosmajian, Haig A. (1983). *The language of oppression.* Lanham, MD: University Press of America.

Botwinick, Jack (1984). *Aging and behavior* (3rd ed.). New York: Springer.

Boulding, Kenneth (1985). *The world as a total system.* Beverly Hills, CA: Sage Publications.

Brandt, Ellen (1990, June). Witnesses to a century. *Highways,* 26–28.

Brewi, Janice, & Brennan, Anne (1982). *Mid-life: Psychological and spiritual perspectives.* New York: The Crossroad Publishing Co.

Breytspraak, Linda M. (1983). Toward a conceptual framework for analysis of the development of the self in the later years. In Patricia Morrow (Ed.), *The meanings of old age: A collection of papers on humanities and aging* (pp. 147–158). Columbia, MO: Missouri Gerontology Institute, University of Missouri/Columbia.

Bridges, William (1980). *Transitions: Making sense of life's changes.* Menlo Park, CA: Addison Wesley.

Brim, Orville G. Jr., & Abeles, Ronald P. (1975). Work and personality in the middle years. *Items: Social Science Research Council, 29,* 3, 29–33.

Brockman, Elin S., & Hales, Dianne (1990, June). Women who make a difference. *Family Circle,* 15–17.

Brown, Robert McAfee (1980, September). Making friends with time. In *A.D.,* pp. 16, 18.

Browning, Don S. (1972). *Generative man: Psychoanalytic perspectives.* Philadelphia: Westminster Press.

Brunner, Jerome (1986). *Actual minds, possible words.* Cambridge, MA: Harvard University Press.

Bryer, Kathleen B. (1979). The Amish way of death: A study of family support systems. *American Psychologist, 34*(3), 255–261.

Buber, Martin (1965). *Between man and man.* New York: Collier.

Buhler, Charlotte (1969). Loneliness in maturity. *Journal of Humanistic Psychology, 9*(2), 167–181.

Buhler, Charlotte (1977). Meaningfulness of the biographical approach. In L.R. Allman & D.T. Jaffe (Eds.), *Readings in adult psychology: Contemporary perspectives.* New York: Harper & Row.

Buhler, Charlotte, & Massarik, Fred (Eds.). (1968). *The course of human life: A study of goals in the humanistic perspective.* New York: Springer.

Buie, James (1988, October). "Me" decades generate depression. *APA Monitor, 19*(10), 18.

Bullock, Allan & Stallybrass, Oliver (Eds.). (1977). *The Harper dictionary of modern thought.* New York: Harper & Row.

Burdman, Geral Dene Mair, & Brewer, Ruth M. (1978). *Health aspects of aging.* Portland, OR: A Continuing Education Book.

Burson, Nancy (1990, July). Final days. *New Woman,* 68–71.

Butler, Robert N. (1968). The life review: An interpretation of reminiscence in the aged. In B. Neugarten (Ed.), *Middle age and aging.* Chicago: University of Chicago Press.

Butler, Robert N. (1970). Looking forward to what? The life review, legacy, and excessive identity versus change. In Ethel Shanas (Ed.), *Aging in contemporary society.* Beverly Hills, CA: Sage.

Butler, Robert N. (1971, December). Age: The life review. *Psychology Today, 5*(7), 49, 51, 89.

Butler, Robert N. (1975). *Why survive? Being old in America.* New York: Harper & Row.

Butler, Robert N. (1977, March). Coping with the midlife crisis. *Dynamic Maturity, 12*(2), 11–14.

Butler, Robert N. (1980). Ageism: A foreword. *Journal of Social Issues, 36*(2), 8–11.

Butler, Robert N. (1983). Aging, research on aging, and national policy: A conversation with Robert Butler. *American Psychologist, 38*(3), 300–307.

Butler, Robert N., & Gleason, Herbert P. (Eds.). (1985). *Productive aging: Enhancing vitality in later life.* New York: Springer.

Butler, Robert, & Lewis, Myrna (1976). *Love and sex after sixty.* New York: Harper & Row.

Butler, Robert, & Lewis, Myrna (1982). *Aging and mental health: Positive psychosocial and biomedical approaches* (3rd ed.). St. Louis, MO: C.V. Mosby.

Butterfield-Picard, Helen, & Magno, Josefina B. (1982). Hospice the adjective, not the noun: The future of a national priority. *American Psychologist, 37*(11), 1254–1259.

Bytheway, B., Keil, T., Allatt, P., & Bryman, A. (Eds.). (1989). *Becoming and being old: Sociological approaches to later life.* London: Sage.

Campbell, Joseph (1988). *The power of myth.* New York: Doubleday.

Caplan, G. (1964). *Principles of preventive psychiatry.* New York: Basic Books.

Capps, Donald, Capps, Walter H., & Bradford, M. Gerald (Eds.). (1977). *Encounter with Erikson: Historical interpretation and religious biography.* Santa Barbara, CA: Scholars Press.

Carlsen, Mary L.B. (1973). A four-year retrospective view of the educational experience of a group of mature women undergraduate students (Doctoral dissertation, University of Washington). *Dissertations Abstracts International, 35*(1), 153A.

Carlsen, Mary Baird (1988). *Meaning-making: Therapeutic processes in adult development.* New York: Norton.

Charme, Stuart L. (1984). *Meaning and myth in the study of lives: A Sartrean perspective.* Philadelphia: University of Pennsylvania Press.

Choron, J. (1964). *Modern man and mortality*. New York: Macmillan.

Cicero, Marcus Tullius (1909). Treatise on old age. (E.S. Shuckburg, Trans.). In C.W. Eliot (Ed.), *The Harvard Classics* (Vol. 9). New York: P.F. Collier & Sons.

Clayton, Vivian (1975). Erikson's theory of human development as it applies to the aged: Wisdom as contradictive cognition. *Human Development, 18*:119–128.

Cliffe, Martha (1982). Erikson links stages of infancy, old age. *APA Monitor, 13*(6), 7.

Coatsworth, Elizabeth (1976). *Personal geography*. Boston: Stephen Green Press.

Cohler, Bertam J. (1982). Personal narrative and life course. In Paul B. Baltes & Orville G. Brim, Jr. (Eds.), *Life-span development and behavior* (Vol. 4, pp. 205–241). New York: Academic Press.

Colarusso, Calvin A., & Nemiroff, Robert A. (1981). *Adult development: A new dimension in psychodynamic theory and practice*. New York: Plenum Press.

Cole, T.R., & Ellor, J.W. (1990). Editorial statement. *Generations, 14*(4), 4–5.

Cole, Elbert C. (1989). Elements of a model ministry by, with and for older adults in the congregations. Unpublished paper, adaptation of work by Paul Maves. Kansas City, MO: Shepherd's Centers of America.

Coleman, Barbara (1988, October). Dubious protection: Guardianship under fire. *AARP News Bulletin, 29*(9), 2, 15.

Coles, Robert (1970). *Erik H. Erikson: The growth of his work*. Boston: Little, Brown.

Coles, Robert (1988, May). Our time for giving. *50-Plus, 88.*

Comfort, Alex (1976). *A good age*. New York: Crown Publishers.

Cooper, John Charles (1975). *Fantasy and the human spirit*. New York: Seabury Press.

Costa, Paul T. Jr., McCrae, R.R., & Arenberg, D. (1983). Recent longitudinal research on personality and aging. In K. Warner Schaie (Ed.), *Longitudinal studies of adult development*. New York: Guilford.

Crystal, John, & Bolles, Richard (1974). *Where do I go from here with my life?* Berkeley, CA: Ten Speed Press.

Curtin, Sharon R. (1972). *Nobody ever died of old age*. Boston: Little, Brown.

Davidson, Glen W. (1984). *Understanding mourning: A guide for those who grieve*. Minneapolis, MN: Augsburg Publishing.

Deits, Bob (1988). *Life after loss: A personal guide dealing with death, divorce, job change and relocation*. Tucson, AZ: Fisher Books.

Disabled Independent Gardeners Association (1989). Brochure describing their services. 1632 Sutherland Avenue, North Vancouver, B.C., Canada V7L 4B7.

Donahue, W., Hunter, W.W., Coons, D.H., & Maurice, H. (Eds.). (1958). *Free time: Challenge to later maturity*. Ann Arbor: University of Michigan.

Downs, Hugh, & Roll, Richard (1981). *The best years book: How to plan for fulfillment, security, and happiness in the retirement years*. New York: Delacorte Press.

Dumont, R.G. & Foss, D.C. (1972). *The American view of death*. Cambridge, MA: Schenkman Publishing Co.

Dychtwald, Ken, & Flower, Joe (1989). *Age wave: The challenges and opportunities of an aging America*. Los Angeles: Jeremy P. Tarcher.

Eastman, Peggy (1989, April). America's "other drug problem" overwhelms thousands, experts say. *AARP News Bulletin, 30*(4), 1–3.

Edwards, Beverly (1990, August). "Whiz kids:" The Computer Sams prove that bits and bytes are not just for the Nintendo generation. *Highways, 24*(8), 48–50.

Efran, J. S., Lukens, R. J., & Lukens, M. D. (1988, September/October). Constructivism: What's in it for you? *The Family Therapy Networker, 12*(5), 26–35.

Eisdorfer, Carl (1974). The role of the psychiatrist in successful aging. In Eric Pfeiffer (Ed.), *Successful aging*. Durham, NC: Center for the Study of Aging and Human Development, Duke University.

Eisdorfer, Carl (1983). Conceptual models of aging: The challenge of a new frontier. *American Psychologist, 38*(2), 197–202.

Eisdorfer, Carl, & Cohen, Donna (1984). *The loss of self*. New York: New American Library.

Eisler, Riane (1987). *The chalice and the blade*. San Francisco: Harper & Row.

Ellison, Jerome (1978). *Life's second half: The pleasures of aging*. Old Greenwich, CT: The Devin-Adair Co.

Ellor, James W. (1990). On knowing in gerontology. *Generations, 14*(4), 5–6.

Embler, Weller (1966). *Metaphor and meaning*. DeLand, FL: Everett/Edwards, Inc.

Erikson, Erik (1961). The roots of virtue. In J. Huxley (Ed.), *The humanist frame*, pp. 147–165. New York: Harper & Brothers.

Erikson, Erik H. (1963). *Childhood and society* (2nd ed.). New York: Norton.

Erikson, Erik (1968). *Identity, youth and crisis*. New York: Norton.

Erikson, Erik (1974). *Dimensions of a new identity*. New York: Norton.

Erikson, Erik (1978). *Adulthood*. New York: Norton.

Erikson, E.H., & Erikson, J.M. (1978). Introduction: Reflections on aging. In S. Spiker, K. Woodward, & D. Van Tassel (Eds.), *Aging and the elderly. Humanistic perspectives in gerontology*. Atlantic Heights, NJ: Humanities Press.

Erikson, E.H., Erikson, J.M., & Kivnick, H.Q. (1986). *Vital involvement in old age: The experience of old age in our time*. New York: Norton.

Erikson, Joan M. (1988). *Wisdom and the senses: The way of creativity*. New York: Norton.

Esposito, Joseph L. (1987). *The obsolete self: Philosophical dimensions of aging*. Berkeley: University of California Press.

Estes, Carroll L., & Binney, Elizabeth A. (1989). The biomedicalization of aging: Dangers and dilemmas. *The Gerontologist, 29*(5), 587–596.

Feifel, Herman (Ed.). (1959). *The meaning of death*. New York: McGraw-Hill.

Feifel, Herman (Ed.). (1977). *New meanings of death*. New York: McGraw-Hill.

Feinstein, David, & Krippner, Stanley (1988). *Personal mythology: The psychology of your evolving self*. Los Angeles: Tarcher.

Feldman, David (1980). *Beyond universals to cognitive development*. Norwood, NJ: Ablex Publishing.

Fenell, David (1988, October). Long-term marriages and new marriages: Comparing perceptions. Workshop presented at AAMFT Convention, New Orleans, LA.

50 Plus Magazine (1981). Leisure and your retirement. New York: Retirement Living Publishing Co., Inc.

Fingarette, Herbert (1962, Fall). On the relation between moral guilt and guilt in neurosis. *Journal of Humanistic Psychology, 2*(1), 75–89.

Fingarette, Herbert (1963). *Self in transformation*. New York: Basic Books.

Fisher, Kathleen (1985). Aging called developmental stage as researchers honor Institute. *APA Monitor, 16*(7), 12.

Fisher, Kathleen (1986, January). Demographics beckon young to maturing field. *APA Monitor, 18*, 19.

Flanagan, J.D. (1978). A research approach to improving our quality of life. *American Psychologist, 33*(22), 138–147.

Fowler, James W. (1984). *Becoming adult, becoming Christian: Adult development and Christian faith*. San Francisco: Harper & Row.

Fowler, James, & Keen, Sam (1978). *Life maps: Conversations on the journey of faith*. Waco, TX: Word Books.

Frankl, Viktor (1969). *The will to meaning*. New York: World Publishing Co.

Freedman, Richard (1978). Sufficiently decayed: Gerontophobia in English literature. In S. F. Spicker et al. (Eds.), *Aging and the elderly: Humanistic perspectives in gerontology*. Atlantic Heights, NJ: Humanities Press.

Friedan, Betty (1985). The mystique of age. In R.N. Butler & V.P. Gleason (Eds.), *Productive aging*. New York: Springer.

Friedman, Maurice (1972). *Touchstones of reality: Existential trust and the community of peace*. New York: Dutton & Co.

Friedman, Maurice (1985a). Healing through meeting and the problematic of mutuality. *Journal of Humanistic Psychology, 25*(1), 7–40.

Friedman, Maurice (1985b). *The healing dialogue in psychotherapy*. New York: Jason Aronson.

Frijda, Nico H. (1988, May). The laws of emotion. *American Psychologist, 43*(5), 349–358.

Gardner, John W. (1964). *Self-renewal: The individual and the innovative society*. New York: Harper & Row.

Gardner, Howard (1982). *Art, mind, and brain: A cognitive approach to creativity*. New York: Basic Books.

Gatz, Margaret, & Pearson, Cynthia G. (1988). Ageism revised and the provision of psychological services. *American Psychologist, 43*(3), 184–188.

Gatz, M., Popkin, S.J., Pino, C.D., & VandenBos, G.R. (1985). Psychological interventions with older adults. In J.E. Birren & K.W. Schaie (Eds.), *Handbook of the psychology of aging* (2nd ed.). New York: Van Nostrand Reinhold.

Genevay, Bonnie (1979). Ties that bind: The aging family and treatment. *Family Therapy, 3*(4), 16–17.

Ghiselin, B. (1955). *The creative process*. New York: Mentor.

Gilmore, Susan (1989, August). Hey neighbor! *The Seattle Times/Seattle Post-Intelligencer*, 6–14, 25.

Ginzberg, Eli (1968). *Manpower agenda for America*. New York: McGraw-Hill.

Goldman, Connie (1985). *I'm too busy to talk now: Conversations with American artists over 70*. Washington, DC: Connie Goldman Productions.

Goldman, Connie (1987). I'm too busy to talk now: Conversations with creative people over 70. Washington, DC: Connie Goldman Productions.

Goldman, Connie (1988). *Late bloomer: Stories of successful aging*. An informational inspirational cassette and booklet based on the Late Bloomer radio series. Fairfax Station, VA: Connie Goldman Productions.

Goldman, Freda H. (1965). *A turning to take next: Alternative goals in the education of women*. Boston: Center for the Study of Liberal Education for Adults, Boston University.

Goodman, Lisl Marburg (1981). *Death and the creative life: Conversations with prominent artists and scientists*. New York: Springer.

Greer, Kate (1988, November). What's happening to American families. *Better Homes & Gardens*.

Grollman, Earl A. (Ed.). (1974). *Concerning death: A practical guide for the living*. Boston: Beacon Press.

Gross, Ronald (1982). *The independent scholar's handbook: How to turn your interest in any subject into expertise*. Reading, MA: Addison-Wesley.

Gruber, Howard (1984). Preface. In M. Basseches, *Dialectical thinking and adult development*. Norwood, NJ: Ablex.

Hadley, Robert G., & Brodwin, Martin G. (1988, November). Point of view: Language about people with disabilities. *Journal of Counseling and Development, 67*(3), 147–149.

Hall, G. Stanley (1922). *Senescence: The last half of life*. New York: Appleton & Co.

Hansson, Robert (1989). Old age: Testing the parameters of social psychological assumptions. In S. Spacapan & S. Oskamp (Eds.), *The social psychology of aging*. Newbury Park, CA: Sage.

Harris, Diana K. (1988). *Dictionary of gerontology*. New York: Greenwood Press.

Harris, L., & associates (1975, 1981). *The myth and reality of aging in America*. Washington, DC: The National Council on Aging.

Havighurst, Robert J. (1972). *Developmental tasks and education* (3rd ed.). New York: David McKay.

Hawthorne, Maggie (1977, August 26). Skelton his own best audience. *Seattle Post-Intelligencer*.

Heilbrun, Carolyn (1988). *Writing a woman's life*. New York: Norton.

Henig, Robin Marantz (1985). *The myth of senility: The truth about the brain and aging*. Washington, DC: American Association of Retired Persons.

Holmes, T.H., & Rahe, R.H. (1967). The social readjustment rating scale. *Journal of Psychosomatic Research, 11,* 213–218.

Hommell, Penelope A. (1989, April/May). House aging committee releases first guardianship standards. *The Aging Connection,* p. 1.

Hooyman, Nancy (1986). *Take care: Supporting older people and their families.* New York: Free Press.

Howe, Reuel L. (1962). *The creative years.* Greenwich, CT: Seabury Press.

Howe, Reuel L. (1963). *The miracle of dialogue.* New York: Seabury Press.

Janis, Irving L. et al. (1969/1971). *Stress and frustration.* New York: Harcourt, Brace, Jovanovich.

Jung, Carl (1960). The stages of life. *The collected works of C.G. Jung* (Vol. 8). Princeton, NJ: Princeton University Press.

Jung, Carl (1963). *Memories, dreams, reflections.* New York: Pantheon Books.

Kahn, R.L. (1975). The mental health system and the future aged. *Gerontologist, 15,* 24–31.

Kalish, Richard A. (1979). The new ageism and the failure models: A polemic. *The Gerontologist, 19*(4), 398–402.

Kalish, Richard A. (1985). *Death, grief, and caring relationships* (2nd ed.). Monterey, CA: Brooks/Cole Publishing Co.

Kane, Rosalie A. (1989). The biomedical blues. *The Gerontologist, 29*(5), 583–584.

Karp, David A. (1988). A decade of reminders: Changing age consciousness between fifty and sixty years old. *The Gerontologist, 28*(6), 727–738.

Kastenbaum, Robert (1973). Epilogue: Loving, dying, and other gerontologic addenda. In C. Eisdorfer & M.P. Lawton (Eds.), *The psychology of adult development and aging.* Washington, DC: American Psychological Association.

Kastenbaum, Robert (1978). Essay: Gerontology's search for understanding. *The Gerontologist, 18*(1), 59–63.

Kastenbaum, Robert (Ed.). (1979). *Between life and death.* New York: Springer.

Kastenbaum, Robert (1986). *Death, society, and human experience* (3rd ed.). Columbus, OH: Charles E. Merrill.

Kastenbaum, Robert (1987). Gerontology. In G.L. Maddox et al. (Eds.), *The encyclopedia of aging.* New York: Springer.

Kastenbaum, Robert (1988). *Successful aging: The secret of how to be a late bloomer.* Fairfax Station, VA: Connie Goldman Productions.

Kastenbaum, Robert, & Aisenberg, R.B. (1972). *The psychology of death.* New York: Springer.

Kastenbaum, Robert, & Kastenbaum, Bernice (1989). *Encyclopedia of death.* Phoenix, AZ: Oryx Press.

Katz, D., & Braly, K.W. (1933). Racial stereotypes of 100 college students. *Journal of Abnormal and Social Psychology, 28,* 280–290.

Katz, Marvin G. (1990). Older persons find help, new friends by "turning on"—their computers. *AARP Bulletin, 31*(1), 1, 10–11.

Kaufman, Sharon (1987). *The ageless self: Sources of meaning in late life.* New York: New American Library.

Keen, Sam (1988, December). The stories we live by. *Psychology Today, 22*(12), 43–49.

Kegan, Robert (1982). *The evolving self.* Cambridge, MA: Harvard University Press.

Kegley, Jacquelyn Ann K. (1989). *Paul Tillich on creativity.* New York: University Press of America.

Keith, Jennie (1982). *Old people as people: Social and cultural influences on aging and old age.* Boston: Little, Brown.

Kemp, Bryan (1985). Rehabilitation and the older adult. In J.E. Birren & K.W. Schaie (Eds.), *The psychology of aging* (2nd ed.). New York: Van Nostrand Reinhold.

Kemper, D.W., Deneen, E.J., & Giuffre, J.V. (1987). *Growing younger handbook.* Boise, ID: Healthwise, Inc.

Kemper, D.W., Mettler, M., Giuffre, J., & Matzek, B. (1986). *Growing wiser: The older person's guide to mental wellness.* Boise, ID: Healthwise, Inc.

Kertzer, David I. (1989, July/August). Lasting rites. *The Family Therapy Networker, 13*(4), 20–29.

Kimmel, Douglas C. (1988). Ageism, psychology, and public policy. *American Psychologist, 43*(3), 175–178.

Kitwood, Tom (1990, June). The dialectics of dementia: With particular reference to Alzheimer's Disease. *Ageing and Society, 10*(2), 177–196.

Klagsbrun, Samuel C. (1982). Ethics in hospice care. *American Psychologist, 37*(11), 1263–1265.

Kleyman, Paul (1989). End of Pepper era leaves rich memories but uncertainty on long-term care. *The Aging Connection, 10*(3), 1, 3.

Koestenbaum, Peter (1976). *Is there an answer to death?* Englewood Cliffs, NJ: Prentice-Hall.

Korchin, Sheldon J. (1976). *Modern clinical psychology.* New York: Basic Books.

Kubler-Ross, Elizabeth (1969). *On death and dying.* New York: Macmillan.

Kubler-Ross, Elizabeth (Ed.). (1975). *Death: The final stage of growth.* New York: Simon & Schuster.

Kuhn, Maggie (1974, June). Grass-roots gray power. *Prime Time.*

Lakoff, George, & Johnson, Mark (1980). *Metaphors we live by.* Chicago: The University of Chicago Press.

Langer, E., & Rodin, J. (1976). The effects of enhanced personal responsibility for the aged: A field experiment in an institutional setting. *Journal of Personality and Social Psychology, 34*, 191–198.

Langer, Ellen (1989). *Mindfulness.* Menlo Park, CA: Addison-Wesley.

Lawton, George (Ed.). (1943). *New goals for old age.* New York: Arno Press and the New York Times.

Lawton, M. Powell (1973). Clinical psychology? In C. Eisdorfer & M.P. Lawton (Eds.), *The psychology of adult development and aging.* Washington, DC: American Psychological Association.

Lazarus, Arnold (1971). *Behavior therapy and beyond.* New York: McGraw-Hill.

Lazarus, Arnold (1976). *Multimodal behavior therapy.* New York: Springer.

Lazarus, Richard S., & DeLongis, Anita (1983). Psychological stress and coping in aging. *American Psychologist, 38*(3), 245–254.

Lazarus, Richard S., & Folkman, Susan (1984). *Stress, appraisal, and coping.* New York: Springer.

Lazarus, R.S., & McCleary, R.A. (1949). *Journal of Personality, 18*, 171.

Lear, Frances (1989). Editorial essay. *Lear's, 1*(6), 168.

Lehman, Harvey (1953). *Age and achievement.* Princeton, NJ: Princeton University Press.

Lerner, Max (1982, September 1). Sorry Skinner—It's all in your mind. *New York Post.*

Lerner, Max (1990). *Wrestling with the angel: A memoir of my triumph over illness.* New York: Norton.

LeShan, Eda (1986). *Oh, to be 50 again!: On being too old for a mid-life crisis.* New York: Times Books.

Levin, Eric (1989). Turning point. *Life, 12*(13), 50–52.

Levin, Robert (1989). Putting it in perspective. *Generations, 13*(3), 65–68.

Levin, Robert, & Weil, James (1989). Doing well and doing good. *Generations, 13*(3), 4–5.

Levinson, Daniel J. (1978). *The seasons of a man's life.* New York: Knopf.

Linkletter, Art (1988). *Old age is not for sissies.* New York: Penguin Books.

Lippmann, Walter (1922). *Public opinion.* New York: Harcourt Brace.

Liss-Levinson, William S. (1982). Reality perspectives for psychological services in a hospice program. *American Psychologist, 37*(11), 1266–1270.

Loder, James (1981). *The transforming moment.* San Francisco: Jossey-Bass.

Loevinger, Jane (1976). *Ego development: Conceptions and theories.* San Francisco: Jossey-Bass.

Lyman, Karen A. (1989). Bringing the social back in: A critique of the biomedicalization of dementia. *The Gerontologist, 29*(5), 597–605.

Maddox, George L., et al. (Eds.). (1987). *The encyclopedia of aging.* New York: Springer Publishing.

Maddox, George L., & Busse, E.W. (Eds.). (1987). *Aging: The universal human experience.* New York: Springer.

Maehr, M.L., & Kleiber, D.A. (1981). The graying of achievement motivation. *American Psychologist, 36*(7), 787–793.

Mahoney, M., & Gabriel, T. J. (1987). Psychotherapy and the cognitive sciences: An evolving alliance. *The Journal of Cognitive Psychotherapy, 1*(1), 39–59.

Maier, Henry (1969). *Three theories of child development.* New York: Harper & Row.

Mair, J.M.M. (1976). Metaphors for living. In J.K. Cole & A.W. Landfield (Eds.), *The Nebraska symposium on motivation, personal construct psychology.* Lincoln: University of Nebraska Press.

May, Rollo (1975). *The courage to create.* New York: Bantam Books.

May, Rollo (1981). *Freedom and destiny.* New York: Norton.

McGoldrick, M., & Gerson, R. (1985). *Genograms in family assessment.* New York: Norton.

McLeish, John A.B. (1976). *The Ulyssean adult: Creativity in the middle and later years.* New York: McGraw-Hill.

McLeish, John A.B. (1983). *The challenge of aging: Ulyssean paths to creative living.* Vancouver, BC: Douglas & McIntyre.

Mettler, Molly, & Kemper, Donald W. (1986). Growing wiser: Building a positive view of old age. *Aging Network News, 3*(3).

Miller, Arthur (1982). *In the eye of the beholder: Contemporary issues in stereotyping.* New York: Praeger.

Milletti, Mario A. (1984). *Voices of experience: 1500 retired people talk about retirement.* New York: Teachers Insurance and Annuity Association, College Retirement Equities Fund.

Mishkoff, Henry C. (1985). *Understanding artificial intelligence.* Dallas, TX: Texas Instruments.

Modern Maturity (1987). Name-calling: Letters to the editor, 30(4), 7.

Molinari, Victor, & Reichlen, Robert (1985). Life review reminiscence in the elderly: A review of the literature. *International Journal of Aging and Human Development, 20*(2), 81–92.

Monroe, Margaret E., & Rubin, Rhea Joyce (1983). *The challenge of aging: A bibliography.* Littleton, CO: Libraries Unlimited.

Montagu, Ashley (1981). *Growing young.* New York: McGraw-Hill.

Montaigne (1986). *The complete essays of Montaigne* (D.M. Frame, Trans.). Palo Alto, CA: Stanford University Press.

Moody, R. Jr. (1975). *Life after life.* Covington, GA: Mockingbird Books.

Mosak, Harold H. (1979). Adlerian psychotherapy. In R.J. Corsini (Ed.), *Current psychotherapies* (2nd ed.). Itasca, IL: Peacock.

Moustakas, Clark (1977). *Turning points.* Englewood Cliffs, NJ: Prentice-Hall.

Myers, Jane E. (1989). *Infusing gerontological counseling into counselor prepartion: Curriculum guide.* Alexandria, VA: American Association for Counseling and Development.

Nakashima, George (1981). *The soul of a tree.* New York: Kodansha International.

National Institute on Aging (1986). *Age words: A glossary on health and aging.* NIH Pub. No. 86-1849. Wash., DC: U.S. Govt. Printing Office.

Neugarten, Bernice (Ed.). (1968). *Middle age and aging: A reader in social psychology.* Chicago: The University of Chicago Press.

Neugarten, Bernice (1972a, Spring). Robert W. Kleemeier Award Lecture (Houston, Texas, October 28, 1971). *American Psychologist,* 9–15.

Neugarten, Bernice (1972b). Personality and the aging process. *The Gerontologist, 12*(1), 9–15.

Neugarten, Bernice (Ed.). (1982). *Age or need? Public policies for older people.* Beverly Hills, CA: Sage.

Neugarten, Bernice (1983). Health care, medicare, and health policy with older people: A conversation with Arthur Flemming. *American Psychologist, 38*(3), 311–315.

Neugarten, Bernice, & Gutmann, David L. (1968). Age-sex roles and personality in middle age: A thematic apperception study. In Bernice Neugarten (Ed.), *Middle age and aging: A reader in social psychology,* pp. 58–71. Chicago: The University of Chicago Press.

Nichols, Michael P. (1986). *Turning forty in the eighties: Personal crisis, time for change.* New York: Norton.

Nichols, Roy, & Nichols, Jane (1975). Funerals: A time for grief and growth. In Elizabeth Kubler-Ross (Ed.), *Death: The final stage of growth.* New York: A Touchstone Book.

Nickerson, Eileen T., & O'Laughlin, Kay (Eds.). (1982). *Helping through action: Action-oriented therapies.* Amherst, MA: Human Resource Development Press.

O'Donnell, Walter E. (1966, February). "Babied" parents. *Family Circle, 66,* 89, 92.

Older Women's League (1987). The picture of health for midlife and older women in America. A Mother's Day report. Washington, DC: OWL.

Olson, Robert W. (1980). *The art of creative thinking.* New York: Harper & Row.

Ott, Margaret Saunders (1982, June). Don't break the rhythm. *Whitworth College Today, 50*(4), 4.

Overholser, Renee V., & Randolph, Elizabeth (1976, October). A University of Wisconsin doctor's report: Secrets of how to live longer. *Family Circle, 84,* 90, 91.

Pacheco, Catherine Chapman (1989). *Breaking patterns: Redesigning your later years.* New York: Andrews & McMeel.

Painter, Charlotte (1985). *Gifts of age: Portraits and essays of 32 remarkable women.* San Francisco: Chronicle Books.

Palmer, Parker J. (1989, September/October). Learning is the thing for you: Renewing the vitality of religious education. *Weavings, 4*(5), 6–19.

Parkes, C.M. (1972). *Bereavement: Studies of grief in adult life.* New York: International Universities Press.

Peck, Robert (1956/1966). Psychological developments in the second half of life. In E.I. Anderson (Ed.), *Psychological aspects of aging.* Washington, DC: American Psychological Association. [Reprinted in L.D. Kleinsasser & D.B. Harris (1966). *The middle years: Development and adjustment* (pp. 157–164). Center for Continuing Liberal Education, Pennsylvania State University.]

Peck, M. Scott (1978). *The road less traveled.* New York: Simon & Schuster.

Pfeiffer, Eric (1974). *Successful aging: A conference report.* Durham, NC: Center for the Study of Aging and Human Development, Duke University.

Piper, Alan, & Bronte, Lydia (Eds.). (1986). *Our aging society: Paradox and promise.* New York: Norton.

Polanyi, Michael, & Prosch, Harry (1975). *Meaning.* Chicago: The University of Chicago Press.

Polster, Erving (1987). *Every person's life is worth a novel.* New York: Norton.

Portwood, Doris (1978). *Common sense suicide: The final right.* New York: Dodd, Mead.

Prado, C.G. (1986). *Rethinking how we age: A new view of the aging mind.* Westport, CT: Greenwood Press.

Puner, Morton (1974). *To the good long life: What we know about growing old.* New York: Universe Books.

Randolph, Elizabeth (1989, December 19). Four-footed therapists work with the elderly. *Family Circle,* 186.

Riley, M.W., Foner, A., & Waring, J. (1988). Sociology of age. In N.J. Smelser (Ed.), *Handbook of sociology.* Newbury Park, CA: Sage.

Rodin, J., & Langer, E. (1977). Long-term effects of a control-relevant intervention among the institutionalized aged. *Journal of Personality and Social Psychology, 35,* 897–902.

Roe, Anne (1956). *The psychology of occupations.* New York: Wiley.

Rosenblum, Gail (1989, January). A new job, a new life. *New Choices,* 27–34.

Rosenmayr, Leopold (1985). Changing values and positions of aging in Western culture. In J.E. Birren & K.W. Schaie (Eds.), *Handbook of the psychology of aging* (2nd ed., pp. 190–215). New York: Van Nostrand Reinhold.

Rosenzweig, M.R., & Porter, L.W. (Eds.). *Annual review of psychology* (Vol. 32, pp. 439–476). Palo Alto, CA: Annual Reviews.

Rosner, Stanley, & Abt, Lawrence E. (Eds.). (1972). *The creative experience.* New York: A Delta Book.

Rothbart, Harold A. (1972). *Cybernetic creativity.* New York: Robert Speller & Sons.

Rothenberg, Albert (1988). *The creative process of psychotherapy.* New York: Norton.

Rozental, S. (Ed.). (1967). *Niels Bohr: His life and work as seen by his friends and colleagues.* New York: Wiley.

Sarton, May (1988). *After a stroke: A journal.* New York: Norton.

Savings Bank of Puget Sound (1985, February). Cashing in on late-life leisure (Newsletter). Joan Gaines, Creative Director.

Sayers, Dorothy (1938). Are women human? Address given to Women's Society. In Rosamond Kent Sprague, *A matter of eternity: Selections from the writings of Dorothy L. Sayers.* Grand Rapids, MI: Eerdmans.

Schaie, K. Warner (1988). Ageism in psychological research. *American Psychologist, 43*(3), 179–183.

Schank, Roger C. (1988). Creativity as a mechanical process. In Robert Sternberg (Ed.), *The nature of creativity: Contemporary psychological perspectives.* New York: Cambridge University Press.

Schmidt, Robert (1989, June 14). Individual health aging: Achieving a personal program for maintaining a healthy lifestyle throughout the life span. Workshop presentation for "Wellness and Aging: The Next Ten Years," American Society on Aging, regional seminar, Seattle, WA.

Schmidt, R.M., Wu, M., & Williams, G.Z. (1988) Health watch, a longitudinal perspective study of healthy aging in 2200 individuals. In Allan L. Goldstein (Ed.), *Biochemical advances in aging 1988.* New York: Plenum.

Schwartz, Arthur N. (1975). An observation on self-esteem as the linchpin of quality of life for the aged: An essay. *The Gerontologist, 15*(5), 470–472.

Scott-Maxwell, Florida (1968). *The measure of my days.* New York: Knopf.

Seligman, Martin (1988, August). G. Stanley Hall lecture at the APA Convention. Reported by James Buie.

Selye, Hans (1978, March). On the real benefits of eustress. Interview by Laurence Cherry. *Psychology Today,* 60–70.

Sennett, Dorothy (1988). *Full measure: Modern short stories on aging.* St. Paul, MN: Graywolf Press.

Shanas, Ethel (Ed.). (1970). *Aging in contemporary society.* Beverly Hills, CA: Sage Publications.

Shatkin, Susan (1986, October). Meditation: Practice tied to longevity, health in nursing homes. *APA Monitor, 17*(10), 28.

Shem, Samuel (1978). *The house of God.* New York: Dell.

Shields, Cleveland G. (1990). Family therapy, research can help family caregivers. *AAMFT Family Therapy News, 21*(1), 5.

Shlechter, Theodore M., & Toglia, Michael P. (Eds.). (1985). *New directions in cognitive science.* Norwood, NJ: Ablex.

Siebert, Lawrence Al (1983, August). *The survivor personality.* Revised paper based on presentation to the Western Psychological Association convention, San Francisco, April 1983.

Simmel, Georg (1950). *The sociology of Georg Simmel.* Edited and translated by Kurt H. Wolff. New York: Free Press.

Simonton, Dean Keith (1990). Creativity in the later years: Optimistic prospects for achievement. *The Gerontologist, 30*(5), 626–631.

Simos, Bertha (1979). *A time to grieve: Loss as a universal human experience.* New York: Family Service Association of America.

Skinner, B.F. (1983, March). Intellectual self-management in old age. *American Psychologist, 38*(3), 239–244.

Skinner, B.F., & Vaughan, M.E. (1983). *Enjoy old age: A program of self-management.* New York: Norton.

Smith, Huston (1965). *Condemned to meaning.* New York: Harper & Row.

Sowa, John F. (1984). *Conceptual structures: Information processing in mind and machine.* Menlo Park, CA: Addison-Wesley.

Spacapan, Shirlynn, & Oskamp, Stuart (Eds.). (1989). *The social psychology of aging.* The Claremont Symposium on Applied Social Psychology, Newbury Park, CA: Sage Publications.

Sperbeck, David J., & Whitbourne, Susan Krause (1985). Reminiscence in adulthood: A social-cognitive analysis. In T.M. Shlechter & M.P. Toglia (Eds.), *New directions in cognitive science.* Norwood, NJ: Ablex.

Spicker, S.F., Woodward, K.M., & Van Tassel, D.D. (1978). *Aging and the elderly.* Atlantic Highlands, NJ: Humanities Press.

Stephens, Ray (1989a). Recalling Pepper: Elderly America loses its man with a mission. *AARP Bulletin, 30*(7), 14, 16.

Stephens, Ray (1989b). Who will be "Mr. Aging?" *AARP Bulletin, 30*(7), 1, 5.

Sternberg, Robert J. (Ed.). (1988). *The nature of creativity: Contemporary psychological perspectives.* New York: Cambridge University Press.

Storandt, Martha (1983). Psychology's response to the graying of American. *American Psychologist, 38*(3), 323–326.

Strachey, Lytton (1918). *Eminent Victorians.* Garden City, NY: Garden City Publishing.

Strickland, Bonnie R. (1989). Internal-external control expectancies: From contingency to creativity. *American Psychologist, 44*(1), 1–12.

Strouse, Jean (1986). The real reasons. In W. Zinsser, (Ed.), *Extraordinary lives* (pp. 163–195). Boston: Houghton Mifflin.

Tamke, Susan (1978). Human values and aging: The perspective of the Victorian nursery. In S.F. Spicker, K.M. Woodward, & D.D. Van Tassel (Eds.), *Aging and the elderly: Humanistic perspectives in gerontology.* Atlantic Heights, NJ: Humanities Press.

Taylor, Calvin W. (1988). Various approaches to and definitions of creativity. In Robert J. Sternberg (Ed.), *The nature of creativity: Contemporary psychological perspectives* (pp. 99–121). New York: Cambridge University Press.

Tolstoy, Leo (1960). *The death of Ivan Ilych and other stories.* New York: NAL/Penguin.

Tournier, Paul (1972). *Learn to grow old.* New York: Harper & Row.

Troll, L., Israel, J., & Israel, K. (1977). *Looking ahead: A woman's guide to the problems and joys of growing older.* Englewood Cliffs, NJ: Prentice-Hall.

Tyler, Leona (1978). *Individuality: Human possibilities and personal choice in the psychological development of men and women.* San Francisco: Jossey-Bass.

Tyler, Leona E. (1983). *Thinking creatively.* San Francisco: Jossey-Bass.

Uris, Auren (1979). *Over 50: The definitive guide to retirement.* Radnor, PA: Chilton Book Co.

Vandenbos, G.R., DeLeon, P.H., & Pallak, M.S. (1982). An alternative to traditional medical care for the terminally ill. *American Psychologist, 37*(11), 1245–1248.

Vedder, Clyde B. (1965). *Problems of the middle-aged.* Springfield, IL: C.C. Thomas.

Viorst, Judith (1986). *Necessary losses.* New York: Fawcett Gold Medal.

Von Oech, Roger (1983). *A whack on the side of the head.* New York: Warner.

Waggoner, Neva (1989). *Richly blessed.* Phoenix, AZ: Imperial Litho/Graphics.

Warrick, Pamela (1986). *Older volunteers: A valuable resource.* Washington, DC: American Association for Retired Persons.

Weiner, Bill (1980). *Quiet desperation: Plain talk on life and death.* Secaucus, NJ: Lyle Stuart.

Wheelis, Allen (1973). *How people change.* New York: Harper & Row.

White, T.H. (1987). *The once and future king.* New York: The Berkley Publishing Group.

Wiesel, Elie (1966). *The gates of the forest.* New York: Holt, Rinehart & Winston.

Willing, Jules Z. (1981). *The reality of retirement: The inner experience of becoming a retired person.* New York: William Morrow.

Wilson, Verne (1985, October). Stanley Chapple—He continues to serve. *Voice of Washington Music Educators, 31*(1), 8–9.

Wortmann, C.B., Loftus, E., & Marshall, M. (1981). *Psychology.* New York: Knopf.

Wrenn, C. Gilbert (1983, February). The fighting, risk-taking counselor. *The Personnel and Guidance Journal, 61*(6), 323–326.

Wrenn, C. Gilbert (1989). Preface. In Jane Myers, *Infusing gerontological counseling into counselor preparation: Curriculum guide.* Alexandria, VA: American Association for Counseling and Development.

Yutang, Lin (1935). *My country and my people.* New York: Reynal & Hitchcock.

Yutang, Lin (1937). *The importance of living.* New York: John Day.

Zinsser, William (Ed.). (1986). *Extraordinary lives: The art and craft of American biography.* Boston: Houghton Mifflin.

Zukav, Gary (1979). *The dancing Wu Li masters: An overview of the new physics.* New York: William Morrow.

INDEX